The Great Han

The Great Han

RACE, NATIONALISM, AND TRADITION
IN CHINA TODAY

Kevin Carrico

UNIVERSITY OF CALIFORNIA PRESS

University of California Press, one of the most distinguished university presses in the United States, enriches lives around the world by advancing scholarship in the humanities, social sciences, and natural sciences. Its activities are supported by the UC Press Foundation and by philanthropic contributions from individuals and institutions. For more information, visit www.ucpress.edu.

University of California Press
Oakland, California

© 2017 by Kevin Carrico

Library of Congress Cataloging-in-Publication Data

Names: Carrico, Kevin, author.
Title: The great Han : race, nationalism, and tradition in China today / Kevin Carrico.
Description: Oakland, California : University of California Press, [2017] | Includes bibliographical references and index.
Identifiers: LCCN 2017010809 (print) | LCCN 2017013220 (ebook) | ISBN 9780520967687 (ebook) | ISBN 9780520295490 (cloth : alk. paper) | ISBN 9780520295506 (pbk. : alk. paper)
Subjects: LCSH: Costume—China—History—21st century. | Nationalism—China—History—21st century. | Racism—China—History—21st century. | Race—History—21st century. | Ethnicity—China—History—21st century. | Politics and culture—China—21st century.
Classification: LCC GT1555 (ebook) | LCC GT1555 .C37 2017 (print) | DDC 391.00951--dc23
LC record available at https://lccn.loc.gov/2017010809

Manufactured in the United States of America

26   25   24   23   22   21   20   19   18   17
10   9   8   7   6   5   4   3   2   1

It is only as an aesthetic phenomenon that existence and the world are eternally justified.

—FRIEDRICH NIETZSCHE, *The Birth of Tragedy*

CONTENTS

ILLUSTRATIONS

ACKNOWLEDGMENTS

Although this book bears only one name on its cover, its story is considerably more complex. *The Great Han* is not only the product of years of engagement with Han Clothing Movement participants, but also of decades of learning from others, and I would like to thank a few of the people who have made this possible.

I have benefited greatly from working with engaged educators from a young age in Maryland and Pennsylvania. Among them, I would particularly like to thank John Davison, Jane Dunlap, Dan McWilliams, Neil Mufson, and Kurt Winkler for fostering my interests in language and culture. I would also like to acknowledge the memory of Betty Tjossem, who organized my first trip to China nearly two decades ago, in the spring of 1998.

My studies in Chinese language, history, and society were greatly enriched by the faculty at Bard College. I would particularly like to thank Li-hua Ying, who introduced me to both the excitement and the challenges of the Chinese language. Alan Klima showed me the potential of anthropology as a fundamentally fun discipline. Robert Culp, meanwhile, not only helped me to recognize the joys of research as an undergraduate, but has also over the past two decades gone far above and beyond the demands of an undergraduate advisor.

This project was first developed at Cornell University, working with a reliably supportive and thought-provoking dissertation committee. Steven Sangren introduced me to the exhilaration of anthropological theory, and any theoretical contributions that this book might make bear his indelible mark. Magnus Fiskesjö's passion for knowledge across disciplines and regions has been a constant source of inspiration since we first met a decade ago, and he has been endlessly supportive of this project from start to finish. Mabel Berezin's insights on sociological theory, nationalism, and far-right movements in other regions have helped me think comparatively about developments in China. Huang Hong's Cantonese class was not only fun, but also usefully helped me understand what people were saying during research in Guangzhou. And Robin McNeal's work on China's past in the present has been deeply influential upon this project. I would also like to thank classmates, friends, and staff at Cornell for all of their support throughout graduate school, including Miishen Carpentier, Donna Duncan, Inga Gruss, Zachary Howlett, Margaret Rolfe, and Lesley Turnbull.

In the early stages of this project, I also benefited greatly from the chance to participate in the Association for Asian Studies Dissertation Workshop in 2010 on the theme of Popular Culture and Social Change. Feedback from contributing faculty and fellow participants enriched the development of this project. I would particularly like to thank David Szanton for organizing this workshop for emerging scholars.

The ethnographic research upon which this book is based was generously funded by the United States' Department of Education's Fulbright-Hays Doctoral Dissertation Research Abroad Program. From 2010 to 2011, I was fortunate to be affiliated with Sun Yat-sen University's Comparative Literature Section, the most intellectually innovative academic department that I have had the honor of knowing during my time in China. There, I would like to particularly thank Ai Xiaoming, whose academic and activist work has been a constant source of inspiration, as well Ke Qianting, Huang Haitao, and Tracy Chen. Thanks as well to Zhao Dayong, whose witty insights shaped my thinking throughout research.

A first draft of this book was developed during my postdoctoral fellowship at Stanford University's Center for East Asian Studies from 2013 to 2014. I would like to thank Thomas Mullaney for his support and thoughtful advice on transforming a dissertation into a book. I would also like to thank friends and colleagues at the Center for East Asian Studies, especially Kristin Kutella Boyd, Rebecca Corbett, John Groschwitz, LeRon Harrison, Marna Romanoff, and Connie Tse.

This manuscript was completed during my postdoctoral fellowship at the University of Oklahoma's Institute for US-China Issues from 2014 to 2016. In Norman, I had the chance to work with Peter Gries, whose book *China's New Nationalism* first inspired me to pursue academic work. At a time when I saw few reasons to be optimistic about an academic career, Pete's enthusiasm and support helped me continue onward. I would also like to thank Miriam Gross, Rhonda Hill, Lauren Lee-Lewis, Ronda Martin, Mark Raymond,

Matt Sanders, Noah Theriault, and David Stroup. I would also like to extend my appreciation to Susan Tabor and Lierin Probasco of Oklahoma City Community College's Division of Social Sciences for the opportunity to share my passion for sociology with the broader Oklahoma City community.

This manuscript was finalized at my new home in the Department of International Studies, Modern Languages and Cultures, at Macquarie University, in Sydney, Australia. I would like to thank my colleagues in Chinese Studies here, including Shirley Chan, Sijia Guo, Ni Li, Hui Ling Xu, and Lan Zhang. I have appreciated the thoughtfulness and thoughtful engagements of my colleagues across the department and beyond, including especially Rodrigo Acuna, Chris Houston, Sung-ae Lee, Brangwen Stone, Estela Valverde, and Chris Vasantkumar. Teaching relief to finalize revisions to this manuscript was generously provided by a Macquarie Early Career Research Grant, for which department chair Ulrike Garde has been an inspiring mentor. And the Faculty of Arts' Emerging Scholars Scheme, organized by Clare Monagle, has provided an ideal environment to exchange ideas with other researchers in the faculty. I must also express my sincere gratitude to the broader community of China scholars in Australia, who have been so welcoming to me as a new arrival, especially Geremie Barmé, Jonathan Benney, Gloria Davies, Chongyi Feng, Benjamin Garvey, Gerry Groot, Bruce Jacobs, and Christian Sorace.

Sections of Chapter 5 have been previously published as "Producing Purity: An Ethnographic Study of a Neotraditionalist Ladies' Academy in Contemporary China" in the collection *Cultural Politics of Gender and Sexuality in Contemporary Asia*, edited by Tiantian Zheng (2016). These sections are reproduced here with permission from the University of Hawaii Press. Sections of Chapter 6 have also been previously published as "The Manchu in the Mirror: The Emptiness of Identity and the Fullness of Conspiracy Theory" in the collection *Emptiness and Fullness: Ethnographies of Lack and Desire in Contemporary China*, edited by Susanne Bregnbæk and Mikkel Bunkenborg (2017). These sections are reproduced here with permission from Berghahn Books.

Many thanks to those who read and commented on chapters and chapter sections, including Yinghong Cheng, Allen Chun, Richard Handler, Loretta Lou, and Hoon Song. Special thanks are reserved for William Callahan, Peter Gries, and James Leibold, who generously read and shared their thoughts on the entire manuscript. All have made this a better book. Any remaining errors are, of course, solely my own.

At the University of California Press, I would like to thank Reed Malcolm, who has provided me with a truly seamless publishing experience. Zuha Khan has also been greatly supportive in organizing and finalizing the manuscript from start to finish. I also deeply appreciate the thoughtful comments from my two peer-reviewers, whose insights have enriched the final manuscript.

Last but not least, I would not have written this book nor pursued this career without the support of my family. I would particularly like to thank my parents Joseph and Rebecca Carrico, as well as my grandparents and extended family, for encouraging and supporting my studies throughout all of these years. I cannot even begin to express in words my gratitude to my wife, Leaf Carrico, who is not only a wonderful companion and my best friend, but also reliably the most thoughtful critic of my work. And finally, thanks to my son, Teddy Carrico, whose presence illuminates my life on a daily basis. Before I start my next book, I look forward to many more action-packed afternoons at the playground.

Kevin Carrico
Sydney, Australia
April 23, 2016

Introduction

NATIONALISM

"You can't have nationalism [*minzu zhuyi*] without a race [*minzu*]. That's what we want to do: promote Han racial nationalism [*Han minzu zhuyi*]."

Yu is a network technician from rural Shandong Province, living in the Pearl River Delta. We met a number of times over dinner during my time in China, usually at a dangerously spicy Chongqing-style hot pot restaurant near his apartment in Guangzhou. We would order six beers at a time, and after a few rounds, Yu reliably became the most talkative of any of my interlocutors. This evening, as the 2011 Lunar New Year approached, Yu was explaining to me his understanding of nationalism. In doing so, he placed particular emphasis upon the idea of *minzu*: *minzu* means "race" or "nationality" in Chinese, while at the same time forming the core of the Chinese term for nationalism (*minzu zhuyi*).

> The multiracial nationalism we have now in China, with 56 races as part of a larger "Chinese race" [*Zhonghua minzu*], is a big scam. It was imposed upon us by the Manchus, forcing us Han, the core of China from the beginning of time, into submission. All that this nationalism has done is weaken China. You can't just destroy the distinction between civilization and barbarism [*hua yi zhi bian*], incorporate a bunch of barbarians into our nation, and then expect a strong nation. All this talk of "wealth and power" [*fuqiang*] nowadays is empty and meaningless without Han nationalism.

Yu is a member of China's Han Clothing Movement (*Hanfu yundong*), a youth-based nationalist movement that has emerged over the past decade and a half in urban China. The movement is dedicated to "revitalizing" the Han majority, an extremely diverse ethnic group[1] constituting roughly 92 percent of China's population. Toward this goal of revitalizing the Great Han, the movement promotes a supposedly eternal ethnic outfit known as Han Clothing (*Han minzu fuzhuang* or *Hanfu*), characterized by broad sleeves and flowing robes decorated with brilliant colors. This book is based in field-work with members of the movement in locations across China: based primarily in Guangzhou and Shenzhen in the southern province of Guangdong, my travels throughout China from 2010 to 2011 also provided a chance to discuss this movement with participants in Zhengzhou, Beijing, Chengdu, Kunming, Suzhou, and Haikou. From one city to the next, I listened to the concerns and aspirations of movement participants like Yu, seeking to understand why they had become invested in this particular movement at this particular historical moment.

As suggested by its name, clothing is essential to the Han Clothing Movement. This is not any ordinary attire: Han Clothing is imagined to be the eternal apparel of the Han, woven into narratives of history and identity extending from the mythical progenitor figure of the Yellow Emperor to the Han people of today. Clothing, while central to movement representations, thus remains primarily a medium for the movement's main message of nationalism: an unyielding fascination with the idea of the Han Chinese nation.

There is widespread agreement in the academic literature that nationalism is the core ideology in China today.[2] Yet beyond this consensus, the reasons for nationalism's appeal and affective power are considerably less clear. Building upon Benedict Anderson's theory of nations as imagined communities, I unfold my experiences with the Han Clothing Movement in the following chapters to examine precisely how imagined communities are imagined, and particularly how the emotions characteristic of nationalist investment are produced and reproduced over time.

> Without a race [*minzu*], there cannot be any nationalism [*minzu zhuyi*]. That is why the nationalism that we promote is Han nationalism [*Han minzu zhuyi*]. That's the only proper route for China: to acknowledge that we Han are the only real Chinese. It is only when we revitalize Han culture, Han customs, and Han rituals that we will be able to experience again the real China: the land of rites and etiquette [*liyi zhi bang*].

This notion of "the real China" promoted by Han Clothing Movement enthusiasts, a fantasy land of traditional rites and etiquette over and against their everyday experience of the actually existing real China, is central to understanding the emotional power of nationalism. Nationalism, in my analysis, is neither a natural, primordial bond nor a reflection of print-capitalist development nor a simplistic ideology forced upon the people by a "ruling class." Rather, I propose a structural-psychoanalytical reinterpretation of the national experience as perpetually split between the appeal of boundless imaginings and the disappointments of an inherently bounded reality. Characterized by a perpetual experiential gap, which drives emotional investments in the imaginary national ideal, the sole remedy to the disappointment of this gap becomes a reinvestment in these ideas, seeking a solution in the source of the dilemma. I thus define nationalism in the analyses that follow as a fantasy-based, paradoxical, and thus self-perpetuating cultural-imaginary system.

But for Yu, nationalism was the one and only truth, even if, or precisely because, its promises were so distant, while also seeming so close. Just before raising his glass, signaling that it was time for us both to finish our beers in one quick gulp, he repeated: "Han nationalism is our only path forward. Cheers."

RACE

Considerable debate exists in academic circles as to whether the concept of "race" is relevant to the Chinese experience of identity. This debate operates on two levels. The first controversy surrounds the idea of a Sinocentric cultural universalism, wherein Chineseness would be primarily a matter of culture: according to this theory, anyone who adopted Chinese culture could then become "Chinese." Within this model of history, racial thought is then viewed as a Western invention later imported into China, and thus foreign. This culturalist-universalist narrative provides hope of a pleasant alternative to a racialized view of the world, an alternative that can be discovered and embraced on the other side of the world. Yet for all its appeal, this idealized narrative has been thoroughly deconstructed by Frank Dikötter in his *Discourse of Race in Modern China*, in which he demonstrates the intertwinement of ideas of culture and biology in the distinction between Chinese and barbarians (*hua yi zhi bian*) from premodern times to the present.[3]

The second controversy revolves around the ambiguity of the signifier *minzu*, which is used to mark identity in the Sinophone world. In the People's Republic of China, the focus of this book, *minzu* has been officially translated as "nationality," referring to the Stalinist theory of nationalities composed of common territory, language, economy, and psychological nature.[4] Recent proposals from scholars in China have called for a softening of this language, moving toward the ostensibly depoliticized idea of *zuqun* or "ethnic groups"[5] as a means of achieving the very political mission of denying subaltern rights: softening language while maintaining a hardline policy. Further adding to the confusion, the issue of Chinese ethnic terminology is not at all clarified by the fact that the 56 *minzu* currently recognized in China are also considered to be part of a larger meta-*minzu*, the *Zhonghua minzu* or "Chinese nationality" or "race," in an arrangement that Fei Xiaotong and Xu Jieshun have argued constitutes "diversity in unity" or "plurality and unity."[6]

To Yu, these debates that have shaped academic discussions of race and identity in China in recent decades were fundamentally meaningless. In his understanding, there had once been an absolute distinction between Chinese and barbarians (*hua yi zhi bian*) that maintained the purity of the Han Chinese race and Chinese culture, extending from the prehistorical reign of the Yellow Emperor to the end of the Song Dynasty (960–1279 C.E.). With the Mongol invasion in the Yuan Dynasty (1271–1368 C.E.) and the subsequent Manchu invasion in the Qing Dynasty (1644–1911 C.E.), this distinction had collapsed, contaminating Chinese culture and as a result producing the omnipresent challenges of Chinese modernity. In an imaginative reframing of the "century of humiliation" (*bainian guochi*) that constitutes the core of official nationalist narratives in China, the depredations of early modernity were to be blamed not only on those whom Yu called the "Western barbarians" (*Xi yi*), but also on such conquering barbarian stranger kings as the Mongols and the Manchus. In Yu's experience, these invaders from the past had now been joined in their depredations by races from around the world to leave him feeling out of place in his own home.

Yu had moved to the south from rural Shandong at the age of sixteen to earn money for his family. Although he has developed quite a successful career in network technology, and despite the growth and excitement unfolding around him, he told me on a number of occasions that he was thoroughly disappointed with everything. Nothing he saw here in this metropolis, he told me, could ever be as impressive as the memories from his childhood in the countryside: behind the flashing neon lights and fancy sports cars, he said, there was nothing deeper, indeed, nothing even substantively real, in city life. He glowingly recounted Chinese New Year celebrations from his youth: although food and entertainment were simple, the celebrations had the feeling of being a genuine festival. And by contrast, despite the glitz and extravagance that often goes into Chinese New Year celebrations nowadays, he told me that it never feels quite like a real Chinese New Year celebration: it is as if something is missing. This search for what is missing for Han Clothing Movement participants is the topic of this book.

After a few drinks, Yu's attention would inevitably shift to the discussion of African immigrants in his new home city of Guangzhou. That evening, engaging in a play on words on the Chinese term for prejudice (*qishi*), Yu exclaimed that his views were not an example of "*qishi*," which literally means to have an imbalanced view, but rather examples of "*zhengshi*," meaning to look at something directly and correctly. And in this direct gaze at the China before him today, what he saw was not pretty:

> There are parts of Guangzhou, you know, like Xiaobei, that are overrun by these black devils [*hei gui*]. I've been there, have you? You have to leave before nightfall, to be safe. I've seen people laying there in the street, these big black devils, passed out with a needle in their arm, foaming at the mouth. If they don't have money to buy their drugs, they'll beat you and rob you. And if they need a woman, they'll just grab one off the streets and do with her as they please. They'll share her with their friends and give her AIDS. Places like this, like Xiaobei, they're in China, right? There's no debate about whether Xiaobei is part of China. But the people of China have to avoid Xiaobei for their own safety. This is our home country, and we can't go there.

Yu brushed aside my question about whether he had ever actually gone to Xiaobei, or had only read about it online.

Although the clear distinction between civilization and barbarism had collapsed in modernity, Yu still firmly believed that the Han was a relatively pure race, with unchanged biological markers. In the chapters that follow, I thus translate the Chinese term *minzu* as "race" in situations in which Han Clothing participants are imagining the Han in a racial manner. Despite my own view that races do not exist, I cannot deny the power of racial thinking among movement members. It is precisely such imagining of an essential, unchanging Han-ness deep inside that led Yu and others like him to believe that it would be easier than most races for the Han to recapture its authentic tradition once it managed to cast off the influence of various foreign impurities.

Yu was obsessed with the idea of Chinese women having sex with African men, and shared with me on no less than three separate occasions the "true" tall tale of an innocent local Chinese woman who had fallen in love with a

Nigerian. According to Yu, during their courtship, this Nigerian had told this young woman that he was very wealthy. Trusting him, and completely disregarding her family's opposition, she followed him back to Nigeria. There she discovered that his definition of wealth was ownership over a few "grass huts" in his village. Then, Yu claimed, her boyfriend informed her that according to his village's customs, she would be required to sleep with all five of his village chiefs. As a result, she had four children over a span of five years in Nigeria, only two of which were in fact fathered by her boyfriend. Eventually, in order to escape this situation, she applied for help from the Chinese Embassy in Nigeria, which Yu claims brought her back to Guangzhou. Despite having escaped Nigeria and returned home, Yu told me that she still suffered from nightmares and posttraumatic stress disorder.

Likely because I am a white male from the United States, Yu assumed throughout his racist rants that I was a brother in arms, and that it would only take a few more conversations or a few more beers for me to air my "true opinions" on the matter of race, despite my repeated disagreement with his statements. During our talks, Yu would often tell me that "the America of today will never again be able to become a purely white nation." I would inevitably shrug my shoulders in indifference to this prospect. In response, Yu would sigh in frustration and shake his head.

Yet unlike my home country, Yu still saw a chance for China to become a pure Han nation: a China for Han only. This was, he told me, his goal in joining the Han Clothing Movement. Towards this goal, he believed that Chinese nationalism needed to abandon its modernist fixation on a geobody and globalization, sacrificing "barbarian" minority lands and international exchanges in order to realize a newfound racial and cultural purity. There was not an issue of culturalism versus racial thinking in Yu's view of the world: culture and race were one and the same. The continued existence of a Han race, despite the barbarian onslaught in recent centuries, provided the essential foundation for a return to a pure Han nation, based in pure Han tradition.

TRADITION

Later that evening, Yu asked me, as someone who has spent years in China, what advice I might have for his country: "What could we improve?" Having been asked similar questions countless times, and noticing that most people are never particularly happy with any answer that I provide, I tried at first to avoid the conversation altogether, safely suggesting that any problems that the Chinese people faced would be resolved by the Chinese people, not by me. Yet Yu insisted. Expecting a sympathetic audience from a network technician, I opened up slightly and told Yu how my email had been inaccessible without a virtual private network since my arrival in China the previous year, and suggested that the ever-expanding controls on the Internet and other media could perhaps be relaxed to allow free discussion of the many contentious issues in contemporary society. When I finished, Yu paused, took in a deep breath, and then provided me with a lengthy and notably irritated response: having briefly overcome my hesitation to respond, his response soon reinforced my initial hesitation.

Yu proceeded to inform me that there were "riots" in Tibet in 2008, and that the "Western media" played a dangerous game by spreading rumors and flat-out lies throughout these events. The one and only real truth, he told me, is that the Tibetans were making trouble and attacking the innocent Han. These Tibetans and Uyghurs and other minorities want to be independent, he told me, but this is thoroughly impractical, as they are just as uncivilized as the Africans he loathed. "They can't even take care of their own economy and economic development, and they want to be independent? What kind of a country would that be?" The Han Chinese, he told me, are thus in Tibet only to do good: in a reincarnation of the civilization-barbarism distinction under a developmentalist guise, Yu saw the Han central government altruistically funneling money into an underdeveloped region whose people simply had no idea how to take care of themselves. Yet the "Western media" misrepresented the Chinese people's sincere and well-intentioned efforts to help these helplessly simple people, characterizing their goodwill mission as an invasion. On account of such misrepresentations, Yu argued, he believed the state had the right to block whatever websites it pleased.

In reality, as was the case with many of Yu's post-truth narratives, the truth was considerably more complex. The Great Firewall that blocks websites originated long before the protests and crackdown in Tibet in 2008, and has lasted long after, but such facts were in no way about to complicate Yu's beliefs. After all, he had earlier asserted that it would be perfectly fine to abandon Tibet to realize a pure Chinese culture, but was now arguing fervently in favor of China's continued occupation. Then, at one ominous point in our exchange about Tibet, he leaned in to say earnestly, "Let me tell you, this is just my own opinion. I'm not a leader, I'm just me. But if I was the leader, I would gather up all of those people who rioted in Tibet and Xinjiang, and I would execute them. Shoot them [*qiangbi*]! Problem solved."

Unwilling to let indiscriminate capital punishment for ungrateful minorities stand as his most extreme point of advocacy that evening, Yu then proceeded to develop a traditionalist justification of the state censorship I had ever-so-hesitantly criticized. Taking a step back, he acknowledged that the censorship system creates an environment in which there are many issues and problems about which average people are unaware, but then insisted that this is not in fact a problem. Citing the five cardinal relationships in Confucianism, he suggested that there are naturally different levels of people, and that those on the bottom must obey those above in order for society to function properly: a son must obey his father, just as a wife must obey her husband, just as the ruled must obey their rulers. I would hear similar traditionalist ideological frameworks of an ideal harmonious society repeated countless times during my research.

"There is heaven," he said, "and there are the people. Between them is the son of heaven. People are unable to communicate with heaven, because they are too far removed. Only the son of heaven can communicate with heaven." And then, looking me straight in the eye, he declared "Hu Jintao is the son of heaven." There were many issues that in his opinion the common people did not need to worry about, and indeed did not even need to know: the son of heaven and his colleagues, he reassured me, have all of the information that they need in order to make the right decisions. My doubts about censorship, he concluded, were simply the result of my lack of knowledge of traditional Chinese culture. "You still don't understand China," he said with a smirk, raising his glass again.

The Han Clothing Movement is organized around the concept of tradition, promoting a very particular vision of traditional clothing, traditional ritual, and accompanying traditional lifestyles, incorporating everything from etiquette to gender roles. Each of these aspects of tradition is portrayed as authentic and natural, a seemingly eternal truth. Yet as Yu's invocation of then-leader Hu Jintao as the son of heaven belies, these constructions of tradition are anything but natural. The discussion above highlights the experiential gaps existing within Yu's vision of the Han race and the Chinese nation: invented traditions, another core topic in this book, function as a means of closing that gap and attempting to aestheticize the mundane and everyday in the direction of an elusive ideal image.

Yu reassured me later that evening, after a few more drinks, that one day everyone would wear Han Clothing, and that these Internet restrictions and other forms of censorship and control would become obsolete: there might need to be Internet controls in the United States, he added, to stop everyone from trying to immigrate to China. That moment, he asserted, would mark the true rise of China as a great power, or the realization of his "real China." The following chapters trace this process of reconstructing national and racial identity through the media of tradition.

ON THE QUESTION OF CRITICAL ANTHROPOLOGY

As suggested by the vignettes above, this ethnography runs counter to the currents in contemporary anthropology, insofar as I disagree with the beliefs of my informants and engage with these beliefs in a critical matter. This is an approach with which many of my colleagues in both anthropology and China studies may disagree. In the field of anthropology, the denunciation of the colonial past and the discipline's role therein has produced an environment in which critique can seemingly only be applied to "the West," while postmodernism and cultural relativism promote an uncritical ethnographic stance in which the anthropologist is to serve primarily as a cultural transcriber, renouncing analysis and certainly all critique. Correspondingly, in the highly politically charged field of China studies, identification with romanticized ideas of China (not dissimilar to ideas embraced by movement participants) combined with increasing state pressures on research have produced hesitation among some scholars in the field to address sensitive matters of politics, history, and ethnicity directly. Identifying fully with one's area of study (or at least the official representation thereof), the goal of such superficially friendly work becomes the task of representing a politically correct viewpoint known as "China's perspective" to the world against various perceived villains, such as "cultural hegemony," "global capitalism," or "imperialism."

Such well-trodden analytical approaches were certainly possible in the preparation of this volume. I could have argued, for instance, that Han Clothing is a valiant native response to the cultural imperialism and homogenization of globalization, working against capitalist hegemony to reassert China's voice and tradition on the world stage. I also could have easily provided an abundance of quotations from interviews to support this viewpoint, arguing that Han Clothing is in fact the sole authentic representation of a true Chinese tradition in the present. And I could have very easily taken movement discourses and movement histories at face value as truths to share with the world, interpreting these histories as of course having equal truth value to any other historical narratives, even forming an exciting new ontology. All of the pieces of such an analysis were there, and they would have been very easy to put together. The result would undoubtedly be a feel-good text casting me as a benevolent representative[7] communicating for the "Han people" on the "world stage."

The problem with such an approach, however, is that I would find it not only thoroughly dishonest but also immensely patronizing. A rapidly growing field of contemporary scholarship focuses upon finding and criticizing "Orientalist" imaginings and mystifications of "the other," endlessly rediscovering the discoveries of Said's original work.[8] Such scholarship, purportedly engaged in a politically progressive project of liberating "the East" from "Western knowledge production," not only ironically reproduces and reinforces the East-West binary that it claims to want to overcome, but furthermore provides a theoretical buttress for conservative and even xenophobic nationalism. Yet, even more importantly, such scholarship completely overlooks the fact that beyond distorted knowledge production across the East-West binary, all people across the world are engaged in similarly imaginary and mystifying relationships with their own national communities: these imaginary relations to the self are a central focus of the analyses that follow.

Thus, rather than tailoring my analyses to avoid critical engagement and hence avoiding easy accusations of "Orientalism" or collusion with seemingly ubiquitous "anti-China forces," I argue instead that the condescending suggestion that phenomena in China must be removed from critical analysis and handled uniquely delicately is in fact the epitome of Orientalism and anti-China thinking. On a daily basis, people discuss, question, and challenge many of the assumptions underlying "our" existence in "the West." Do races exist? How has whiteness been constructed as the default identity? How do mythologies of George Washington and other founders shape our (mis) understanding of national history? How does the representation of our racial past and present reproduce real inequalities? And what exactly is going on in the minds of Tea Party participants? Although not always well received, such critical analysis usefully pushes against the boundaries of conventional thinking and sheds new light upon our world. To hold China or any other country to a different critical standard is then a thoroughly Orientalist approach, insofar as it is based in the infantilizing assumption that "they" are not ready for critical reflection, and must rely upon "our" continual praise and support, which we so benevolently provide. Such an approach is not only a disservice to academic work but also a disservice to the people of China, benefiting only the advocates of this self-serving moralization divorced from fundamental realities on the ground. This book then, in the tradition of Allen Chun's deconstruction of "Chineseness"[9] and Ghassan Hage's study of Australia as a "white nation,"[10] develops a critical analysis of the idea and experience of identity, while at the same time attempting to understand identity's undeniable and deep appeal.

Considering the passions of nationalist identification examined in my analyses, it has not surprised me that these analyses have at times aroused precisely such passions in discussions and presentations. And considering the dedication that Han Clothing Movement participants have repeatedly demonstrated towards the movement, my interpretation of their ideas, beliefs, and practices will likely be disappointing to many. Yet I want to emphasize here that the viewpoints featured in this book are in the end products of a deep empathy with participants' perspectives and motivations for joining this movement, factors which I have traced in detail in the chapters that follow. My empathy, however, extends neither to the results of participation nor to the often outlandish beliefs produced therein. It is logically possible to be empathetic with the trials and dilemmas that someone is facing, while nevertheless strongly disagreeing with their proposed solutions to these dilemmas. This is the situation in which I have found myself: I can thus only hope that the Han Clothing enthusiasts with whom I have worked over the past eight years might recognize the empathy in my critique, insofar as I have strived to understand the world through their eyes, despite my disagreement with the products of this worldview.

METHODOLOGY

The Han Clothing Movement has made a few prior appearances in the scholarship on contemporary China. Antonia Finnane's *Changing Clothes in China: Fashion, History, and Nation* includes a brief discussion of early aspects of the movement in relation to the globalization of fashion and local identity.[11] Jyrki Kallio's *Tradition in Chinese Politics: The Party-State's Reinvention of the Past and the Critical Response from Public Intellectuals* also includes a brief but fascinating discussion of the movement as an example of Han nationalism and traditionalist politics in China today.[12] And the most thorough study of the movement thus far is James Leibold's article "More than a Category: Han Supremacism on the Chinese Internet.[13] Leibold's analysis focuses upon a fascinating incident in late 2008 in which a Han Clothing Movement partici-pant by the name of "Great Wind of the Han" (*Dahan zhi feng*) publicly slapped a well-known scholar of Qing history, Yan Chongnian, during a book signing. Leibold's study sheds important light upon the more extremist senti-ments of the Han Clothing Movement. Yet as Leibold notes in his discussion of Han Clothing, "the movement encompasses a very diverse group of indi-viduals who find different sorts of meaning and enjoyment in the category of Han."[14] By engaging in long-term fieldwork and incorporating ethno-graphic materials to consider the complex daily life experiences, dilemmas, and attachments of Han Clothing Movement participants, this book aims to build upon prior analyses to provide a novel account of the broad diversity of individuals within this movement, as well as the common modes of national-identificatory enjoyment that bring them together.

In his analysis of contemporary Chinese nationalism, Peter Gries has argued that "to understand Chinese nationalism, we must listen to the Chinese."[15] Accordingly, in this project I have taken the time to listen to participants in the Han Clothing Movement. This study is based primarily in a year of in-depth fieldwork with Han Clothing Movement participants in urban China, extending from the summer of 2010 to the summer of 2011. My research base was in the Pearl River Delta cities of Guangzhou and Shenzhen. Although located at quite a distance from the historical homeland of "the Han" in the central plains, both of these cities are home to the largest, best-established, and most active branches of the Han Clothing Movement in China today, and their relative proximity in Southern Guangdong Province allowed me the opportunity to work with movement participants in both cities.

My research activities in Guangdong consisted primarily of participating in movement events, visiting Han Clothing stores, and spending time with Han Clothing Movement participants outside of movement events. Group and individual interviews were primarily unstructured and completely open-ended discussions. I also conducted a series of research trips to meet with Han Clothing enthusiasts and associations in other cities with active move-ment organizations, such as Zhengzhou, Kunming, Chengdu, Haikou, Dongguan, and Beijing. Combined with my work in Shenzhen and Guangzhou, this collection of cities extended geographically across China: from the urban sprawl of the Pearl River Delta in the south, to the historically rich yet currently economically impoverished region of Zhengzhou in the north, to the ethnically diverse city of Kunming in the west, to the center of national politics in Beijing, my research trips provided samples of a broad spectrum of living environments and personal experiences for thinking through the motivations and aspirations of movement participants. Finally, a touristic journey through the Dali region provided an opportunity to think comparatively about minority representation and Han identity construction. Both prior to and following my fieldwork, this research was further supplemented by immersion in the online virtual worlds of the Han Clothing Movement.

In the chapters that follow, all participants are referred to by pseudonyms, and composite characters have been formed in some cases to ensure that no informant can be identified based upon my descriptions.

THEORETICAL APPROACH AND LAYOUT OF THE BOOK

My theoretical approach in the following analyses is not amenable to succinct summarization, as I remain resistant to theoretical identification. However, for interested readers, the main inspirations for my analytical framework are to be found in Lacan's analyses of subjectivity, Luhmann's theory of social systems, and Sloterdijk's spherological framework.

First, I locate the ideal forms of nationalist, racial, and other forms of identification around which the Han Clothing Movement is structured in the Lacanian imaginary register, meaning that these forms of identification are based in the "assumption of [a] specular image" of the "ideal-I,"[16] thereby constituting the nationalist-identificatory ego in fictional fantasies of being: as I say in Chapter 1, no nation or group organizes itself around mundane and banal descriptions. Yet at the same time, no nation or group can transcend mundane and banal realities, creating a fundamentally complex and even paradoxical relationship to the self. As a result, these fantasies are and remain fantasies: both Lacanian analyses of subjectivity as "alienating identity"[17] and Luhmannian studies of society as difference[18] build upon the Saussurian division of signifier and signified to highlight this perpetual gap at the core of being and society that is the focus of the analyses that follow. As Luhmann observes, the modern nation-state is constituted in an "organizing difference" insofar as "the politician has to be able to say more than he can do."[19]

The resulting impossible "demand for realization" reproduces the political-identificatory system just as the search for complete and ideal being perpetually reproduces the Lacanian imago.[20]

Caught in this impossibility of their ideals of "the Han" and "China," I interpret the various activities of the Han Clothing Movement as an attempt, following Sloterdijk's analyses of spheres in human history,[21] to construct ideal spaces as immunological spheres within a disintegrating social realm that does not match participants' ideals of what China is supposed to be. Accordingly, we see the movement's image of Han-ness and Chinese-ness only ever fleetingly realized in moments that aim to transform society yet can only exist through their complete spherical segregation from society, thereby reproducing the dilemma of the gap in its ephemeral solution and further fueling the passion of identity thinking.

The chapters in this study are organized thematically, developing this argument. The first section of this book, composed of the first three chapters, examines the concepts noted in this book's title, namely race, nationalism, and tradition. The first chapter, "Imaginary Communities," combines materialist and ethnosymbolic approaches to nationalism to develop a theory of nations as not only imagined but indeed imaginary communities, systematically trapped in the gap between fantasies and realities: the "real China," in this reading, is an imaginary object of identification that never in fact existed. The second chapter, "Han Trouble and the Ethnic Cure," deconstructs the ideas of Han-ness and tradition, demonstrating the minority origins of the Han and the contemporary origins of tradition. The gap highlighted in these conceptual reviews is developed through ethnography in the third chapter, "The Personal Origins of Collective Identity," which presents four case studies of Han Clothing Movement participants' everyday lives in cities across China, tracing in particular how personal aspirations and dilemmas are expressed and imaginarily resolved through fantasies of a coherent, glorious, and eternal majority identity promoted by the movement.

Having established the distance between imaginary identities and experience, as well as the corresponding demand for realization, the second section of the book, composed of the final three chapters, traces the movement's creation of immunological microspheres to reconstruct their sacred visions of Han-ness, Chineseness, and tradition in a profane environment. The fourth chapter, "Reenacting the Land of Rites and Etiquette: Between the Virtual and the Material," traces this reconstruction of identity through three primary media of representation: ethnic clothing, ritual, and photography. Each medium enacts a growing abstraction from participants' living environment: ironically, the eternal image of tradition finds its most stable embodiment via the most modern of technologies, the digital camera. The fifth chapter, "The Manchu in the Mirror," examines the widely believed claim within the movement that the formerly powerful Manchus who ruled over China in the Qing Dynasty (1644–1911 C.E.) continue to exercise power in the present. Unraveling these paranoid conspiracy theories of Manchu genocide against the Han, conspiracy theory and identity are shown to be two sides of the same coin, with conspiracy theory serving as a final guarantor for the processes of identity construction central to the Han Clothing Movement. The sixth chapter, "Producing Purity," analyzes the reconstruction of gender roles under the legitimizing rubrics of "culture" and "tradition." Building upon fieldwork in a traditionalist "Ladies' Academy" dedicated to transforming modern city women into proper and traditional "ladies," I proceed to analyze the implications of the Han Clothing Movement's simultaneously constraining and fulfilling identity visions for its future as a movement, arguing that its seeming solutions to the dilemmas of the present can only, in the end, generate further dilemmas.

Finally, in the conclusion, "Neotraditionalism in China Today," I expand this theoretical framework to interpret a series of distinct yet related neotraditionalisms and nationalisms in contemporary China: traditional education, Confucian constitutionalism, New Leftism, and the construction of new "old towns." This conclusion provides a basis for reflecting upon the Han Clothing Movement as one example of much broader trends in contemporary Chinese society, striving to realize identity through an imaginary image, and seeking the true path of the future in an imagined past.

ONE

———

Imaginary Communities

FANTASY AND FAILURE IN
NATIONALIST IDENTIFICATION

HOW IS THE NATION, as an imagined community, imagined? Where and how do the passions that are characteristic of nationalist identification emerge, and how are they sustained? And what are the political, social, and personal effects of these imaginings? How, in sum, can we begin to understand the complexity of the human relationship to notions of nation, race, and the underlying concept of identity? These questions, which frame the analyses that follow, were on my mind when I met a group of Han Clothing movement enthusiasts in the southern metropolis of Shenzhen to celebrate the Mid-Autumn Festival in 2010. Having conducted online research on this group prior to my arrival, there were a few facts of which I felt fairly certain. First, the Han Clothing Movement was dedicated to promoting a purified vision of Chinese tradition and contemporary identity, devoid of any polluting "foreign" influences. I was leaving the United States in the summer of 2010 during the rise of the Tea Party to conduct research in China with a group that might be called the Green Tea Party. Second, members of this group, in promoting this purified vision, were not shy about using inflammatory rhetoric with regard to those whom they called "barbarians," meaning either China's minority nationalities or the broad and quite diverse group of people, constituting the remainder of the global population, described conventionally in China as "foreigners." And third, these preceding two facts were indicative of a final fact, namely, that the Han Clothing Movement was a fairly extreme nationalist group, dedicated to celebrating a particular vision of China.

A considerably more complex picture emerged, however, that autumn afternoon when I sat down with movement enthusiasts in Shenzhen. The unpredictable autumn weather, prone to sudden downpours, led the organizers to move an outdoor celebration indoors to a small, dimly lit teahouse buried deep among the skyscrapers of Futian District. After everyone introduced themselves and the conversation started to pick up, I expected to hear fairly straightforward nationalist narratives, which would consist of excessive praise for one's nation and people, alongside equally passionate criticisms or denunciations of other nations and people. And over the course of the afternoon, I did indeed hear plenty of passionate denunciations of other nations and people. However, considering that members of the Han Clothing Movement are racial nationalists dedicated to celebrating the idea of China, I was consistently surprised by just how much time they spent complaining about China.

A man in his late twenties who came from the rural province of Anhui led me through a formulaic set of questions with which any "foreigner" in China will be familiar: How long had I been in China? Did I like it? What were the main differences between China and "the West"? Did I like moon cakes? Who does? But then when we reached a pause in the conversation, my new friend suddenly asked, "How much do you know about traditional Chinese culture?" Answering his own question before I could, he highlighted four components of tradition, namely clothing, food, housing, and transport (*yi shi zhu xing*), which he asserted were the core of Han traditional culture and thus of Chinese traditional culture.

Considering that we were both attending a Han Clothing event, he began appropriately from clothing. Clothing, he told me, was elaborate and beautiful in the imperial era, and proper attire was a central component in ordering society. Establishing a metaphorical relationship between the individual body and the social body, he asserted that only when clothing was in order could society be in order. But Chinese nowadays, he noted, wear "Western clothes" made from unnatural synthetic fibers. Men wear sneakers and "Western" suits (literally *xizhuang*), he claimed, that never quite fit them correctly, and women, he asserted, walk around with their breasts and buttocks hanging out, in clear violation of proper dress, and greatly damaging national dignity. This Han Clothing gathering, he reassured me, would finally provide me the chance to see real "Eastern clothes," in contrast to "Western clothes."

Another central component of Chinese culture, he continued, is food. Chinese cuisine is rich and diverse, extending from the delicate cuisine of Shanghai to the numbing spice of Sichuan to the refined gastronomy of Guangdong. And throughout history, the social experience of sharing a meal has created lasting bonds between people. Yet he quickly added that food nowadays is not always safe, and one must be careful what one eats. There is the infamous gutter oil, meaning discarded restaurant oil removed from disposal sites, reprocessed, and endlessly reused, potentially causing cancer through repeated ingestion.[1] There are genetically modified foods, which he informed me have been sent to China by the US government[2] in order to make the Han extinct, despite my clearly articulated skepticism on this point. And there are even fake eggs, he noted, made from the mixture of various chemicals to resemble egg whites and yolks. "The fake eggs look prettier than real eggs on the outside, but on the inside they're made of aggressive cancer-causing agents," he added, as we glanced warily at the dishes before us, which had long before grown cold.

Returning to the tranquil past, he affirmed the architectural skills of his ancestors: "Nowadays, we think that we are more advanced than them. But in many ways, they were much smarter than we are, and had answers to many questions that are now lost." Citing the canals supposedly created by Yu the Great to control flooding of the Yellow River in prehistorical creation myths, he told me with a look of certainty that these canals and riverbeds remain strong to this day: truly superhuman feats that even the party-state with its massive engineering projects could never achieve. Ancient homes, he added, were built using interlocking logs, providing unparalleled structural stability: one could remain safe from earthquakes and any other external threats, a protection no longer afforded by contemporary structures. Pointing to the skyscrapers beyond the window, he asked, "How long will those buildings last? Apartments fall apart nowadays before you've even finished paying them off."

Already seeing the pattern of his monologue, I was not surprised when he followed his final comments about the importance of quiet solitude and meditative wandering within traditional Chinese culture with a simultaneously frustrated yet longing question: "Where can anyone find time or space to do that today?" Then, with a sigh, he told me that "the China out there today, the China that you are visiting, that is absolutely not the real China" (*bu shi zhenzheng de Zhongguo*).[3]

Suddenly, I was left trying to make sense of a member of a nationalist group informing me that his nation was at the moment not real. No preliminary research had given me even a hint of preparation for this unexpected comment. But this seemingly paradoxical statement upon closer examination came to reveal the fundamentally paradoxical core of the nationalist experience embodied in the Han Clothing Movement, which drives its affective attachments. Briefly reviewing this monologue, we see two completely different worlds emerging as inverted images of one another: the undeniable and uncontainable grandeur of the national past, with its elaborate clothing, healthy food, secure abodes, and peaceful quiet, standing in stark contrast to the bared buttocks, contaminated food, collapsing buildings, and chaotic and cramped cityscapes of the present. Although these two worlds are presented and indeed naturalized as a distinction between an ideal past and an imperfect present, these two worlds in fact represent the distinction between nationalist-identificatory fantasy and lived experience, laying bare the irresolvable split and corresponding tension between ideality and experiential reality that both structures and reproduces the identificatory experience. This book aims to illuminate these conflicted elementary structures of nationalist identification, autopoeitically producing and reproducing the nation as the difference between images and their never completely realized experience, in a perpetually enthralling process falsely essentialized as a stable identity.

THE ELEMENTARY STRUCTURES OF NATIONALISM: IDENTITY AS FANTASY

These impromptu reflections upon the "real China," although unexpected at first, in fact illuminate a central logic of nationalist-identificatory thought: a logic frequently on display in practice, yet largely overlooked in analyses. Scholarship on nationalism in recent decades frequently employs the concept of "imagined communities," based upon Benedict Anderson's influential eponymous volume, in which he famously proposes a redefinition of the nation "in an anthropological spirit" as "an imagined political community."[4] Yet if a nation is an imagined community, how is this community imagined?

Anderson's answer posits that the emergence of imagined communities is intertwined with the rise of "print capitalism," referring to the mass circulation of novels and particularly newspapers, also known as one-day bestsellers.[5] The simultaneity of space and time expressed in these media, as shown in the examples of a newspaper's front page or a novel's fictional

Manila dinner party, then produces a sense of "homogeneous, empty time" that structures national thinking.[6] The homogeneous time generated through these media is then reproduced on a daily basis through consumers' "mass ceremony" of reading newspapers, in which, according to Anderson, "each communicant is well aware that the ceremony he performs is being replicated simultaneously by thousands (or millions) of others of whose existence he is confident, yet of whose identity he has not the slightest notion."[7] Anderson's analysis of the nation thus envisions groups engaged in daily experiences of commonality, brought about by shifts in capitalist production, which create a sense of homogeneous, empty time.

This refreshingly novel interpretation of nationalism relies upon a conventionally materialist framework, wherein an imagined community is produced primarily through transformations of infrastructure that in turn affect the superstructure. As revealing and compelling as this analysis may be, one is nevertheless left to wonder whether national experience is really quite so bland and, indeed, devoid of imagining. Peter Sloterdijk has noted that the one phenomenon in the contemporary world that should truly astonish us all is the existence and perpetuation of these "large political bodies."[8] Is "homogeneous, empty time" then the real cornerstone of national identification, which fans the flames of nationalist affect the world over? Is national imagining composed primarily of imagining fellow members and one's communion with them, or is this perceived communion just the beginning of the imagining, which extends further into feats, images, and ideals far beyond the abilities of the individual and indeed any real collective? In his article "Internationality," Jonathan Rée examines these questions in a memorable comment upon Anderson's framework, observing that "it is surely only the coolest of nationalists who will pride themselves on belonging to a nation of newspaper readers."[9] Anderson's theory, which famously begins from the quandary of the passions of nationalism, does not in the end fully account for these passions: nationalism is indeed a daily phenomenon,[10] but it is not as a result necessarily quite so banal.

Such an analytical framework structured around repetitive ceremonies and empty calendrical time misrepresents the human relationship to imagined communities as ironically lacking in imagination, while at the same time misrepresenting fundamental characteristics of human interactions with media and the calendar. First, the act of reading a newspaper is not primarily a ceremony, but more importantly a conduit for distinguishing information and noninformation[11] and correspondingly receiving information on topics of interest and personal investment: an interaction between media and the mind. It is then not so much a ritualized imagining of a community of fellow readers as a structuring of this community around commonly recognized events, themes, and concerns, often in fact detached from readers' everyday lives. Second, in contrast to the notion of "empty calendrical time," we should note that calendars are not empty grids of equal dates, but rather textured grids featuring peaks and plateaus. Such peaks include annual holidays, such as Thanksgiving, in which one recounts and even reenacts American national mythologies, or major historical moments, such as centennials or bicentennials, in which the representation of national identity becomes a matter of primary importance,[12] or national megaevents in which national identity talk is greatly intensified.[13] Modern calendrical time is then anything but empty and monotonous. Third, just as media stories in the information age provide stimuli to think, reflect, imagine, discuss, and (increasingly) comment and share, so calendars also provide space upon which their owners can write, filling in empty blocks of space with their own content, whether burdensome or enjoyable: two categories of content that are also primary in lived experience, as the calendars on our home refrigerators and office walls attest. Such nuances of affective experience, however, are missing from the materialist imagined communities framework.

To overcome such omissions and develop a framework better suited to the imaginings and intensities of the imagined community, Rée playfully and usefully proposes redirecting the study of nationalism towards the field of the Lacanian imaginary to seek out the "wild longings and weird fantasies" therein.[14] In Lacanian terms, the imaginary is the locus of fantasy, which consists of images of wholeness that are "captating," a neologism that explicates the simultaneous processes of captivation and capture in the human relationship to these imaginary images.[15] Even a quick glance into such a nationalist imaginary reveals, unsurprisingly, that there is no nation in the world organized around mundane ideas or represented through bland imagery; instead, the essential ingredients of national imagery are, as Anthony Smith observes, "myths, symbols, and memories of ethnic origins, election, homeland, and the golden age"[16] alongside romanticized national characteristics, redemption and revenge for past injustices, and an ideal national order imagined as an essentialized wholeness. Rather than a relationship to fellow citizens generated through a daily ritual, then, imagined communities are produced through identifications with shared or contested but always imposing visions of what makes "us" who we are. And rather than the "homogeneous, empty time" portrayed as a central characteristic of the national experience, these identifications are structured around an often romanticized past and a promising future, marked in the present by cyclical peaks of excitement embodied in rituals of celebration: national days, national spectacles, mythical and historical commemorations, and count-downs to future accomplishments. Such attention to the imaginary and affect-laden nature of imagined communities, highlighting the zealous investments, wild fantasies, and obsessive identifications structured around a reliably grandiose national symbolic chain, then brings us closer to account-ing for the unrelenting passion of the nation form: the passion from which Anderson's analyses famously begin.[17]

Although fantasy is not a prominent component of Anderson's theoretical toolbox, its presence can nevertheless be detected in his examples, such that we might fruitfully reconsider his history of nationalism through the vantage point of desire. In his chapter "Creole Pioneers," Anderson examines the frus-trations created for "creoles" born of Spanish migrants in the new territories overseas. A sense of fellowship emerged around the "shared fatality of trans-Atlantic birth"[18] due to the resulting exclusion of these figures from positions of official importance in the Spanish bureaucracy. This exclusion and the thwarted aspirations that it produced in turn generated a logic that eventually provided the foundation for nationhood: for if the Creole born in the Americas was not a true Spaniard and was thus blocked from occupational passage to the metropole, then, the Creole pondered, the Spaniard born in Spain was also not a true American.[19] Accordingly, if the Spaniard has Spain, then the Creole should have his or her own home, a space in which he or she would be free from exclusion, a condition to be reserved for others, and hence better able to realize his or her aspirations, ideal life, or indeed, fantasies. The nation was thus from its inception in these elementary national structures a space of fantastic imaginings, an imaginarily secure sphere of one's own in which one would be able to realize one's aspirations. But most importantly in cultural-historical terms, as Anderson notes, the creoles engaged in this imag-ining possessed the political, cultural, and military means to enact this fan-tasy, leading to the establishment of the nation as a social institution founded in and enacting desire. Nations are then externalizations of personal identifi-catory desires that have become institutionalized and are then in turn inter-nalized as a supposedly existing reality, and thus as a social institution.[20]

This social institution, constructed in and through the imaginary,[21] has since spread across the world as a particularly resonant mode of structuring identifications and aspirations. On the other side of the globe, the empire-turned-nation of China has been organized over the past century around a number of diverging aspirations and fantasies expressed through the nation form: from a new Republic and New Culture to New Life, to Liberation and a People's Republic, to a Great Leap Forward, to a Cultural Revolution, to stability and development, to reunifying the motherland, to a century-long Olympic dream, to the awakening of a dragon, to the more recent focus upon five millennia of culture and tradition and the rise of a new great power, to, most recently, Xi Jinping's articulation of the China Dream (*Zhongguo meng*) and a "new silk road" and the myriad discussions that these concepts have generated.[22] Reading a state-run newspaper, viewing a news website, or watching television news in China is by no means a mundane ritual, despite its reliable and even almost formulaic predictability: one opens onto rapidly rising skyscrapers, skyrocketing GDP figures, speeding trains, aircraft carriers, space launches, smiling children, reports on drives to eliminate corruption and realize a "civilized citizenry," chest-thumping editorials claiming to represent the "voice of China," countdowns to the next national megaevent, and culturalist performances wrapped in romanticized discourses of "my country" (*wo guo*), five millennia of culture and tradition, unity, stability, harmony, development, rise, and inevitable celebration—familiar images from the nationalist imaginary. Expanding upon studies that revealingly analyze motivations of Chinese nationalism and national identity in the nation's relationship to such significant others as the United States, Taiwan, and Japan,[23] these internal images of the national self and national mission bring our attention to the equally important binary relationship between citizens and another significant other that frames the analyses that follow: the national imaginary itself.

Therefore, despite my reservations regarding aspects of Anderson's analytical framework, his attention to the role of media and communication in general is important for any analysis of imaginary communities and their national symbolic chains. Ziad Fahmy's articulation of "media capitalism" as an expansion of this framework beyond print media[24] provides a useful approach for analyzing the construction of the image of China, wherein the unique "Chinese characteristics" of the media produce a national-symbolic chain all too reliably drenched in splendor. As Niklas Luhmann observes, the mass media plays an essential role in self-schematization,[25] meaning the inevitably self-simplifying (yet also self-aggrandizing) process of forming an identity. Yet in the reception of national propaganda, the vision of the ironic and detached consumer who believes nothing in the state media beyond the date and the weather report is just as misplaced as the vision of the naïve consumer who simply believes and internalizes everything presented to him or her. Rather, a more accurate perspective can be found between these two untenable options through the vantage point of imaginary communities and collective fantasies, wherein the state media is neither a producer of reality nor a completely illegitimate fraud, but rather a central player in shaping aspirations, expectations, and emotions towards the nation and one's place therein: in Groys' terminology, they are "the designers of the unconscious,"[26] even if one's experience reliably fails to correspond to these designs.

Yet this issue of correspondence reminds us that although the aforementioned aspirations and fantasies are the cornerstone of imaginary communities, they remain at the same time their primary dilemma as a source of perpetual experiential difference. By incorporating individuals into larger than life fantasies that are envisioned as their own identity, national imaginaries capture people's imaginations, intertwine the self with these images, and heighten expectations to points unlikely to ever be realized. As a result, as we saw in the opening monologue contrasting a fantasy "real China" and the real China, these boundless imaginings unavoidably undermine themselves in practice, thereby producing the emotion characteristic of nationalist identification.

THE ELEMENTARY STRUCTURES OF NATIONALISM:
IDENTITY IN EXPERIENCE

The "creoles" featured in Anderson's history of nationalism eventually succeeded in realizing their national dream, moving beyond the seemingly arbitrary exclusion to which they had been subjected by the metropole. Yet despite their substantive contributions to the development of the nation as a form of social organization, the history that followed in the newly established nations of the Americas reminds us that not all was well in their new homes. For even after the emergence of the nation with its seeming reassurance of a proper and secure home of one's own for oneself and one's descendants, boundaries and limits to what one can achieve naturally remain plentiful, as do sources of disappointment, social contention, disharmony, exploitation, violence, and repression. This inevitable twist of fate within fantasy highlights the central contradiction of nations as imaginary communities: although such communities may be boundless in their imaginings, they inevitably have their limits in reality,[27] such that the fantasies upon which they are founded remain unattainable.

In contrast to the expansive grandeur of nationalist imaginaries described in the previous section, the second elementary structure of nationalism is then the limiting banality of everyday national experience. While nations are imagined, they are also lived; while nations are ideas, they are also geographic and existential spaces; while nations are thought as magnificent and always fulfilling fantasies seemingly detached from the mundane nature of everyday life, they are also experienced as an always considerably less fulfilling reality in which one lives out one's inevitably mundane everyday life. The organization of nations around such wonderful ideas as liberty, fraternity, equality, dignity, tradition, unity, or communism, which meant to create a world not only more just but indeed "beautiful,"[28] calling forth individuals as their object of identification, virtually guarantees that the experience of national reality will be a disappointment: while these national imaginaries are always greater than the self, temptingly appear to include oneself, and thus fulfill the self, they are also always greater than the nation-space itself and one's existence therein. If the national imaginary is expressive of a fantastic national pleasure principle that constantly raises our hopes beyond ourselves, the material world and its daily experience then produce an equally powerful national reality principle, a row of jagged rocks upon which one's waves of hopes constantly crash. A complete account of the nationalist experience thus must combine Smith's ethnosymbolic approach, capturing the imaginary nature of the imagined community, with Anderson's materialist approach, capturing the routine nature of the repetitively unfolded newspaper, drained of passion: whereas the nationalist imaginary that appears to include us is populated by "myths, symbols, and memories of ethnic origins, election, homeland, and the golden age,"[29] at the end of the day we are all just sitting on our couches reading our newspapers, or rather tablets, far removed from any myth or golden age. And although national ideals are indeed about far more than mundane rituals and homogeneous, empty time, we cannot forget that our life experience is indeed characterized by precisely such mundane rituals and homogeneous, empty time.

Therefore, while emphasizing the dominance of the imaginary in social institutions[30] and the corresponding significance of fantastic imaginaries in structuring the idea of the nation and constituting its appeal, I have no intention of providing a reductionist postmodern analysis in which "signifiers" or "language games" or "ontologies" somehow shape or in the last instance determine the world, or where a heroic "radical imaginary" is able to transform this world: after all, if this was actually the case, the world would undoubtedly be a far more pleasant place than it is, yielding to humanity's seemingly infinite optimism rather than the inevitable "dictatorship of the real."[31] Instead, I argue that while national imaginaries play an essential role in shaping one's thinking about the world, this world as experience inevitably fails to ever even begin to approach these imaginaries. For example, the greatness (*weida*) that is a characteristic trope of nationalist self-description in contemporary China, as seen in the monologue described above, produces passions and identifications in its ideal form, but can only ever undermine itself in practice: after all, is one's life ever truly "great"? Living in a nation is thus an experience in which one lives within national imaginaries, in that they contribute to one's sense of self (the "real China"), while also living outside of national imaginaries, in that the complexity, uncertainty, and dilemmas of one's lived experience never in fact correspond to these romanticized ideals (the reality of contemporary China). The fantasies expressed through the identificatory imagined community can only be maintained in and as the imaginary, a site of structural difference within identity perpetually blocked from crossing over into the actual experiential environment.

Such an experiential gap in existence is a cornerstone of social and cultural theory that has not, however, been applied to the question of nationalist identification. A century ago, Ferdinand de Saussure refuted the widespread assumption of an unproblematic relationship between a word and the thing to which it refers by articulating the distinction between the signifier and the signified.[32] Words and that which they describe do not naturally go together: our descriptions of a "nation" do not coherently correspond to its reality. Building upon this gap, Jacques Lacan proceeded to take this logic a step further in his analysis of the human relationship to fantasy, combining this linguistic insight with the psychodynamics of Freudian theory. Beyond noting the distinction between the signifier and the signified, Lacan importantly highlights the manner in which the signifying chain of language, existing as it does prior to any individual's entry into this chain, hovers over the signified and indeed over society in general, essentially taking on a life of its own.[33] The bar between the two items in Lacan's graph no longer serves only to highlight a previously overlooked distinction, but even more importantly a hierarchy wherein the signifier reigns over and above the signified, as well as a fundamentally impassable barrier.[34] Within the nationalist-identificatory experience, the wild associations of the nation form this imaginary-symbolic chain that precedes the individual, such that humans come to recognize, imagine, and express themselves through this chain of myths, heroes, ideal, cultures, and other fantasies. At the same time, although the use of this chain is premised upon the idea of identity, correspondence between the self (or the world) and this symbolic chain is never able to be realized. The basic motivation of national desire, then, is the search for an always unattainable and imaginary wholeness precluded by this founding division.

Accordingly, the images and signifiers surrounding the idea of the nation constitute a quite stable signifying chain of imagining, fusing the imaginary and the symbolic, whose representations precede residents and structure their self-understanding, presenting images of coherent wholeness often rendered as "culture," "tradition," or "national characteristics." Residents born into this national space inherit and actively invest themselves in these ideas as if they were entirely natural, unconstructed, and indeed their very own as their "culture" or "values." For example, as discussed above, state media images of China may portray rapidly rising skyscrapers, skyrocketing GDP figures, reports on drives to eliminate corruption, and celebrations of China's ancient civilization and the revitalization of traditional values; however, a citizen in actual experience is equally likely to face such growing challenges as rising living costs and housing prices, the continual expansion of corruption throughout the political system and society, and as described in the monologue at the start of this chapter, a sense of alienation from contemporary society and exclusion from perceived national ideals. As such, in a variation on Saussure and Lacan's graphs of the signifier and the signified, I propose that the relationship between national ideas and lived reality within the national space, the tension at the core of nationalism's affect and passion, can be represented as:

$$\frac{\text{National ideal}}{\text{Lived reality}}$$

This graph signifies the dual identity of nations as, on the one hand, ideas or fantasies, and on the other hand, actual spaces in which people live on a daily basis, a contradictory duality that makes national identity unique both as a signifier and as a signified experience. For while people envision themselves as living within this national signifier, with all of the wild and fantastic

FIGURE I. Sign in a Guangzhou underpass reads "vitality, happiness, harmony, and advancing forward."

associations that have accompanied it from its inception, they at the same time live in an actual geographical and experiential space thus labeled that nevertheless fails to correspond to the images present within this signifying chain, generating an alienating tension between image and substance at the core of nationalist experience, which is in turn structured around a self-perpetuating fantasy of fusion, or what we usually call identity.

The tension of this identificatory fantasy, which allows identity to both carry our greatest hopes and bear our greatest disappointments, can be seen in the dialogue from which this chapter began. The idea of China therein is associated on the one hand with elaborately tailored clothes that wrap individuals in an image of grandiosity, exquisite dining options that create ties to the past and in the present, secure abodes that safely shelter individuals from the potential risks of the outside world, and quiet, meditative reflection worthy of a sage. Yet on the other hand, this idea in practice is associated with bared buttocks and ill-fitting clothes, potentially poisonous or otherwise polluted sources of sustenance, over-priced homes that not only fail to provide security but indeed do not even last as long as mortgage payments, and a chaotic, cramped cityscape in which no refuge is provided. The nation is thus both more and less than itself. Adorno's analysis of the contradictions inherent within the concept of freedom, part of his critique of identity thinking, is instructive for considering the complex and even tortured human relationship to the national symbolic chain:

Emphatically conceived, the judgment that a man is free refers to the concept of freedom; but this concept in turn is more than is predicated of the man, and by other definitions the man is more than the concept of his freedom . . . The concept of freedom lags behind itself as soon as we apply it empirically. It is not what it says, then. But because it must always be also the concept of what it covers, it is to be confronted with what it covers. Such confrontation forces it to contradict itself.[35]

In a similar sense, one might say that the nation is not what "it" says (through the imaginary national symbolic chain, composed of people's communications about and imaginings of "the nation"). It lags behind itself, and is thus similarly forced to be perpetually contradictory in practice: as Sloterdijk has observed, "what is 'authentic' will always be something else."[36]

The nation as a space and experience is then both far more and far less than its imaginings and representations, a disjointed schema perpetuating a gap "between what things claim to be and what they are."[37] The pessoptimism that William Callahan intriguingly analyzes in his study of contemporary nationalism in China and its images of the past[38] is then not only a distinction between the century of humiliation and the promise of the future approached through the present, but also a continually reenacted divide in the present between the expectations of the nation and the realities of experience, producing a perpetual affective roller-coaster that drives the passions characteristic of nationalism. Yet it is precisely through this gap, insofar as "nonidentity is the secret telos of identification,"[39] that the idea of the nation is reproduced and reinvested as an object of identification and longing.

THE ELEMENTARY STRUCTURES OF NATIONALISM: IDENTITY AS A PARADOXICAL SYSTEM

Insofar as the gap between imagining and experience becomes the central tension of nationalism, it is also its driving force. Identification raises individuals upwards beyond their mundane daily lives as a fantasy of inclusion, yet at the same time brings them crashing back down into their daily lives in their experiential exclusion from this fantasy. Yet when one wants to believe in an entity and its power, for whatever reason, even counterevidence can be transformed into an affirmation and reinvestment in the sanctity of this power. Such a self-reproducing pattern can be seen in the longstanding tradition of theodicy, which was founded in the gap between the imagining of a just, loving, and all-powerful god and the actual experience of the world over which this god purportedly reigned: a world always containing what can only be characterized as ungodly elements. While this gap has throughout the centuries raised unavoidable questions about god's justness, love, and power, the inquiries thus produced reliably assumed that the only possible answer was to be found in the source of the original dilemma, as demonstrated by the fact that theodicy literally means "to justify god" (*theos dike*).[40] The dilemmas of experience producing doubts about the image of a loving god were then to be read as anomalies so as to reaffirm the imagining of a loving god, who naturally brought much-needed reassurance amid these very dilemmas of experience[41] by providing a sacred canopy of meaning;[42] the result was a self-reproducing thought system in which counterevidence to imaginings could only plausibly reproduce and reinforce these imaginings, finding the solution in the original problem. Since the downfall of god as the central subject of history and his replacement by the nation, a form of identificatory theodicy or identiodicy has similarly emerged from the gap between the heavenly imagining of the nation and the actual experience of this national space: a space that also inevitably contains highly discordant elements.

Despite their appeal, national narratives do not determine reality; yet despite their fundamental unreality, they continue to have an inherent appeal. In fact, I argue that it is precisely in their unreality that their appeal lies: the nation is a sacred form spread over a profane world, and the profane's resistance to the sacred intensifies the desire to weld one's identity to reality.[43] As in the practice of theodicy, identiodicy pushes back against the evidence, continually provided by the experiential reality of this profane world, of the unreliability of the ideally fulfilling yet always experientially unfulfilled national fantasy, reinterpreting continued disappointments, misfortunes, and injustices as anomalies that are not in fact properly part of the nation, notwithstanding their existence within the realm represented as national space. The common end goal of both theodicy and identiodicy is then to reaffirm an experientially untenable ideal, against all evidence, out of a desire to continue to believe: by finding the solution within the original source of the dilemma, the paradox is reproduced, and a perpetually inconclusive and unstable process is thereby misrepresented as a natural essence.

The elementary structures of national identity, combining both fantasy and experience, then form a simultaneously self-deconstructing and self-reproducing paradoxical system driven by affect and desire, and founded upon its own impossibility. This system is perpetuated, on the one hand, through the national imaginary, which is constantly expanding and intensifying in its contradictory relationship with reality, and on the other hand, through the individual, for whom the imaginary community is simultaneously supplement and lack. The relationship between the two is complex, perpetually troubled, and mutually reinforcing. Although many of us, in the process of becoming adults, submit to the fact that we will never become president nor succeed as a professional athlete or rock star or astronaut, nations as instituted systems of identity imaginings are not bound by the same humility: fantasy is, after all, their very foundation. As a medium of desire, the nation is unique by right of the sheer size of its promises and the hopes and investments that it creates, attaining a magnitude that is comparable only to religious mythologies and extreme political doctrines, with which the nation is in fact often intertwined.[44]

And thus, whereas it would appear most logical that the fulfillment of nationalist ideals or goals would be central to the national project, if the foregoing argument has proven anything decisively, it should be that the national experience is anything but logical; instead, it is an affect-laden and desire-based "community of feeling"[45] founded upon and fueled by imagining, passions, and even, unexpectedly, disappointment. Within this systematization of affective and thus voluntary servitude, the barrier between ideals and existence remains perpetually unable to be crossed; yet this does not stop one from trying. In fact, it is precisely this irresolvable contradiction, namely, the "antagonism between a tendency towards reality and towards illusion"[46] or a will to illusion[47] as identity[48] that drives and deepens the continued passionate attachment to this community among its members: the greater the distance between ideals and reality, the more that one becomes invested in these ideals as sources of support, confidence, and fulfillment. Insofar as the imaginary community exists only in the minds of individuals, while at the same time relying for its appeal upon the imaginary transcendence of the environment in which these individuals actually live, it is never to be found in individual experience. Yet the grandiosity of the national symbolic system produces investments that are only reaffirmed, strengthened, and expanded through the fundamental discordance of the system as a whole, meaning that even in its own failure, the imaginary community continues to live on affectively as a fantastic supplement to its own nonrealization, perpetuating nonidentity via the promise of identity.

Nations are then modes of collective organization through which people envision goals or ideals, but do not realize them:[49] the output of this national system, namely, its inevitable failure to live up to its imaginings, then functions in turn as its input,[50] driving its perpetuation. The lack of experiential fulfillment from essential national images constitutes at once the core contradiction and the driving force of nationalist sentiment, resulting in a reinvestment in and growing proliferation of these images: the elaborate and beautiful clothing, rich cuisine, secure and stable homes, and peace and quiet articulated in the opening monologue are simultaneously constituted as a desire, a disappointing lack, and an imaginary supplement. Returning then to my original expectations of nationalist discourse consisting of excessive praise for one's nation and people and equally passionate criticisms or denunciations of other nations and people, I have found that one is just as likely to hear an enthusiastic nationalist complain about his or her nation ("Things aren't going in the right direction") as celebrate his or her nation: yet either way, powerful sentiments and imaginings, eager to make one's nation great again, are certain to be present. These controlling sentiments illuminate Jonathan Rée's comment that although one might like to think that a nation belongs to oneself, as suggested by the stock phrase "my nation" (or in Chinese, *wo guo*), it would in fact be far more accurate to describe oneself as belonging to one's nation:[51] as much as one possesses nationality, the ideals and patriotic duties associated with this identity similarly possess oneself, capturing one's emotions in a captating cycle of imaginings, experiential disjunctions, and further imaginings, such that one is always seeking a chance to strive yet again towards its perpetually elusive realization.

After the articulation of the imagined community of the nation through the development of the printing press as described by Anderson, it has been precisely these sentiments that have kept these printing presses, and the affective attachments articulated and distributed therein and in the newer realm of cyberspace, in operation. The unshakeable sense of "That's not it"[52] inevitably leads the invested individual to the persistent question "Where is it?" The only possible answer provided to this question within the nationalist-identificatory system is to be found within this system itself, fueling the further production of imaginings and investments. The cultural media proposed by the Han Clothing Movement in response to this founding identificatory dilemma, labeled as "tradition" and imagined to provide a bridge from the contemporary reality of China to the "real China," are the focus of this book.

CONCLUSION

In this chapter, I have proposed a new approach to analyzing and understanding the nationalist experience, moving beyond the standard discussion of nations as imagined communities to an examination of imaginary communities as expressions and objects of desire. This shift seeks to account for the passions and investments that are central to national identification by considering the nation as a vehicle of fantasy, through which individuals come to seek collective fulfillment and transcendence from the mundane and often imperfect nature of their personal lives. Yet besides highlighting the overlooked imagining that constitutes the imagined community, this line of analysis further highlights the imaginary community's fundamentally dual and thus self-reproducing nature: the nation is experienced both as an imaginary space of seemingly limitless possibilities and as a space of mundane and inherently limited daily experience. This central contradiction of nationalism and identity, namely, the failure of experience to correspond to national fantasy, does not, however, detract from the passionate attachments to the national ideal, but instead only further reinforces these ideals as a perpetually elusive but also perpetually appealing goal. The result is a continually self-deconstructing yet also self-reproducing system, wherein the disappointment resulting from the heightened expectations promoted by the nationalist imaginary results in a reinvestment in and intensification of this nationalist imaginary, toward the goal of making this imaginary real.

I found that revitalizing the "real China," as articulated by my acquaintance in this early exchange, was a point of constant fascination and longing for participants in the Han Clothing Movement. Yet for all of the talk of China, the key to this goal of revitalization could only be realized through the centerpiece of the movement, the Han, perceived by movement participants be the completely unproblematic equivalent of the Chinese nation itself. The next chapter thus turns from the nationalist question of the real China to movement participants' uncertain experience of majority identity, a dilemma which I call Han trouble. Within this narrative, contemporary China can only be a downtrodden imitation of its ideal self because the Han remains a downtrodden imitation of its imagined former self: by articulating an ethnic identity for the formerly blank and unmarked default nationality, movement participants find themselves at the center of China's always elusive process of national rejuvenation.

TWO

Han Trouble and the Ethnic Cure

BEHIND THE SEEMINGLY STABLE CONCEPT of national identity, the preceding analyses have traced infinite gaps that systematically reproduce the national ideal as a purportedly essential yet never realized imaginary reality. Expanding this framework, this chapter proceeds to examine two core and intertwined manifestations of proper and real Chineseness according to Han Clothing Movement participants: the Han race and its traditions. Just as the cycle of fantastic imagining and reality present in nationalist identity complicates the idea of the nation, so the processes involved in the movement's production of Han-ness and tradition provide a novel vantage point for analyzing these concepts.

Han-ness, officially constructed as unmarked in relation to "minorities," is ironically reconstructed in movement discourses according to the representational tropes through which minorities are typically represented in mainstream Han culture. In a process that I call ethnicization, movement participants thus draw upon imaginings of already disempowered minority figures as a means to further empower the majority. This repressed borrowing at the core of the movement's articulation of Han-ness in turn explains movement participants' eager self-differentiation from, and active hostility to, China's minority nationalities as "barbarians."

Tradition, also imagined to be unchanging and essential to the Han, is in reality actively constructed as a fantasy inversion of the present, while at the same time appearing as a stabilizing and even eternal source of identity. Tradition's appeal then lies in its simultaneous combination of active identity construction combined with its appearance as a natural, unconstructed reality passed down from one generation to the next.

34

Before unfolding these analyses, a brief history of the Han Clothing Movement will provide context for this reexamination of Han-ness and tradition in the construction of the movement's "real China."

A BRIEF HISTORY OF THE HAN CLOTHING MOVEMENT: HAN-NESS, TRADITION, AND THE REVITALIZATION OF CHINA

According to enthusiasts of the Han Clothing Movement, the dilemma of today's China, meaning its fundamental unreality, was on full display in the fall of 2001, when leaders from across the Asia-Pacific Region gathered in the city of Shanghai for an Asia-Pacific Economic Cooperation (APEC) Ministerial Meeting. Just a month after the attacks of September 11, this event's theme was, appropriately, "meeting new challenges in the new century." Unbeknownst to organizers and participants, however, one photo opportunity at this meeting was soon to produce a movement that would meet the new challenges of this new century by seeking answers from past centuries.

At each APEC meeting throughout the years, attendees have been given "local dress" from the host region, in a well-documented and cringe-worthy tradition that begin in 1993 when Bill Clinton handed out "bomber jackets" during a summit in Seattle.[1] Accordingly, at the 2001 meeting, leaders gathered for a photo opportunity in a traditional-looking outfit referred to as "the outfit of the Tang" (*tangzhuang*). Curious photos of the leaders collectively smiling in their newly acquired outfits, and of George W. Bush, Jiang Zemin, and Vladimir Putin chatting earnestly in the "outfit of the Tang," quickly spread across official media, the Sinophone Internet, and around the world as representations of China and Chinese tradition.[2] One problem, however, emerged within this representation: the outfit of the Tang was not in fact a product of the distant era known as the Tang Dynasty (618 C.E.–907 C.E.), often celebrated as one of the pinnacles of traditional Chinese civilization. Despite the seeming precision of this name, the "outfit of the Tang" is in fact a vague term used to refer to a variety of Chinese-style clothing, a concept first constructed by Chinese overseas during the late Qing Dynasty in relation to "Western clothing" (*xizhuang*). More specifically, the outfit on display at APEC was known as the *magua*, an originally Manchu style of clothing that spread throughout broader Chinese society during the Manchu

FIGURE 2. Enthusiasts wearing Han Clothing in Beijing.

dominated Qing Dynasty (1644–1911 C.E.).[3] Ninety years after the fall of the Qing, Chineseness was thus being represented on a national and global stage in this case through what could be viewed, in a nationalist and essentialist lens, as the clothing of a peripheral or "barbarian" people at best, or even for some, the imposition of an external conquering power.

Some local viewers thus saw in this kitschy photo opportunity a disturbing attempt to represent and indeed embody Chineseness through disgraceful "barbarian" clothing: *Manfu*, or Manchu clothing, thus provided a spark, to borrow Maoist terminology, which started a Han prairie fire. The answer to *Manfu* was soon found in *Hanfu*, or Han Clothing. According to movement histories, a now untraceable post (or series of posts) was reportedly distributed on a number of popular Chinese BBS forums in response to the APEC photo-op, criticizing the representation of China on the global stage through the Manchu derived *magua*. This post reportedly declared that the most outrageous aspect of this sartorial slight was the simple fact that there was a far more suitable choice for representing China: a traditional style of clothing, purportedly first created at the time of the mythical figure the Yellow Emperor and worn for millennia by the Han, the core of Chinese civilization. This clothing, portrayed in sketches attached to the post, was characterized by broad sleeves and flowing robes decorated with brilliant colors and elaborate designs, and was known simply as "Han Clothing," or the traditional clothing of the Han.

The suggestion that the Han, China's previously unmarked majority, also had "traditional clothing" created a sensation online. Soon numerous online discussion boards appeared focused on this new yet ancient idea of Han Clothing. The best known of these forums in which interested parties gathered is Hanwang, or the Han Network, located at the easy to remember addresses www.hanminzu.com and www.hanminzu.org: *hanminzu* here refers to *Han minzu*, the pinyin for "Han nationality" or "Han race." For full dramatic effect, the site has the large character for "Han" displayed prominently at the top of the page, while also rendering the date in years since the birth of the mythical Yellow Emperor, representing 2017 as the 4,728th year of the Yellow Emperor. The site is home to a virtual encyclopedia of commentaries on Han Clothing and culture, covering such aspects as sartorial design, history, traditional literature, calligraphy and art, philosophy and religious belief, politics, military affairs, ritual and etiquette, architecture, and medicine. Other sites that have also left their mark upon the development of the Han Clothing Movement amid a series of online internecine squabbles include Chinese Traditional Sartorial Culture, Heavenly Han National Culture, Chinese Revitalization, Baidu's Han Clothing forum, Hanweiyang, Hanyifang, and the Chinese National Studies website.[4]

Such online forums, as virtual gathering points for like-minded individuals, gradually became the platform for Han Clothing's transition from virtual sketches to material reality, as well as for the movement's attempted social reconstruction of reality toward its imagining of the real China. Some enthusiasts began using these sites to exchange ideas on how to make one's own Han Clothing, and to share personal photos of actual pieces of Han Clothing sewn in accordance with online sketches, externalizing what had previously only been an illustrated mode of fantasy. In an even more significant step, these forums were also the sites on which enthusiasts first posted photos of themselves wearing Han Clothing in public spaces. The most famous of such initial attempts was by Wang Letian of the city of Zhengzhou in Henan Province, who posted photographs of his 2003 journey under the pseudonym "Zhuangzhi Lingyun": this name is not only a Chinese idiom meaning "great aspirations," but also interestingly the Chinese title for Tom Cruise's 1986 blockbuster film *Top Gun*. Like the sketches described above,

Wang's "maverick" photographs had an awakening effect upon viewers: the images were distributed widely on Han Clothing websites, and his actions were imitated in the weeks that followed in numerous Chinese cities, objectivizing Han Clothing as an actually existing reality in sites across the country, so that the fantasy ideals captured in these newly sewn material forms could in turn be recognized and internalized as a more authentic articulation of one's self. In this movement from ideas to materials to images to the self, what we now know as the Han Clothing Movement was established.

The Chinese name for the Han Clothing Movement, *Hanfu yundong*, highlights the two main elements of this sociocultural phenomenon. On the one hand, as suggested by the term *Hanfu* (Han Clothing), the movement is dedicated to a rewriting of Chinese history around the central figure of the Han and a reinvention of Han traditions in the present. On the other hand, as indicated by the term *yundong* (movement), this social group is a movement in the Maoist sense insofar as it is dedicated to reshaping the world in its particular aesthetic image.[5] Local Han Clothing associations, rather than surrounding the cities from the countryside (*nongcun baowei chengshi*), instead wage a guerilla warfare of imaginaries from within the enemy's territory, surrounding disillusioning urban reality with transcendent fantasy.

Hanfu (Han Clothing)

Beginning from the "Han Clothing" (*Hanfu*) aspect of the Han Clothing Movement, movement narratives engage in the type of rewriting of history that has characterized the founding of each new dynasty, all of the way from the Qin rewriting of history[6] through the Chinese Communist Party's renarration of history around "class struggle"[7] and subsequently patriotism.[8] The subject of history in this case, however, is the Han. Han Clothing first emerged in the era of the Yellow Emperor who, as a mythical progenitor of the Han race, is naturally located at the beginning of history and is thus also the inventor of clothing himself. In the dynasties that followed, movement narratives assert that members of the Han race uniformly wore Han Clothing throughout these eras until the arrival of the Qing. As such, Han Clothing is envisioned as having been present at all of the great moments in Chinese history: the establishment of the empire under Qinshihuang, the emergence and expansion of the Silk Road, the flourishing eras of the Han and the Tang dynasties, the invention of the compass and paper, and all of the moments in between. There is no clear history indicating that there was any such apparel in existence under the name Han Clothing, but as an imaginary tradition[9] envisioned as having been present at and thus providing links to the many celebrated moments in Chinese history, Han Clothing thus becomes a tradition intertwined with greatness.

Yet precisely as a result of this greatness, Han Clothing Movement narratives also need to explain how this clothing style came to be forgotten by history and replaced by alien and thus inferior forms of clothing—a forgetting that even extends to official cases of national representation, as seen at APEC. The main historical turning point within Han Clothing Movement narratives of modern Chineseness is not, as in official histories, the Treaty of Nanking in 1842 or the founding of the Chinese Communist Party in 1921. Rather, movement narratives focus upon the conquest of China by the Manchu Qing Dynasty in 1644, when Prince Dorgon led his banner armies past the Shanhai Pass to conquer China. Alleging that the Manchu rulers were determined to break the Han's spirit and completely subordinate the Han to alien Manchu dominance, movement narratives re-create the famous Qing queue order of 1645, in which all male subjects were required to shave their hair into the distinctive queue style, as a queue-cum-clothing order (*tifa yifu*) that eliminated Han Clothing by force: in a variation on the well-known choice between keeping one's hair and keeping one's head, those who insisted upon wearing Han Clothing, according to this narrative, were slaughtered by the new Manchu ruling class.

Myth is rendered here as historical memory. Historian Edward J. M. Rhoads, tracing sartorial policy in the Qing Dynasty, notes that the adoption of Manchu clothing was only required of the male scholar-official elite: "The great majority of Han men were free to continue to dress as they had during the Ming."[10] Similarly, no Han women were required to adopt Manchu dress.[11] Although sartorial policy was then in reality not a matter of great concern for the Qing, the imagined forcible suppression of "Han Clothing" in this era serves as a crucial explanatory foothold for contemporary subjects' unfamiliarity with this invented tradition, attributing this disappearance to predatory outsiders. And at a deeper level, as I will discuss in more detail below, this pseudohistorical disappearance of Han Clothing furthermore narratively structures the challenges of China's modern history around the medium of Han Clothing, linking the perceived downfall of China from its imperial status as a "land of rites and etiquette" to this imaginary moment of the suppression of Han Clothing. Beyond explaining Han Clothing and its disappearance, this myth then in a case of multilayered synecdoche makes

Han Clothing and its fate, as representative of the Han and its fate, the key to understanding China and its fate: both its perceived glorious past, as well as the long, winding, and often tortuous road of modern history.

Yundong (Movement)

In response to the dilemma of the present, participants seek to actively promote their aestheticized vision of Han-ness against the disappointments of reality. The primary drivers of these Han-centric efforts have been associations established in cities across the country since 2003, focused particularly in the urban coastal areas, but also existing in the interior. Examples of cities with one or more Han Clothing Movement associations include Shenzhen, Dongguan, Guangzhou, Foshan, Xiamen, Hangzhou, Shanghai, Suzhou, Nanjing, Wuhan, Hefei, Zhengzhou, Jinan, Beijing, Tianjin, Xi'an, Chengdu, Chongqing, and Kunming. These associations, in my experiences in numerous cities, are composed of young and fairly well-educated professionals, with a roughly 1:1 proportion of men and women participating.[12] Associations host weekend gatherings either once or twice a month, or in some cases weekly, to bring together like-minded people and promote traditional Han culture. Such weekend activities can take the form of visits to museums, temples, teahouses, or parks, the reenactment of traditional rituals, promotional efforts seeking visibility and potential converts in crowded shopping districts, participation in ethnic clothing shows, traditional music concerts, and self-produced variety shows. Whatever the event may be on any given week, Han Clothing is an essential fixture at movement activities, serving as a representative of Han tradition and the beauty of the "real China."

The goals of the Han Clothing Movement are primarily based in a confidence that revitalizing Han Clothing and associated traditions through these events will in turn revitalize traditional culture, returning to the ancient ideal of the "land of rites and etiquette" (*liyi zhi bang*) and thus realizing the real China. Participants therefore demonstrate a considerable amount of patience with regards to the movement's goals, avoiding the type of political action that would provoke an antagonistic response from the authorities: there is no annual meeting nor broader organizational planning, and most are content to simply wear Han Clothing, engage in traditional rituals and related activities, and promote these ideas to others. The "movement" aspect of the movement thus exists in a notably reserved relationship with the Chinese government, which works to the movement's advantage. Discussing "what was to be done" to raise Han Clothing's profile during the 2010 Asian Games in Guangzhou, the local group's consensus was simple and straightforward: "We should do nothing!" Such political reticence in relation to the anaconda in the chandelier,[13] combined with the movement's embrace of the type of insular nationalism and political conservatism that is currently at the core of Chinese state ideology, makes the Han Clothing Movement a unique case in contemporary China as a nationwide social movement that even goes so far as to violate the official ethnic policy of "diversity" while still being largely officially tolerated.

Despite this emphasis upon the scattered local promotion of traditional culture, surrounding reality with aestheticized fantasy, there have been occasional moments over the past decade in which the Han Clothing Movement emerged onto the national stage, prompting broader discussion. In 2006, a student in Wuhan completing his doctoral studies proposed that he be allowed to wear Han Clothing to his graduation, as an external embodiment of Chinese culture and as a recognition of the importance of Chinese culture in the academic world.[14] Although this move generated media and online discussion at the time, few have followed in this student's footsteps in the years since. In March of 2007, Ye Hongming, a representative to the National People's Congress, suggested that Han Clothing be recognized as China's "national clothing."[15] His proposal stated that "the Han nationality [*Han minzu*] is the core of the Chinese nationality [*Zhonghua minzu*]; the Han language [*Hanyu*, Chinese] is the national language [*guoyu*] of China; thus, to acknowledge Han Clothing [*Hanfu*] as our national clothing [*guofu*] on the one hand represents our Han nationality's traditions while on the other hand embodying our historical cultural transformations."[16] Although successfully rendering explicit the majoritarian assumptions within the official discourse of unity within diversity (*duoyuan yiti*), this proposal otherwise had no real-world effects. Soon thereafter, an online petition addressed to the Beijing Olympic Committee and signed by a hundred scholars sought Han Clothing's designation as the Chinese team's official outfit at the 2008 Beijing Olympics' opening ceremony.[17] This petition was ignored. And again in 2013 and 2014, participants in the National People's Congress proposed legislation on Han Clothing, again with no results.[18]

The Han Clothing Movement is then not a movement in the conventional sense of the term. Its main area of focus is not in the unpredictable

FIGURE 3. Image of China's fifty-six nationalities.

and cutthroat world of Chinese politics: attempts to elevate Han Clothing to national clothing have repeatedly produced zero results. The real focus of the Han Clothing Movement, as noted above, is the daily aestheticized struggle against the disillusioning dictatorship of the real, developing in cities across the country on a daily basis. The foundational ideas in this fight are the Han and their tradition, which are assumed to provide the foundations for a rediscovery of the "real China." Yet as I argue in the analyses that follow, each of these ideas is intertwined with its polar opposite: the ethnic rearticulation of the Han majority relies upon imaginings of minorities; the ideals of the past are primarily inversions of the present; and the "real" China toward which participants strive is primarily an imaginary, redeeming image of China developed in response to the disappointments of reality. The Han-ness, tradition, and Chineseness heralded by members of the Han Clothing Movement are thus both symptoms of and fleeting, illusory cures for increasingly pressing ethnic, social, and national dilemmas in China today, generating a self-reproducing system typically referred to as "the Han" and "China."

FIGURE 4. The Han within the national family (close-up of figure 3).

HAN TROUBLE: RECONSIDERING
ETHNIC RELATIONS

Early in my fieldwork, a group of friends in Guangzhou shared a PowerPoint presentation detailing the lengthy history of Han Clothing and the recent rise of the Han Clothing Movement. One of the first images in the presentation featured members of the official fifty-six nationalities of China, fittingly posing in the shape of the numeral "56." Each figure in the image is conveniently marked by a distinct form of ethnic clothing, one of the primary media through which identity is represented in China today.[19] This panorama of distinct outfits, shaping the "magic number" of ethnicity,[20] 56, is furthermore held within the uniting embrace of a shadow in the shape of the People's Republic, projected upon a sea of vibrant green grass. Signaling their presumed joyful situation within the bosom of the nation, each nationality's representative displays a smile and waves enthusiastically towards the viewer.

My informants, however, did not smile back. Instead, they zoomed in on the image to show me the true object of their interest: their designated representative from "the Han" in this ethnic panorama. If we look carefully, amid the sensory-stimulating sea of vibrant and colorful costumes, we will find the designated Han figure dressed quite unimpressively in a T-shirt, shorts, and sneakers.

Far removed from the costumes surrounding him, as well as even the superficially ascetic yet heroically aesthetic garb of the Maoist era, such a banal representation was not, however, unexpected: it is precisely through such normal and nonexotic representations that the Han majority is constructed as the civilizational standard, both modern and unmarked. This image in fact perfectly embodies the relational or boundary-based theory of ethnicity, first articulated by Fredrik Barth in his introduction to the collection *Ethnic Groups and Boundaries*, and highly influential upon studies of ethnicity in China. In brief, Barth argues against the once common-sense idea that ethnic groups are discrete cultures with unique characteristics developed in isolation from one another, showing instead how ethnicities evolve in interaction between peoples, producing ascriptive and exclusive groups only through their relations with one another.[21] Ethnic groups thus are not composed of unchanging ethnic characteristics, nor are they maintained through the transmission of characteristics over time; rather, ethnic identity depends upon the establishment and maintenance of boundaries between a group and others. In light of these findings, Barth states that "the critical focus of investigation [of ethnic groups] from this point of view becomes the ethnic *boundary* that defines the group, not the cultural stuff that it encloses."[22] This mode of analysis importantly moves beyond the essentialist understanding of identity, highlighting its inherently relational nature.

Such a relational understanding of identity has been highly influential upon analyses of ethnic representation along the majority-minority binary in China in recent decades. Within standard representations, state-defined minorities are invariably portrayed, without a hint of subtlety, as simple and primitive people.[23] According to the burdensome orthodox Morganian-Marxist-Stalinist framework of evolutionary history in which difference is inscribed in post-1949 China, there are five stages of history (primitive communism, slave society, feudalism, capitalism, socialism/communism), and the various minority nationalities are distributed along these historical stages in the present, as "living fossils" (*huo huashi*) of past forms of social organization.[24] It is because they are imagined as visitors from another simpler era in the present that minorities are so frequently portrayed as "colorful" and "exotic":[25] whether displaying their elaborate costumes or participating in equally elaborate traditional cultural festivals, and whether dancing before CCTV's cameras for the annual Chinese New Year celebration or joining in the "inevitable dancing in a circle"[26] for spectators' enjoyment, typical representations of China's minorities are lacking in neither color nor customs. Dancing, celebrating, and living in a bygone era, minorities are portrayed as "simple people" whose lives have yet to be impacted by the disconcerting course of history.

Portraying and speaking of minority lifestyles in this manner does not of course reflect the lived realities of China's non-Han populations, but rather constructs a particularly flattering image of the majority by contrast. Thus, when China's minorities are portrayed as primitive, ancient, or "closer to nature," as they inevitably are, the Han majority is by contrast portrayed along this boundary as advanced and modern elder brothers;[27] when minorities are portrayed as being occupied by "festivals, costumes, and the inevitable dancing in a circle,"[28] the Han are busy "doing things" at the "forefront of development and civilization."[29] When minorities are portrayed as "exotic," the Han majority is characterized as normal; and when minorities are envisioned as "marked" (by exotic customs or costumes), the Han majority is by contrast constructed as "unmarked."[30] Through a binary, boundary-based relationship with "the minorities," a reliably flattering "majority discourse"[31] is produced, wherein the Han is placed teleologically at the forefront of China's development, embodying both modernity and civilization.

None of this will be unexpected or even in any way novel to readers familiar with ethnic representation in China today. Instead, what was unexpected that day in Guangzhou was my informants' frustrated response to this standard image of ethnic relations with which we are all so familiar. The sight of the Han, purportedly the vanguard of the nation, standing amid a gathering of exquisitely dressed nationalities in a T-shirt and sneakers, and thereby representing modernity in relation to primitive minorities, raised a quandary that I would hear repeated throughout my research: "Is this what the Han really looks like? This is not the real Han. All of the other nationalities have their own ethnic clothing. What about the Han?" Just as the unreflective directness of this kitschy image reveals the official framework of identity, so the directness of this question reveals the concerns driving the Han Clothing Movement.

Considering the flattering ways in which the binaries of ethnic representation work in favor of the Han, why were my informants so outraged? To understand this response, it is necessary to introduce another relationship into the relational study of identity. Barth's insights, as well as the analyses and critiques of ethnic representations that have followed in his footsteps, importantly denaturalize once taken-for-granted majority-minority representations by highlighting their construction around relational binaries, as well as allowing us to recognize the inequality that is essentialized and thus symbolically and actually reproduced through such binary representations. Yet in its focus upon the relationship between ethnicities, this framework overlooks another equally important relationship, highlighted by my informants' response to the standard image of the Han described above: the boundary between members of an identity group and the idea of that identity, or more specifically their relationship to their "own" representation, a relationship that is never straightforward or untroubled. This is the "cultural stuff" that Barth's boundary-based analyses usefully de-essentialized; yet the de-essentialization of "ethnic characteristics," although theoretically significant, certainly has not resulted in such imagined ethnic characteristics being any less significant in people's practical understanding of themselves and their world. Focusing solely upon the relationship between ethnicities in the production of ethnic identity, such as the majority-minority relationship in Han-ness, thus produces a theoretical blind spot: the equally complex and significant relationship of those labeled "Han" to the content of "Han-ness."

In light of this perspective, the attention given in recent decades to the ways in which ethnic representations are constructed in favor of an advanced, modern, and "unmarked" Han overlooks an important fact: being advanced, modern, and normal is often painfully boring, as the Han representative in the colorful ethnic photograph above could undoubtedly attest. In the relationship between nationalities within the official ethnic structure, it is the lack of ethnicity that makes the Han the default majority. Yet in the relationship of members of this group to its representation, it is precisely this lack of ethnicity that ironically undermines the presumed power of this label for its subjects, dethroning what would otherwise be the master signifier[32] of identity. My interlocutors' inquiry regarding the standard representation of

FIGURE 5. A propaganda poster advocating "solidarity" reflects conventional majority and minority representations via clothing and skin color, Haikou.

Han-ness—namely, "is this what the Han looks like"—significantly brings this experiential factor back into consideration, expressing their relationship to Han-ness and their desire to make the unmarked, disenchanted, and modern Han newly marked, enchanted, and most importantly enjoyable.

As a person identified by the label "Han" in contemporary China, one derives from this label no unique characteristics to be preserved, no unique markings to display, no clothing to admire or to be admired in, and no Han show in which the majority can be placed on display before a captivated audience: modernity, normality, and unmarkedness after all do not make for a very exciting show. While these characteristics distinguish representations of the Han from the one-dimensional portrayals of minorities trapped within inconvenient costumes suited only for constant cultural celebrations, they nevertheless present a similarly one-dimensional and thus constraining vision of Han-ness, suited only, in step with the disenchanted atmosphere of the era, for such bland and practical concerns as "doing business" (*zuo shengyi*): the Han man's burden.[33] As the presumed core of the Chinese nation, some members of the Han have come to expect a more compelling vision. I call this conundrum Han trouble,[34] wherein Han-ness is primarily embodied through a bland lack of any performance, constructed in T-shirts and sneakers in relation to colorful and spirited minority images, a flattering binary that nevertheless lacks any "color" on the Han side of the formula.

The question, "Is this what the Han looks like?" as stated by my interlocutors, is thus the most succinct expression of the driving motivations of Han trouble within the movement, as well as the most common, having been repeated throughout my research. For this question clearly presumes its own answer: namely, "No." Yet beyond simply saying "No," as some other equally emotive bestselling nationalist authors are known to do,[35] movement participants are engaged in the task of constructing a new (although purportedly eternal) vision of Han-ness. And surprisingly, this vision, reshaping the relationship between members of the Han and the idea of their identity, draws heavily upon already existent imaginings of minorities as "ethnic," in a process of rearticulating the majority that I call ethnicization.

ETHNIC TRANSFERENCE AND THE MINORITY ORIGINS OF THE HAN

In her study of the origins of the Zhuang and ethnic politics in modern China, Katherine Palmer Kaup meticulously traces the top-down creation of the virtually nonexistent "Zhuang nationality" in Guangxi in the 1950s and its path to the present.[36] The Han Clothing Movement, in its emergence over the past decade, has been engaged in a similar, albeit largely bottom-up project of re-creating the Han. This re-creation of the Han claims to only be revitalizing an eternal and natural tradition derived from an ancient and eternal Han race, intrinsic to its descendants. Yet I argue that this reconstruction is in fact a new creation drawing unexpectedly upon official representations of minorities as references for what characteristics a real ethnic

FIGURE 6. Ethnic clothing for rent, Splendid China, Shenzhen. Sign reads "Pass through cultures and time, experience ethnic style."

identity should possess. The question repeatedly raised by my informants in response to the image of the 56 nationalities—"What about the Han?"—in fact ever so subtly points to minorities as possessing what the Han want, or, according to movement discourses, need. Thus, just when the question of the majority's relationship to its self-image brings us beyond relational binaries of the majority-minority relationship, it also immediately brings us back to this relationship, for in attempting to re-create the Han as "ethnic" (*you minzu tese*), the Han Clothing Movement ironically derives its understanding of the "ethnic" from imaginings of the minority nationalities, the former sole possessors of said attributes.

Considering the consistent representation of minorities through fetishized images of clothing, customs, and dance shows, it is significant to note that this Han-ist movement similarly focuses its attention in representing the Han precisely upon clothing, customs, and performance, articulating the once default majority through acts of ethnic transference. Against the standard image of Han-ness presented in catalogs of ethnic clothing,[37] featuring modern Han citizens in "Western suits," sweaters, sneakers, or jeans that differentiate them from minorities' more "traditional" ethnic clothing, the

Han Clothing Movement promotes an image of the Han draped throughout history in an elaborate, colorful ethnic uniform, similar yet also prior and thus superior to fetishized minority clothing. The purported rediscovery of this component of ethnicization provides an eternal external marker designating one's presumed essential Han-ness, while at the same time imaginarily projecting that marker backwards across the millennia, far prior to the modern emergence of the concept of a Han nationality.

And against the standard image of the Han as unmarked and default, the movement further produces a Han with enjoyable customs and characteristics "just like" the minorities. A careful index is kept within movement circles of properly Han activities, such as engaging in ritual, playing traditional instruments like the *guqin*, writing calligraphy, studying the classics, papercutting, embroidery, and archery, all of which are traditional like imagined minority cultural practices, yet at the same time also clearly civilized and distinguished activities. And against the standard casting of the Han as the viewer of ethnic performances by "minorities," movement participants eagerly promote performances that bring the Han on stage in ethnic shows, a topic discussed in more detail in the final section of this chapter. Yet most revealingly, minorities are frequently discussed among movement participants not only for their customs and clothing but also for their perceived ethnic unity and strength, supposedly derived from the preservation of their way of life. Reminiscent of Baumann's structural reinterpretation of Orientalism, wherein "what is good in us is still bad in them, but what got twisted in us still remains straight in them,"[38] a Han Clothing activist in Guangzhou told me that despite their backwardness, there was one area in which minorities were particularly adept: preserving their cultures and thus remaining united. In this process of ethnicization designed to revitalize the Han, members of the majority ironically identify with and build upon the "ethnicity" of minorities, who are imagined to possess the tradition and customs, and thus the unity, strength, and fulfillment that the Han is perceived as lacking.

If, as Dru Gladney observes, "societies make and mark their majorities and minorities under specific historical, political, and social circumstances,"[39] the members of these majorities and minorities also continually remake, remark, and indeed re-create themselves and their collective identities with shifting historical, political, and social developments. The Han Clothing Movement is one example of such remaking and remarking, highlighting the potentially dynamic relationship between standard ethnic representation and the ethnic subject supposedly denoted therein. Within this relationship, the movement is a product of a founding lack in the modern Han, characterized as default, standard, and unmarked: as is often the case with majorities the world over, that which makes the Han the majority in relation to "the ethnic" also makes it dreadfully plain and boring as an identity. Thus, only by becoming "ethnic," in the distinctly Chinese sense of having ethnic clothing and customs, can members of the Han overcome the blandness of majority identity to truly identify with their ideal image of "the Han." The movement's focus upon Han identity thus takes an unexpected detour through tropes of minority representation, with surprising results: on the one hand, the new and eternal Han is modeled on the minorities from which they differentiate themselves as Han, while on the other hand this ethnic transference and borrowing is repressed through the articulation of an often violent dislike for the "barbarians" from whom the Han learned ethnicity.

In the next section, I turn to an analysis of the Han Clothing Movement's focus upon ancient tradition, which, upon closer examination, is equally unexpectedly derived primarily from the experiences of the present.

THE INVENTION OF TRADITION AS INVERSION OF THE PRESENT

"Did you know that the Chinese people had a cure for cancer centuries ago?" In social science research, the standard assumption in the research process is that the researcher will ask questions, and that people participating in the project, as "informants" or "interlocutors" or whatever term we now use for the people with whom we speak, will respond. Yet more often than not, my interviews began with questions like this, posed by my interviewees towards me. Setting aside for the moment whatever questions I had prepared on whatever topic I may have once considered to be potentially significant, I happily succumbed to these unexpected interjections that methodologically became far more revealing of the hopes, anxieties, and aspirations of participants in the Han Clothing Movement.

Cancer is a fate that haunts us all, and it particularly haunts those of us living in environments of enhanced anxiety regarding the purity of air, foods, and fluids, as is the case in contemporary urban China. I was thus surprised to be informed with such confidence one afternoon that all of this anxiety was misplaced, so long as one was in touch with tradition. The cure for cancer could be supposedly found therein in an item known as *qingaitiao*: a stick that looks like thick incense, made of the plant *Artemisia argyi*, which can be lit and held over areas of the body believed to be afflicted with illness in traditional Chinese medical practice. Undoubtedly sensing my disbelief that the cure for cancer, eagerly sought for decades, was available for 5 yuan (less than US$1) on Taobao, the Chinese equivalent of Ebay, my acquaintance happily provided a concrete example. He knew a woman who had been diagnosed with late-stage lymphoma; her illness had already reached a point at which it was too late for hospital treatment. Yet in his opinion, this lateness had saved her: hospital treatment, he asserted, could do nothing but make the situation worse. Instead, my interlocutor revealed *qingaitiao* to her as an effective, homeopathic, traditional cure for cancer.

Another question: "But how does it cure cancer?" Responding to his own inquiry, he informs me that the cancer-curing properties of *qingaitiao* are to be found in the rhythm at which it burns and releases curing smoke onto the affected area. According to his description, this burning process mimics the rhythm of a mother's heartbeat in the uterus. Playing upon words, he emphasized the phonetic resemblance between the largely meaningless character 艾 at the center of *qingaitiao* and the homophonic character 愛 meaning love. *Qingaitiao* then become little sticks of love, capable of curing even the incurable. Immediately benefitting from this treatment, he told me that his acquaintance had been cured in less than a month. Yet this cure for cancer, this secret that modern medicine has been unable to unlock despite its concerted efforts and vast expenditures, had been largely forgotten in its native land of China due to the rush to abandon cultural roots and embrace "Western medicine." He told me of another family that collected hundreds of thousands of yuan in treatment expenses trying to cure a family member of cancer in a hospital. The treatment was unsuccessful, as it was doomed to be, in his analysis. Yet even in death, he told me, the family still had to bear hundreds of thousands of yuan of debt for the treatment. Whether these stories were true or ideal types for the sake of putting forward an argument, the point that he intended to make was clear: modern medical treatments in hospitals kill, compounding illness and debt, and only traditional, natural, indigenous cures are able to truly save people.[40] Local tradition, in this worldview, is always better than even the most recent developments and innovations.

Yet the imagining of tradition within this worldview remains intertwined precisely with these recent developments, and the "fears, discontents, anxieties, or uncertainties" that they produce,[41] as the example of cancer, the most anxiety inducing of diseases today, clearly demonstrates. Examples of the very "present" nature of the imagined past abound throughout my time in China: I was told during a traditional tea preparation ceremony that the nutritional absorption from tea in the past totaled more than seven times the nutrients absorbed from modern-day, mass-manufactured tea, on account of more advanced production and preparation methods. On another occasion, I was told that there was no pollution in the past: rather than using "chemical" shampoos that make water undrinkable, people in the past washed their hair with tea, in harmony with nature. This harmony extended into society, I was told, insofar as Confucian ethics guided people's thoughts and behavior, thereby ensuring the smooth functioning of society. And sometimes the power of tradition, as suggested by the cure for cancer discussed above, exceeded the human world with which we are familiar, extending into the supernatural. For example, another informant told me on a number of occasions that the people of China in the past could teleport from one location to another simply through the power of their minds. Thanks to this power, ancient maps were just as accurate as contemporary satellite-based maps, because cartographers' spirits were physically able to leave their bodies and view the landscape from above. And in a most revealing example of such anachronism, I was told on two occasions that China's GDP during the Song Dynasty, immediately prior to the hated Mongol takeover and thus at the imagined pinnacle of national glory, constituted a substantial 40 percent of global GDP.

These examples, whether appropriating the undeniably modern concept of national gross domestic product and applying it to the Song era, or envisioning the past as an era so advanced that we perpetually lag far behind its accomplishments, highlight an essential aspect of the movement's imaginings of tradition: just as the re-creation of the Han is based in its fantastic reimagining via ethnicity against the bland and unmarked representations of modern Han-ness, so the image of the past, another object of identity for the movement, is similarly based in the unfulfilled desires of the disappointing present, and in determined opposition to its anxiety-inducing realities. With regards to the question of history at the core of any discussion of the movement's appropriation of the past, despite the fact that Han Clothing Movement devotees are fascinated by the past and its traditions, they did not show any hints of even slightly rigorous research in historical or archaeological matters, focusing primarily upon vague fantastic notions distributed on

Internet forums and occasional references to the *Book of Rites*, which is after all not exactly a measured or reflective portrayal of everyday life in the past. Fantasy was far more important than historical or ethnographic facts, and myth stood in for memory, producing a self-congratulatory image of traditional culture as a transcendent cure for any and all ills of the present, the missing supplement to the pitfalls of modernity.[42]

It is not, however, particularly novel to simply recognize traditions as "invented" or to trace their foundations in the concerns of the present. This much has been clear since the publication of Eric Hobsbawm and Terence Ranger's edited volume *The Invention of Tradition*.[43] Nevertheless, the question of precisely why traditions are invented and why such imaginings of the past have become so influential and powerful within human experience in the present remains largely unanswered. If the primary concerns of the practice of tradition are located in the present, why is the medium of the past used in discussing the issues of today? The Han Clothing Movement's invocation of the national past and "tradition" sheds significant light upon these questions, revealing the power of tradition as simultaneously an unrestricted medium of fantasy (countering reality) and a stabilizing source of identity ("ours"), which serves within this context not only as an invention, as previously observed, but indeed as a therapeutic inversion.

The lack of restrictions upon the imagining of the past, allowing for visions of unrivaled security, lack of illness, and most importantly an all-encompassing wholeness, makes it an ideal medium of fantasy whose expansiveness stands in stark contrast to the all-too-immediate restrictions apparent in the experience of the present, characterized by its anxieties, uncertainties, and instabilities. Of course, this fantasy construction is and can only be a retroactive romanticization, benefiting from distance: any and all societies across time and space are plagued with problems and uncertainties. Consider, for example, the *Analects*, a classic that played an essential role in sociopolitical organization throughout the imperial era that movement enthusiasts romanticize. Yet this romantic vision forgets that the *Analects* were in fact based in the similar imagining and celebration of the glory days of the Zhou Dynasty, a sort of political Garden of Eden in which all of the rites and rituals worked flawlessly to produce an immaculate society.[44] So, even if movement participants were somehow able to travel back in time to the premodern era that they view so fondly, they would undoubtedly still find plenty to complain about, and perhaps yearn to return further back to the splendor of the early Zhou, towards which people in the premodern era were already yearning, and which in the end was also probably not anywhere near as wonderful as we have all been led to believe. The longest standing human tradition may then be the fundamentally imaginary exaltation of lost tradition.

At the same time, in contrast to the all-too-real gap between identity's imaginings and experience, tradition's unbounded imagining, detached from fundamental realities, is importantly denied through its false grounding as "our" past and tradition. In his insightful study of nostalgia as a sociocultural phenomenon, Fred Davis points out that nostalgic memories "reassure us of past happiness and accomplishment and, since they still remain on deposit, as it were, in the bank of our memory, [they] simultaneously bestow upon us a certain current worth, however much present circumstances may obscure it or make it suspect."[45] Although Davis is speaking here of nostalgic memories in actual personal life experiences, his point nevertheless remains of equal relevance to the imaginary national nostalgia promoted by the Han Clothing Movement, wherein the imagined national past is made immensely personal. For in rendering these imaginings as national historical memory, they are represented as realities that actually existed in the same geographical space in which participants currently live, among their common ancestors with whom they share imaginary blood ties, intertwining them with Han identity as the only moment in which a truly Han society reigned, encompassing almost every aspect of life as tradition, and as purely and completely Han. Han-ness thus serves as a subset of Chineseness, able to redeem the latter from its perceived corruption in the present, while at the same time standing in for the latter as its genuine and forgotten equal, a racial-cultural *qingaitiao* curing the ills of the present. In this manner, to borrow a phrase from Stephanie Coontz's illuminating critique of idealized portrayals of the "traditional" American family,[46] "the way we never were" is reimagined as the way we definitely were, and will indeed be again.[47]

THE OUT-OF-CONTROL SNOWBALL THEORY
OF THE HAN

The idealized construction of the past and its traditions then not only provides imaginary solutions to the confounding problems of the present, naturalizing this solution as pure "Han tradition" that has existed and will return. Furthermore, in relation to the present, the false identity thus established with these romanticized imaginings absolves "the Han" from responsibility for the often overwhelming dilemmas of the present, portraying the Han as a victim of contemporary society, rather than said society's core. When discussing ethnicity and the construction of dominant cultures, although the Han is not a singular, coherent group,[48] there is at the same time no denying that the current social, cultural, and political situation in China has been primarily produced by those labeled "Han," insofar as they constitute over 90 percent of the population, are well represented in positions of power, are invariably envisioned as the national vanguard in contemporary China's push towards the elusive ideal of modernity, and despite the performance of a multiethnic nation are presumed to be the "true" Chinese. State-defined minorities, by contrast, are not only plagued by suspicion but have also long been portrayed as "living fossils" who are to be appropriated and transformed by the civilizing powers of this more advanced Han culture. Described at times as resembling a snowball rolling down a hill, "get[ting] bigger the farther it rolls" by capturing and incorporating other nationalities into its culture by right of "the historical trend of the grand unification,"[49] such a portrayal of the Han is a modernist reincarnation of the distinction between culture and barbarism that played such an essential role in understandings of Chinese civilization in the premodern era.

The ethnocentrism and flattery of such a self-portrayal is so obvious as to not require further comment. Yet from another perspective, by embodying the dominant ethos of society in the present through the equation of Hanness and modernity, the idea of the Han is thereby tied not only to the progress and benefits of this process but also to its destabilizing and anxiety-provoking effects, which have become increasingly apparent in recent decades.[50] As seen in the examples above, the present is burdened by its persistent unhinging of essential components of social life precisely at the moment that they come to appear widely available: the development of the seeming megacities of the future has resulted in countless examples of forced and uncompensated "relocation" across the country;[51] the relative abundance of food in the reform era has been undermined by the anxieties surrounding unsanitary and even purposefully hazardous food preparation;[52] the ability to travel and see new places has been undermined by the overwhelming pollution that has come to cloak many of the country's cities and rural areas in recent decades;[53] the modernization of the medical system has proceeded hand in hand with the proliferation of diseases still without a cure; an abundance of information on computers and cellular phones has been undermined by the unrelentingly strict control over media narratives and monitoring of communications;[54] the opportunity to buy an apartment has been undermined by ever-expanding wealth differentials and uncontrolled inflation; and the perceived rise of the Chinese nation on the global stage has been undermined by the rapidly growing lack of trust in and disillusionment with the current system, as well as between people.

Highlighting the self-reproducing distinction between ideas and experiences, the idea of China's "rise" celebrated in the official media has been accompanied at an experiential human level primarily by rising home prices, rising food prices, rising crime rates, rising health risks, and general rising anxieties. As each new accomplishment or possibility emerges within and is distributed throughout contemporary society, it soon thereafter creates new anxieties, challenges, and impossibilities. And as a result, after decades of unwavering evolutionist certainty regarding a "plural" (*duoyuan*) society eventually becoming "one" (*yiti*), the Han snowball rolling down a hill seems, in Han Clothing Movement interpretations, to be collecting dirt and pollution on its exterior, and gathering speed towards the edge of a dangerous cliff.

The identificatory aspect of tradition, celebrating a lost past as the truth of Han-ness, is a simultaneous product and denial of these realities. By alienating contemporary society as an external imposition (a phenomenon discussed in more detail in Chapter 5) and thus a pollution or violation of Han-ness, the Han is presented as the victim of a cruel modernity rather than its enactor, and the wavering certainty of the teleology of modernity, embodied in its idealized future with the Han at the forefront, is replaced by the certainty of a new teleology based in a stable idealized past, with the Han again at the forefront in a counterimage of an eternally simpler and aesthetically pleasing true Han society. Han Clothing Movement narratives look backwards towards a past harmonious sphere of existence where, one might note in light of the previous analysis of ethnicization, "the minorities" with their simple ethnic ways and charming innocence were always already presumed, within the popular imagination, to be located. Rather than living in cramped and disorienting city spaces, or spending their lives in office cubicles or on factory floors, one's true Han ancestors are imagined to have lived in large open spaces in which one could take in the beauty of nature, carefree in one's long, flowing robes; rather than struggling with and suffering through a threatening and polluted environment, one's true Han ancestors were literally one with all in the world and the heavens, living amid the serene quiet of rolling, grassy hills, in unity with a pure and nurturing natural environment, and raising animals and vegetables on organic farms; rather than worrying about what food to eat or to feed to one's children, all was prepared naturally: food came straight from the fields, and children were fed directly from their mother's breast; and rather than living in a constant state of uncertainty and vigilance, one's Han ancestors lived in a disciplined society ordered by a clear hierarchy and accompanying rituals of respect. Life was simpler, purer, more honest, orderly, and bound in fraternal unity: such is the imagined eternal reality of the Han and China.

Mirroring the antiminority sentiment repressing the deployment of ethnic motifs in Han identity construction, within the obviously nostalgic nature of this past constructed in opposition to the present, participants are adamantly dismissive of the idea of nostalgia (*huaijiu*), often used in Chinese media descriptions of the movement,[55] denying that they could in any way be involved in any such nostalgic activities. Consciousness of nostalgia, after all, endangers the power of said nostalgia.[56] Rather, participants assert that their sole purpose is realizing their true identities, against the false revisions and additions of recent centuries. These are the identificatory imaginings of an imaginary community: by envisioning this community as a lost reality proper to the Han, a dual operation of amnesty and fantasy is realized, whereby members of "the Han" are exonerated from having produced the present society with which they are disillusioned (not the real China, produced not by the real Han), while at the same time imagining in its place a "true Han society" that must and most importantly can be recaptured in order to realize, as the following section describes, the "real China."

THE REAL CHINA

The combination of a revitalized Han race and a corresponding redeeming Han tradition, in movement participants' vision, would reinstate the lost essential truth of Chineseness. As noted in Chapter 1, I was repeatedly told throughout my fieldwork that the China of today was not the "real" or the "true" China. And I was repeatedly surprised that the Han-Chinese nationalists with whom I was working ironically spent a considerable amount of their time complaining about the Han and China. Their "real" China, on account of its boundless greatness, could not be found in the disappointing present. This "real" China could only be found in the unfettered identificatory imaginings, built in opposition to the shortcomings of the geographic space and social experiences now labeled China, around which the movement was organized and which it aims to enact. Just as the contemporary mainstream representation of Han-ness is dismissed as false, such that the "real Han" is to be found through a process of ethnicization modeled on state-defined minority representations, and just as contemporary society is dismissed as an anomaly, such that "real Han tradition" is to be found in an imagined past that inverts the troubling realities of the present, so the contemporary reality of China experienced on a daily basis is dismissed as unreal, such that the "real China" is to be found in the acting out of romanticized imaginings of what China should, could, and, in movement narratives, must be. The counterintuitive and indeed paradoxical nature of these examples is not unique to this case, but rather reflects the paradoxical core of national identity, trapped in and affectively driven by the gap between imagining and experience.

This split was expressed most clearly in a poem that is popular among movement participants nationwide, which was read aloud, in unison, at a public gathering of the local Han Traditional Culture Study Group under the blazing Guangzhou sun in August 2011. The poem is reproduced in translation below:

When I climb onto the ancient city walls,
Touch its weathered columns with my hands,
And lean excitedly over its edges to glance into the distant horizon,
I can't help but sense a bitter taste on my tongue,
As I hear a voice from above ask: Do you remember?
You are a descendant of Emperor Yan and the Yellow Emperor.

. . . I have dreamed of returning to the Great Tang,
Wandering around with Li Bai,
Whose sword reflects light so radiantly,
And whose lover is the moon above.
I have seen him hovering beneath the moon, singing towards the skies,
As the strong wind blew his hair and long robes,
He floated like a being from the heavens.
. . . Today, centuries later, as I walk into McDonalds,
Wearing Gucci and singing "My Heart Will Go On,"
I feel a gnawing pain inside,
And hear that voice from above: Have you forgotten?
You are a descendant of Emperor Yan and the Yellow Emperor.

And then I remembered, a pack of brown-haired and blue-eyed hyenas,
Destroyed our temples and our ancestral halls with their warships and their
    cannons.

So today, a century later,
We know freedom and democracy,
But have forgotten our civilization's cardinal ethics.
We have toddler prodigies, who can play piano,
But have forgotten our own musical scales,
We can build the tallest skyscrapers,
But can't find room for even one memorial arch for a moral exemplar,
We wear suits and leather shoes,
But lack our own national clothing.
Where are you, oh land of rites and etiquette?
Where are you, children of the Han?

Fred Davis argues that the essence of nostalgia is best expressed through a symbolic medium,[57] and this poem indeed captures most powerfully in its words the Han Clothing Movement's will to the past. The poem begins by envisioning a figure strolling along the ancient city walls and glancing outwards toward the landscape beyond in the present, a landscape undoubtedly populated with considerably less imposing structures and even a likely abundance of disillusioning sights. As the subject is glancing outwards into this distance, symbolically split between the real China before his or her eyes and the "real China" represented by the city wall beneath his or her feet, a voice suddenly appears to remind the wanderer of his or her magnificent cultural roots: "Do you remember?" This reminder initiates a fantastic journey of "memory" through Chinese history from Emperor Yan and the Yellow Emperor, the mythical first sovereigns and purported direct ancestors of the Han, to a mystical and psychosexually suggestive image of Tang era poet Li Bai floating, grasping his radiant "sword," and singing towards his lover the moon, as if he was able to transcend even the irresistible gravitational forces of this world. Fantasy here becomes national tradition and thus identity.

Yet this fantastic journey comes to a sudden conclusion in the return to the banal and even polluted present, where the tensions between the imagined past and disenchanted experience are represented in the image of a stereotypically "non-Chinese" Chinese singing a pop song from the Hollywood film *Titanic* and preparing to order a quick taste of deep-fried enjoyment from a multinational company. In this moment, the voice that repeatedly haunts the narrator, tauntingly asking "Do you remember? You are a descendant of Emperor Yan and Yellow Emperor," embodies a nationalist-culturalist superego, insofar as it appears to scold the subject for betraying his or her weighty responsibilities as a descendant of Emperor Yan and the Yellow Emperor. This culturalist superego, however, is furthermore intertwined with a nationalist-culturalist id of self-aggrandizing desire, insofar as one's primary responsibility as a descendant of the Yellow Emperor would be nothing less than greatness. This poem's popularity within the movement can thus be attributed to its powerful expression of the central tensions underlying its visions of its imaginary community: enjoyment and shame, pride and uncertainty, and grandeur and decline, themes of a frustrated national narcissism captured most clearly in the closing comparisons of the perceived crude vapidity of contemporary society (the real China, represented by imported political ideologies, cutthroat competition from a young age, banal clothing, and endless skyscrapers) and the idealized images of traditional culture ("the real China," represented by ethics, moral exemplars, cultural purity, and aesthetically appealing national clothing). The longing resulting from these tensions between the national imaginary and actual experience are given voice in the questions posed at the end of this poem: "Where are you, oh land of rites and etiquette? Where are you, children of the Han?"

For movement enthusiasts, the land of rites and etiquette and the children of the Han, missing in everyday experience, are found in the Han Clothing Movement, suturing[58] the unforgiving distance between realities and national imaginings. The Internet provides an ideal space for imagining such alternative realities and identities, to the point that online personas have increasingly begun to take the place of in-person self-presentation in recent years, in a struggle against the very real constraints of the real.[59] This most modern of communication tools has thus ironically provided the foundation for this growing traditionalist movement. Han Clothing itself actually began, as described above, as a series of online sketches in the early part of the past decade, designed to imagine an alternative self-presentation for viewers who could identify with these stunning designs as "Han" and thus as their own. This innovation then opened up a space for people to envision alternative identities for themselves, always comfortably under the legitimizing framework of a purportedly eternal identity and tradition. Forums developed in which a growing collection of enthusiasts took on such names as Dream, Legend of the Phoenix, Six-Veined Sacred Sword, Brother Emperor, Han Blood, Han Love Han, Great Han Wind, and Han Army. One might note that these are not in any way, shape, or form traditional Chinese names. Rather, they are signifiers or virtual avatars made to seem real[60] through the idea of culture, imagined traditions expressing a certain fantastic and mystical vision of personhood in premodern China, which is after all what this movement is really about. The Internet's simultaneous intertwinement with and imaginary transcendence of reality today has made it an ideal testing ground for such visions.

However, alongside the rapid proliferation of Internet images, a desire emerged to move beyond images, and to bring these imaginings into the external reality that they deny: it was thus not long after sketches of Han Clothing first appeared online that a few movement pioneers began preparing apparel based upon these images, and started wearing them in public spaces and eventually hosting regular weekend gatherings. Clear protocol on greetings between members marks the entrance into this alternative, usually secluded, and indeed sacred space: an oppositional miniworld representing the real China. Arrivals reliably greet one another with clearly prescribed hand gestures: rather than patting one another on the back, shaking hands, or exchanging cigarettes, arriving participants would fold their hands together at a distance and bow solemnly and slowly at a forty-five-degree angle toward other participants. From that moment onward, participants use their movement pseudonyms to recast their image, symbolically representing their transition from the world of the ordinary to the extraordinary. The grandiosity of the names by which participants refer to one another, as well as the mastery implicit in the otherwise unattainable act of self-naming, testifies to the enchanted alter egos that participants aim to construct.

Such unwieldy self-aggrandizement, however, exists alongside a strong emphasis upon protocol, reflecting the simultaneously fantastic and stabilizing role of "tradition." Movement rules required participants to have their hair clean and combed, to refrain from wearing sneakers, and to refrain from smoking, for fear of shattering the powerful yet fragile traditional aura produced in these gatherings. Group meals revolved around healthy selections and, on particularly enthusiastic days, vegetarian meals. All events were held completely free of charge, and meals shared among participants were always split evenly, avoiding at once the ubiquity of profit-driven motivations in contemporary society as well as the opaque and burdensome web of *guanxi* produced in the socially instituted fight for the bill. The balance between self-aggrandizement and collective discipline, indicating participants' simultaneous desire for the grandeur and meaning but also the control and order that was lacking in their lives, is tellingly also captured in the figure of an at once aesthetically elaborate yet strictly regimented uniform, around which this movement is organized. From names to clothing to social interactions, the world of Han Clothing gatherings was an inverted image of the wider world in which participants lived, a secure albeit illusory sphere far removed from the banality, uncertainties, and pressures of the present, providing participants with a rare although purportedly timeless sense of meaning, dignity, glory, peace, and control.

The Han Clothing Movement thus denies the reality of mainstream representations of the Han, borrowing from motifs of state minority representation to make the Han "ethnic" and "traditional." The movement furthermore denies the reality and legitimacy of the present, constructing a distant and ideal past that imaginarily inverts the disillusioning present to become the one and only true Han society. And finally, the Han Clothing Movement denies the reality of contemporary urban life in China, imagining in its place a fantastic "real China," a land of rites and etiquette free from the concerns of the present, with the Han, draped in five millennia of tradition, standing at its pinnacle. Here, and here alone, participants find their Han-ness and their real China.

WAYS OF BEING ETHNIC IN URBAN CHINA: PERFORMING THE HAN

This real Han standing at the highest peaks of the real China was on full display at a Chinese Nationalities' Culture Festival (*Zhongguo minzu wenhua jie*) held at Guangzhou's Jinan University in November 2010.[61] Ethnic performances were once the sole purview of China's minority nationalities, with the Han sitting reliably in the audience. The closest that one could come to Han participation in such performances was the quite standard and revealing ritual of inviting a member of the audience to join in the minorities' dances: whether one has visited a nationalities' theme park or an ethnic-themed restaurant, the invitation to join in the festivities onstage is an inevitable part of the process, which is nevertheless portrayed as completely spontaneous. The invitation is met with a mixture of excitement and embarrassed hesitation as mostly Han tourists are brought on stage in order to have a taste of "how the ethnics do it." According to the standard formula observed throughout a lengthy series of such performances over the course of my fieldwork, a few spectators are first brought onstage, usually to dance somewhat awkwardly to the amusement of performers and fellow audience members. After this first group returns to their seats, usually a single man from the audience is brought onstage, and attempts are made to teach him how to dance and thereby court one of the minority women: they invariably refuse him, to the great amusement of the audience.

Participants are inevitably pulled onstage with a look of shyness and embarrassed hesitation, but also with a massive smile. It is after all a rare moment for "the Han" to enjoy these things, free from the other concerns that accompany their modern and unmarked life: yet whereas in some settings, the Han's presumed straight-laced modernity is a source of pride, in other settings, such as an ethnic performance, it is a hindrance. Within this mode of self-representation, Han spectators desire to join in the ethnic celebration, yet because they are burdened with their modern responsibilities and anxieties, they remain unable to take on fully the primitive and rhythmic ethnic movements of the far more versatile minorities: one Han participant imitating minority dance in a performance at Shenzhen's Splendid China park, for example, was mockingly described by the minority performers as "looking like he was having a seizure" (*chou feng*). The feigned hesitancy to participate and the resounding applause and giggles accompanying any such performance testify to the ambivalent power of this ethnic spectacle: the will to ethnicity.

The Han's exclusion from popular ethnic performances was a source of perplexity for Han Clothing Movement activists across the country, and an issue in need of resolution. Accordingly, whereas the ethnic festival at Jinan University had in previous years consisted solely of Han college students dressing as minorities and dancing for other primarily Han college students in the audience, with Han audience members occasionally brought onstage to interact with other Han imitating minorities, local Han-ist enthusiasts had now convinced the organizers to incorporate the Han as Han into their 2010 show. These same enthusiasts in turn invited me to watch and fulfill my usual responsibilities for the local Han Clothing organization: taking a gratuitous number of photographs.

The program featured performances from a number of Han students as "minorities," in a discomfiting style reminiscent of the happy-go-lucky portrayals of minstrel shows. We began the evening with a Yao dance, performed at a rapid tempo with an array of colorful costumes, and a throng of jumping, twirling, and shouting women. Next, we viewed a performance by a group of supposed Mongols, described in the dance's introduction as a particularly "cheerful" race who love to dance. As the Han Clothing devotees sitting beside me giggled in captivation, one "Mongolian" woman twirled rapidly and repeatedly pressed her body provocatively against each of the four men on stage, in step with the beat of the music. At one point, as this young lady stood in the middle of the stage, the music came to a sudden halt. Two "Mongolian" men were located on either side of her, bent over with their hands reaching toward the ground and their buttocks facing in her direction. Suddenly, she gave them each a lively spank as she tilted her head to the side and directed a mischievous smile at the audience. The fast-paced music then started again, as the audience clapped with joy and a flurry of flashes from digital cameras lit the stage.

The next section of the show, the Han Clothing display, maintained the same level of excitement among my acquaintances, yet the tone of the performance was considerably more solemn: there was, for example, no spanking involved. Yet even more revealingly, rather than characterizing this section of the show as a "performance" (*biaoyan*) like the other performances that evening, this section was described solemnly as a "ceremonial display" (*liyi zhanshi*). Set against dramatic music evoking a certain classical grandeur, the host began by saying:

> This is the Han race, also known as the Huaxia. The traditional clothing of the Han people is "Han Clothing." From the moment that the Yellow Emperor exercised control over all under heaven through the establishment of a system of clothing and rituals, Han Clothing has been passed from one generation to the next for over four millennia. It is one of the most ancient forms of clothing in the world. Although many nowadays are unaware of Han Clothing, it has been rediscovered in recent years.

At precisely this moment, the first Han Clothing representative stepped out to a round of applause from the audience. He walked slowly and solemnly from stage left with his hands held together a few inches in front of his waist. When he reached the center of the stage, he turned dramatically to face the audience, and slowly stepped forward toward the front of the stage, with his hands still folded together. Upon reaching the front of the stage, he suddenly extended his arms in both directions with a dramatic look upon his face, displaying his body in a position resembling the Chinese character *da* (meaning "great," as in *da Han* "the great Han"). He stood in this position for a few seconds, staring into the audience that stared back at him, before he ever so slowly began turning around, with his arms still extended, to display both the front and the back of his clothing.

Upon completing this turn, he stared toward the audience again, brought his hands together in front of his chest, and bowed slowly. Gradually rising from his bow, he lowered his hands to his waist, turned and walked slowly to the back of the stage. This process was repeated a number of times, as various members of the local Han Clothing Movement displayed their clothing styles and the narrator explained in detail the name and significance of each type.

The narrator concluded the dramatic display with a correspondingly dramatic closing:

> Han Clothing is not just some retro style. Rather, we are on a search: a search for the beauty of our national clothing, a search for our lost civilization, and a search for a prosperity that was once ours. On today's grand world stage, we hope that our ancient civilization will be able to again illuminate the world with its glory—because we are eternally descendants of the dragon.

The show concluded on this note of illumination and glory for the self-proclaimed descendants of the dragon. As yet another group of Han dressed as minorities appeared on stage for yet another round of lively singing and dancing, the Han Clothing activists sitting with me began shuffling in their seats. Just as quickly as the Han ceremonial display had begun, it had ended. And before the next round of vigorous and colorful minorities had finished their bawdy dance, everyone in my party had stood to leave, and was eager for me to do the same; for once, after all, they had come not to see the minorities' performances, but rather to see the Han ceremonial display.

The discrepancy between the performances that evening, a discrepancy that reflects both the benefits and risks of this majority movement's will to ethnicization, reminded me of an unexpected monologue by a then-senior figure in the Guangzhou Han Clothing Association on the history of the world and the role of "shaking" (*yao*) therein, which I had heard one afternoon a few weeks earlier. Drifting to the topic of "the races" as conversations at Han Clothing gatherings often did, my interlocutor had first asserted that the history of the world was the history of the races striving to develop the world and humankind. Yet there was one exception to this historical rule, she claimed: "the blacks" (*heiren*) in Africa, who in her understanding spent their time "shaking" and dancing in circles. These Africans like percussion because they are simple people, she told me. In this sense, they are similar to China's minorities and are thus completely unlike the Han, who developed rituals and played more sophisticated and subtle instruments like the *guqin*. Drums, she emphasized, are much louder and rougher than the *guqin*, a fact that she interpreted as reflecting the character of the two "races" that she was comparing.

Eventually, she says, the "blacks" brought their "shaking" to the United States, where they created "shaking and rolling music" (*yaogun yinyue*), better known as rock & roll. This shaking was contagious, she told me: it first corrupted "white American culture" (*Meiguo bairen wenhua*), and eventually spread around the world through American cultural imperialism. And now the whole world was shaking . . . with just one exception, namely, the Han. "We Han don't rock/shake," she told me with a contented smile on her face. "We do rituals."

Despite the obviously misguided foundations of this cultural-racial narrative of history, these comments nevertheless accurately portray a fundamental truth of Han nationalist views of the self and others, which was also on display in the discrepancy between performances at the Nationalities Culture Festival. While members of the Han Clothing Movement want to join in the ethnic-cultural party and place themselves on display alongside the other nationalities with ethnicity and tradition, proponents are still avidly determined to maintain their imagined difference and presumed superiority as the sole representative of the "real China" as a land of rites and etiquette. This is a role that, in their belief system, requires a high degree of sophistication and decorum. The performance described above is an excellent example of ethnicization, borrowing representational motifs from China's state-defined minorities to make "Han-ness" tangible and enjoyable. The Han now have their clothing and traditions, embodying Han-ness as a stable, homogeneous, and eternal trait, and their performance, aestheticizing the Han through elaborate and colorful costumes and imposing movements.

Yet insofar as movement participants now have their own Han ethnic characteristics and their tradition, having developed this image from the ethnic model of minority nationalities, the Han faces the potential risk of being thought of as "ethnic" in the original sense of the term, a problematic situation for a majority-supremacist movement. Just like any form of transference, the ambivalent relationship produced by ethnic transference thus generates a number of defense mechanisms to redifferentiate the ethnicized Han from their fellow nationalities: the distinction between Chinese and barbarians is thus an obsessive component of movement rhetoric, expressed all too anxiously and compulsively, belying the ethnic origins of this new yet supposedly ancient vision of Han-ness. So, whereas minorities "dance," Han engage in what is referred to as a "ceremonial display" or "ritual." Whereas minorities' performances consisted of fast-paced music, rapid twirls, and sexual innuendoes, the Han's display consisted of dramatic music, right angle turns and grand gestures, and displays of etiquette. Whereas the peak of the Mongolian performance featured a woman joyfully smacking the buttocks of two men, the Han Clothing set featured a series of considerably less bawdy minipeaks in which individual members of the Han would stand before the audience and extend the limbs of their body on grand display, embodying the idea of the Great Han by literally embodying the shape of the character meaning "great." Throughout these performances, while minorities' bodies moved rapidly and seemingly uncontrollably ("shaking"), Han bodies moved slowly with constant composure and control ("not shaking") in their "ceremonial display," symbolically representing the presumed characters of these races in the eyes of their performers and audience: the Han. And while minorities' links to the past are derived from their presumed simple or primitive nature, the Han's links to the past are by contrast signs of its civilized, timeless, and great essence.

By becoming ethnic with clothing, customs, traditions, and performances, enthusiasts reconstruct the standard and bland image of the Han, adding a new dimension of ethnic enjoyment and national fantasy. Yet alongside this becoming ethnic, there is a continued emphasis upon differentiation from the ambivalent identification with ethnicity through the idea of "China" and thus civilization: borrowing from representations of China's disempowered minority nationalities to further empower the already dominant Han still maintains the majority's elevated status as the sole representative of a longstanding civilization, in which minorities have no place. This combination thus articulates enjoyable ethnicity, once exclusive to the minorities, while maintaining imagined superiority, still exclusive to the Han, thereby producing a vision of Han-ness that might best be called "having one's Han and enjoying it too." The movement's exaltation of "the Han" and its supreme Chineseness is symptomatic of tensions within ethnic representation and contemporary society; yet at the same time, it provides the promise of a cure for these tensions.

THREE

The Personal Origins of Collective Identity

THE PRECEDING CHAPTERS HAVE ANALYZED the structural tensions existing within the concepts of the Chinese nation, Han-ness, and tradition, arguing that these contradictions are essential to understanding the Han Clothing Movement's rise and affective power. The unreal expectations of nationalist identity produce disappointment with mundane everyday reality, reproducing the yearning for the transcendent national ideal. Meanwhile, the default and modern construction of Han-ness leads to Han trouble, which is resolved by adding ethnic characteristics modeled on minority representation while nevertheless carefully protecting the sacred assumptions of Han supremacy. Tradition, presented as an identificatory connection from the past to the present, in actuality celebrates a fantasy past constructed in direct opposition to the present.

These modes of analysis, built upon the mutually constituting relationship between individual desires and culture, were developed through direct observation of and participation in Han Clothing Movement activities in cities across the country. As this book's narrative shifts from a deconstruction of these identity concepts to their imaginary suturing reconstruction in movement practices, this chapter presents in detail the stories of four Han Clothing Movement participants. On the one hand, I trace their experiences within the underwhelming and even disillusioning present, as well as the lacks, anxieties, and uncertainties that they face on a daily basis: for them, as Mark Lilla has commented in his recent work on political reaction, "the present, not the past, is a foreign country."[1] On the other hand, I juxtapose these life experiences with their attempts to elevate themselves above their profane surroundings, imaginarily transcending the alien present through an embrace of the idealized past as the truth of the "great Han." Throughout these analyses, we can see that just as Han-ness is intertwined with minority representation, just as tradition is a product of the present, and just as the "real" China emerges as an imaginary inversion of the real China, so the collective ideals of the Han Clothing Movement and its Han identity are products and expressions not of an intrinsic cultural essence or eternal tradition, but rather of the interactions between personal desires, disappointments, aspirations, and anxieties in the present.

LIANG

I first met Liang at a Chinese New Year gathering in Shenzhen. Along with his Han Clothing, he carried with him a small, fist-sized drum with the traditional character for "Han" painted on its skin, which he proudly displayed and occasionally played before curious onlookers. Liang is a resident of the remote outskirts of Shenzhen in his late twenties who makes the hour-long journey into the center of the city on a regular basis to celebrate his Han-ness. Back at his countryside home, he works as a security guard in a residential community, a job that requires that he patrol his quiet community to make sure that nothing illegal nor untoward is happening. The main problem in Liang's countryside community, however, is not that something illegal might happen; the problem, instead, is that nothing ever happens. This is not just my opinion: Liang described his job as pointless, boring, and very poorly compensated. As he told me humorously on a number of occasions when we would talk late into the night, "I don't have much besides time."

I accompanied Liang over three days at work at the beginning of spring in 2011. Starting the day early in the square in the center of the community, I sat on a bench looking around while the other two members of security on call, one of whom was Liang's supervisor, spent the morning playing extremely animated card games, vigorously chain smoking, and then suddenly crashing and taking naps on benches. My eyes, often the only two eyes actually looking around the community, did not notice anything of particular concern, or even of particular interest, throughout the morning. Then, when ten o'clock arrived, Liang informed me that it was time to "make the rounds." I followed him with interest through some narrow alleyways on the perimeter of the community, hoping that we might come across something, indeed anything, of interest.

The moment of interest arrived quite unexpectedly, however, when Liang stopped at a stand to pick up a bottle of 110-proof *baijiu* liquor. Considering that this potent rice wine that burns the throat and numbs the mind is a drink that is difficult to consume at ten in the evening, I had honestly never considered consuming it at ten in the morning, but Liang either failed to notice my surprise, or completely disregarded it. We promptly proceeded down a side alleyway, where Liang reassured me "My supervisor can't see us here" as he handed me a flimsy plastic cup and proceeded to fill it with the toxic-smelling concoction that was about to give us both a profoundly numbing start to an otherwise not particularly memorable day. Like two teenagers sneaking a cigarette around the corner from school, we sat in the alley talking and drinking for almost an hour, as Liang told me that this spot provided a daily respite from the tedious boredom of his work. Liquor was not always the sole source of distraction, he reassured me, perhaps sensing my concern; sometimes it was comic books, or friends, or some combination of the three. As we wandered back towards the center of the community block, Liang's supervisor was in the midst of a particularly heated card game, and either completely failed to notice our intoxication or did not particularly care. The latter seems most likely, considering that he did not even bother to ask how our "rounds" had gone. We then broke for an early lunch, which was limited in terms of food selection yet quite abundant in terms of the provision of liquor. Thankfully, my notes remained intelligible. The rest of the day passed uneventfully, and undoubtedly many more days followed in this manner.

Liang's unique approach to escapism at work clearly alleviated the boredom of a mundane and even, in his words, "pointless" job. However, it was unable to alleviate the boredom of his life outside of work. Liang was single in his late twenties, a situation of concern in Chinese culture, wherein pressure to delay dating in the course of one's education is ironically followed almost immediately by unrelenting pressure to find a partner, marry, and produce children in one's early twenties. Liang's single status was undoubtedly related to his low salary, which also left him with no choice but to live at his parents' house on the semirural edge of the bustling city of Shenzhen: a situation unlikely to be looked upon favorably by many bachelorettes. Many of his friends and family expressed puzzlement at his failure to "dive into the sea" of entrepreneurship downtown, find a wife, and produce children, the standard narrative for a man of his age. Liang's mother had arranged a number of blind dates with local women, which never quite succeeded: "All they care about is money," Liang told me, "and I don't have much of that." His elder brother, who had already proceeded to his second marriage and hence second child, took on a generally condescending and even mocking tone in most conversations that I observed with Liang.

As his brother and his friends acquired the markers of success and moved beyond the boredom of daily life in the countryside toward the excitement of the city beyond, Liang's life remained removed from the ideal image for someone his age. In a world without any clear direction or fulfillment, Liang sought fulfillment elsewhere, and found it in the Han Clothing Movement.

———

Turning on the television in China today, one is immediately impressed by the sheer optimism of national self-representations. The "rise of China," in which the nation returns to its presumed proper place of respect and reverence in the global hierarchy, is constructed as the proper outcome for the "longest-standing uninterrupted ancient civilization" with "five millennia of culture." Yet how do these rhetorical constructions of nationalist pride relate to people's actual lives? These notions of timeless tradition and a burgeoning newfound respect could not have felt further away on that spring day playing cards and smoking in a community on the edge of Shenzhen, as the early spring sun glared down upon our sweaty brows, pleasantly numbed.

Han Clothing, we must note, reverses this disillusioning trend, closing this otherwise omnipresent gap. During movement events, Liang was able to transcend his very worldly everyday concerns and place himself comfortably at the center of five glorious millennia of culture. Liang took on the fascinating moniker Hongwu's Sacred Sword (*Hongwu Shen Jian*). This name tied him to the heroic historical figure Zhu Yuanzhang, the Hongwu Emperor, who established the Ming after the barbarian Mongol invasion; Liang clearly saw himself playing a similar role in resisting contemporary culture, which he perceived to be a Manchu-dominated abomination. Yet beyond historical metaphors, this name furthermore had a deeper, even mystical meaning: Liang was the personification of Zhu's sacred sword, an unabashedly phallic symbol standing straight up and fighting against the onslaught of mundane, barbarian reality.

As suggested by this name, Liang was a different man at movement events, fully decked out in his Han Clothing. He would often, in fact, be transformed into the center of attention when he played his *guqin* (a stringed musical instrument) for movement enthusiasts and interested passersby. The slow, steady, sonorous tones of the *guqin* would drift ever so gently through the air, temporarily bringing Liang's captivated audience away from the cacophony of the present to a quieter and more peaceful moment in time. Yet even more than his audience, this re-presentation of Liang as the classical musician and sacred sword of a major historical resister of the barbarians also brought him away from the disillusioning present, and far away from his village's central square, allowing him to momentarily transcend his living environment and realize fulfillment in his re-creation through the identificatory metaphor of the "great Han."

YAN

Yan was one of the first Han Clothing enthusiasts whom I came to know on a close personal basis. She had been kind enough to offer to meet at a café near Sun Yat-sen University to discuss Han Clothing early in my research. Arriving an hour and a half behind schedule in full Han regalia, her elaborate outfit contrasted almost immediately with her otherwise quite haphazard personal style. Unlike Liang, Yan could not exactly be described as "single," although she also could not exactly be described as committed. Over the course of my research, she had passionate romances and equally passionate break-ups with a series of potential suitors, and was never shy about discussing her love life at quite random moments. One minute we would be discussing the origins of a purportedly ancient Han ritual, and the next minute she would suddenly be telling me about how she was head over heels in love with a successful man who was also in love with her, but that for some reason they also yelled and fought quite often. Then, at our next meeting, she would tell me how unreliable and incompetent her last boyfriend had been, but how thoughtful and caring a new suitor was: I was never quite sure what to make of these stories, but she seemed no less perplexed.

Approaching her upper twenties, Yan faced many of the same issues as Liang: the dilemma of being single, not particularly economically successful, and failing to stand out to potential suitors amid the crowd of millions of other people around her. Yet there were additional stresses here. As mentioned above, remaining single into one's late twenties in China creates comments and pressure from family and friends for men; yet in the case of women, this perceived "condition" all too often produces a sense of impending crisis. The cult of female youth and virginity renders unmarried thirty-year-old women as *sheng-nü*, which is generally translated as "leftover women," but could also be read considerably more harshly as "female leftovers."[2] Accordingly, Yan's relationship to her single status was far less detached and far more tumultuous than Liang's, on account of pressures from her parents, leading her to move from one potentially promising yet uncertain relationship to another, in search of a solution that never arrived.

Alongside her rocky love life, Yan's business life was no more stable. A college graduate with relatively strong English skills, she worked as a shift supervisor in a factory on the edge of the city. However, her position and salary clearly did not meet her expectations, and her mind typically raced from one business idea to another. She memorably began one of our meetings by asking directly, before we had even sat down, "How many American women do you know?" Puzzled and unable to determine an exact figure, I assured her that I knew quite a few "American women." She then leaned in towards me to ask a follow-up question: among these women whom I knew, how many were "white, black, Indian, or Mexican?" Only increasingly puzzled, I responded that this was equally difficult to calculate, and asked why she was curious. It turned out that Yan was planning to manufacture Han-themed change pouches, which she then wanted to sell on eBay to "Americans" at a decent profit. However, she was curious about the demand for such items, and wanted me to conduct an informal survey of all of the "whites, blacks, Indians, and Mexicans" that I knew to see if they might be interested, and to determine which groups would be most interested in such products. Asking why she had not included Asians in her survey, she sighed, dramatically rolled her eyes, and told me that it was all too obvious that Asians would be interested!

I never managed to conduct Yan's suggested survey of "American women." But thankfully, the next time that I met her, she had moved on to greater goals and aspirations. This time, she wanted to sell what she called "Han-style jackets," which she would have the workers under her supervision produce en masse for the American market.

I was never able to decipher whether Yan's business life was modeled upon her love life, or vice versa, or if perhaps both were products of her uniquely insistent yet inconsistent personality. But whatever the cause may have been, her ideal life appeared always almost within yet continually beyond her reach. In a world without stability and order, as she moved from one initially promising yet ultimately uncertain situation to another, Yan naturally yearned for an elusive order and certainty, and found it in the Han Clothing Movement.

———

In the Han Clothing Movement imaginary of "traditional culture," premodern society was a well-oiled utopian machine that operated seamlessly for millennia without interruption, endowed throughout with order and meaning. The five Confucian relationships (ruler–subject, father–son, elder brother–younger brother, husband–wife, friend–friend) are central to this imaginary. These guidelines, in their obsessive categorization, produced a standardized macrolevel mapping of relationship roles structured around preestablished microlevel etiquette that provided a clear social role for any and all people and flawlessly structured interpersonal relations. In a world in which individuals and their relationships are constantly in flux and one is often unable to find one's path to meaning and stability, the experiential complications of relations between people, whether between parents and children, siblings, friends, or lovers, not to mention the often perplexing relations between ruler and subject, are inverted in an image of another world in which these relationships were clearly ordered and "meant something." As such, this highly standardized mode of social relations can be imagined as liberating even despite its oppressive and obsessive regulations, insofar as it is assumed to seamlessly inscribe the individual into an idealized system far greater than themselves.

As a central figure in her local movement organization, Yan benefited from this idealized standardization of social relationships, which was reenacted to a degree among movement participants. Clear protocol and etiquette mapped interpersonal relationships within movement activities, such that fellow participants would bow to Yan as a sign of respect when she arrived. She was referred to respectfully by her Han Clothing name "Dream," which she always wrote using traditional rather than simplified characters, simultaneously signaling her preference for tradition as well as enacting cultural capital via traditional characters. The stability and sense of veneration that she sought in everyday life via various equally unsuccessful routes were realized through the weekend escape into the Han Clothing universe: no matter how her relationships or business ventures were developing in the real world, Yan could always be certain that she would be treated with dignity at movement events.

The micromanagement of social relations to avoid the ailments of contemporary social life within the movement could at times have highly unexpected consequences. For example, despite their embrace of a communal Han identity, movement participants in Guangzhou avoided the *qingke* ("inviting guests") culture in China wherein one individual in a dinner party pays for the entire party's meals, producing a network of relationships (*guanxi*).[3] Thanks to a suggestion from Yan, participants rigorously implemented the "AA-system" of splitting bills evenly, a move that I have often heard criticized in China as excessively "individualistic" and "Western." When I asked about this practice on numerous occasions, informants expressed exhaustion at the relationships and corresponding responsibilities and burdens developed through the standard approach of one person inviting everyone out to dinner. In contrast to the amorphous and unpredictable power plays that emerge in dinner invitation culture, movement participants envisioned and enacted a more stable approach that ensured clarity with regards to one's relations with others at all times, even happily employing means that were clearly not a "Han tradition" toward this end.

XIA

I first met Xia, who comes from the Shantou region of Guangdong Province, through a friend over lunch one weekend at a not particularly authentic Western restaurant in central Guangzhou: the kind of place where pizzas are served with peas and carrots as toppings. Quiet and reserved by nature, our similar personalities led us to develop an immediate rapport. Yet knowing that I was a visiting scholar at Sun Yat-sen University, Xia repeatedly interjected throughout our conversation that afternoon that she was of "low culture" (*wenhua di*), a common phrase meaning that she had not received much formal education. Upon hearing her life story, I could understand her self-consciousness. Where she came from, she told me, people's understanding of gender was "very backward" (*hao luohou*) and preferences leaned heavily towards sons over daughters. In her home village, a family was expected "by tradition" to have at least two sons in order to avoid becoming the laughing stock of the village. Xia's family had three daughters in a row, of which she was the oldest, before they finally had their first son. Yet this happy resolution to her parent's dilemma became a source of constant real-life dilemmas for her. Once her baby brother had been born, her parents decided that they needed to save money for his education and eventual marriage: as such, Xia was told to drop out of school and work in the fields. Dropping out before completing middle school, Xia had toiled in the family's plot for a few years before her parents proposed that she go to "the city" to make some money. The pressures that her parents had previously faced in their efforts to produce a son to secure their future were thus immediately transferred to Xia, who now had no choice but to sacrifice her own future in order to secure her younger brother's.

Beginning with a series of tiring and low-paying jobs in the makeshift factories of Guangzhou's infamously rough Kangle Village,[4] Xia desperately sought a reliable source of income for her parents to pass on to her baby brother. Moving to the outskirts of the city for the cheapest housing that she could find, she noticed one day that a local karaoke hall was hiring hostesses, and was even providing free room and board. The job provided her with more money to send back home, which of course made her family happy. Nevertheless, she told me that work was exhausting and that she was not satisfied with her life. For readers unfamiliar with the contemporary Chinese social context, work in a karaoke hall can often involve varying degrees of sex work, and is solely the purview of the young and attractive. Although I never broached this topic with Xia, I do know that whatever it was that she was required to do in the karaoke hall, she did not particularly enjoy it. She told me that on an average night she would work until two or three in the morning, at which point she would go back to her dormitory, take a shower and hopefully fall asleep by four o'clock. Living on-site and having no vacation time, the majority of her young adult life was beyond her control, confined to a smoky and likely quite seedy karaoke hall in the service of her baby brother.

One day, when I asked Xia how she became interested in Han Clothing, she surprised me by telling me that as a young girl, she loved to wrap herself in her parents' bed sheets and sing and dance in front of a mirror, pretending that she was a happy dancing minority of the type that she had seen on television. Those carefree and innocent memories from early childhood could not be further removed from her present existence. Yet amid the merciless vicissitudes of life, Xia was able to ever so briefly capture moments of otherwise unattainable peace and dignity through her embrace of Han Clothing. Movement activities often started at eight or nine in the morning, an immensely inconvenient time considering her late working hours; activities were also almost always located at least an hour-long cramped subway ride from her apartment. Nevertheless, she did not allow these realities, or any other realities for that matter, to impinge upon her ideal image: Xia was a frequent and lively participant in local activities, sacrificing her already limited sleep for a chance to participate in a group that provided her with an image of a better life and an otherwise elusive sense of prestige, and for once importantly demanded nothing in return. In a world in which she exercised no real control over her own life, Xia naturally desired a certain dignity and control that was perpetually lacking, and found this in the Han Clothing Movement.

———

Having grown accustomed to the dismissal of fortune-tellers as "liars" (*pianzi*) in contemporary China, I was surprised when members of the Guangzhou Han Clothing Movement mentioned fortune telling as one popular movement pastime. It was also, I must note, one of Xia's favorite movement activities. Usually, one or two movement participants deemed properly trained in the art of fortune telling would use a "Feng Shui compass" (*luopan*) and an ancient coin to answer questions based upon a particular view of cosmology supposedly from the time of the mythical ancestor Fu Xi, derived from the idea of the eight trigrams (*bagua*) articulated in the *Book of Changes*. Sitting in on a fortune-telling session with Xia and other Han Clothing Movement members, I was told that this cosmology was much more ancient and thus much more powerful than "modern science," and was able to unlock the secrets of the world.

Explaining to me how to discover the logic of the world, that afternoon's fortune teller began from the concept of the Supreme Ultimate (*taiji*), describing how this Supreme Ultimate unifies the two modes (*liangyi*) of yin and yang, the sun and the moon, the heavens and earth, and man and woman. These two modes could furthermore be broken down into the four images, which also corresponded to the four seasons, four directions, and four sacred mythical beasts (green dragon, white tiger, red phoenix, and black tortoise). And finally these four images could be further split into the eight trigrams, which formed the basis of fortune telling. The splitting of reality into, in the words of the fortune teller, the good and the bad, was a universal phenomenon that could be overcome through a proper grasp of the eight trigrams. And similar to the splitting of ideals and reality analyzed above, while division is in the nature of all things, it is reassuringly also a dilemma that can always be overcome in a promised greater unity.

Particular steps were necessary for proper fortune telling. One was to have no doubts and believe firmly in the accuracy of the readings. One must also be sure to sleep well, eat well, bathe, and prepare a clean space for fortune telling. One would then raise a question: that day, Xia posed the question "Who will I marry?"—a question undoubtedly at the forefront of many participants' minds. Then, tossing an antique coin six times, the master of ceremonies drew a series of six lines based upon the coin tosses.

Examining the tosses and the relationships between the various lines drawn, with straight lines representing *yang* and broken lines representing *yin*, she was told that she would be happiest in November or December, wherein the diagram showed a promising transition from *yin* to *yang*. The relations between the six lines were then further analyzed in search of patterns of difference and repetition, creating a new series of lines, which were then transferred onto the ideas of heaven, humanity, and earth, and again given labels of yin and yang based upon their patterns. As I followed along through one mystifying layer upon another of interpretation and analysis, I found that it was quite easy to become lost in the seemingly unending series of transfers of symbols that could be read in multiple ways. It was even easier, in my observation, to read into this practice any message that one wanted to find: Xia was of course pleasantly surprised to learn that she would likely meet her suitor between November and December, that he would be a well-respected person with a broad network of friends, but that she needed to avoid pressuring him into marriage too quickly.

The imaginary power and knowledge derived from a few coin tosses completely inverted the lack of control and even helplessness that characterizes life outside of the movement. Auspicious news was of course cause for celebration, but even inauspicious news delivered in this context would provide a warning of which one previously had not been aware. Both provide a previously unattainable power, wherein both the good and the bad are unified into an otherwise elusive fantasy of control. By tapping into the universal division of all things and unlocking their secrets, fortune telling endowed movement participants with the imaginary power to actively transcend these divisions and finally bring together in their grasp that which had been perpetually split: their fantasies and their selves.

TSIN

Arriving in Guangzhou late on a humid August evening, after nearly two days on the road from New York to Guangzhou via Beijing, I made my way through the visually stunning yet also stunningly quiet lobby of a newly built hotel immediately adjacent to the city's airport. Upon checking in, I found that my room included a brand new flat-screen television, as well as a yoga mat and a yoga-themed television station designed to help weary travelers relax. The shower in the bathroom featured two shower heads, with one providing an intense flow of water, and another slightly above providing a pleasant, rain-like feel. A plethora of pillows covered my bed, providing a surprisingly refreshing night's rest, despite the jetlag.

While I was enjoying my rest, one of my future informants on the other side of town watched as residents of her community were sprayed with tear gas and randomly beaten by police. Tsin Village was once a rural, agricultural area on the edge of the city of Guangzhou; its transformation over three decades of reform reflects the path of many similar communities across the country. First, Tsin Village is a story of rapid urbanization. Like many rural areas on the edges of cities across China over the past twenty years,[5] Tsin Village has gradually been surrounded by the ever-expanding city of Guangzhou, such that this "village" is now located directly in the center of the new downtown area, known as Pearl River New City. As this area became surrounded by urban life, the former village became an "urban village" (*chengzhongcun*), switching fields for concrete three to four-story apartment buildings, usually housing migrant workers who have come to labor in Guangzhou's factories, and thereby transforming former agricultural workers into landlords. The result of this urban village buildup in recent decades has admittedly been less than aesthetically and socially pleasing, with narrow and cramped alleyways, haphazardly installed power lines that did not appear even remotely safe, scores of wandering rodents of varying sizes, and perpetual and seemingly irresolvable issues of crime. It would not be improper to describe Tsin Village, as I saw it in 2010 and 2011, as a slum. Nevertheless, residents were not moving to the village for the charming scenery and luxurious lifestyle that it provided: like other urban villages distributed across Guangzhou, this space provided rare housing opportunities for the backbone of the city's development, the underpaid worker, in an environment in which housing has become an increasingly unbearable burden even for professionals.

Second, Tsin Village is a story of runaway corruption. David Bandurski compellingly recounts the history of Tsin (Xian) Village, its land, and its politics in his *Dragons in Diamond Village*.[6] As Tsin made the transition from an agricultural village to an urban village, its formerly collectively held farmland was transferred to the state in 1995 at the price of 600 million yuan.[7] Soon thereafter, the village committee, meant to be the collective voice of the villagers, was replaced by a commercial entity, the Tsin Village Enterprise Group; revealingly, the village's former Communist Party chairman Lu Suigeng became chairman of the new enterprise. The 600 million yuan in transfer funds were supposed to be collectively owned by villagers in the form of shares within the Enterprise Group, but as ever more real estate deals for overpriced high-rises on former farmland were negotiated, villagers watched as the value of their shares remained largely unchanged.[8] Some people indeed needed to get rich first, but while lavish funds were being misappropriated by Lu Suigeng, the now landless farmers were left to rely solely upon renting out apartments to migrant workers. Then in 2009, villagers learned that Lu planned to work with Poly Real Estate to demolish the block of makeshift apartment buildings upon which they relied for a living to develop a new residential district and shopping center.[9] Lu's commercial interest here conveniently coincided with the city government's interest: Tsin Village's location is in fact so central that it happened to be located only three blocks north of the newly built stadium in which the 2010 Asian Games' Opening Ceremony was to be held, and just one block east of the elaborately designed walking street leading to this stadium. This awkward leftover of urban development thus suddenly became an embarrassing eyesore for the city's government, who were eager to tear down the block for redevelopment before the start of the Asian Games in November of 2010 as part of an ambitious city-wide image makeover.[10] Ironically, in the eyes of the "people's government," a massive pile of rubble cleared of all people was a more appealing sight than the realities of urban village life.

Finally, Tsin Village is a story of the lack of any means of redress for wrongs committed by the state against citizens. Beginning in the summer of 2009, village residents unhappy with the planned demolitions repeatedly gathered outside of the offices of the Tsin Village Enterprise Group, petitioned the district government, municipal government, and provincial government, hired a lawyer to represent their interests, and attempted to raise awareness of their situation through the Hong Kong media. None of these steps had any discernible impact. On the evening of August 12, 2010, exactly three months to the day before the opening ceremonies of the Asian Games were to be held a few blocks away, residents had gathered in the village market in protest against its planned demolition. Soon, a phalanx of riot police and demolition workers surrounded the area with helmets, protective shields, and weapons. Charging in, the police beat residents with batons, and chased protestors through the winding alleyways of the village, detaining dozens.[11] At three in the morning on August 13, as I slept in my yoga-themed hotel room, the police released a series of gas canisters in an attempt to clear the area. Moments later, a bulldozer charged forward to tear down the market structure, which had served as a source of meager livelihood for elderly village residents for two decades, but was now being suddenly declared an "illegal" and "unsafe" structure.

My informant in the village, whom I will call Tsin, witnessed this chaos, and recounted the events to me one afternoon immediately before the start of the 2010 Asian Games. Since that terrifying night in August, she told me, the Tsin Village Enterprise Group had strived to make the village uninhabitable: after destroying the market, workers had also proceeded to cut power lines, overturn residents' vending stalls, and demolish the village school. Hired vigilantes had even doused blankets in gasoline and set them alight in the narrow, winding corridors of the village at night. These steps were intended to scare away tenants as well as owners. Evacuated residences were demolished, and the rubble was left unattended, eliminating homes for people while producing new homes for a rapidly growing rat infestation. These unfortunate developments were hidden safely from the outside by checkpoints at the four main entrances to the village staffed by demolition workers dressed in camouflage fatigues, as if prepared for war, and checking the papers of anyone entering or exiting. Massive iron walls that had been built around the area in the weeks following the August confrontation sheltered the village from view, while also reflecting the imaginary community that government officials and investors envisioned for this space once these slums were gone, featuring skyscrapers located on rolling grassy green hills and well-dressed gentlemen playing rounds of golf.

The only respite that Tsin could find from this stressful and indeed warlike environment was in weekend Han Clothing Movement activities, which she attended regularly. She had begun reading about Han Clothing around the time of the initial demolition orders in August 2009, and become more involved after the violence in August 2010. She told me that she found the Han Clothing activities in such natural environments as parks or mountains on the edge of the city particularly relaxing, providing both natural beauty and a predictable stability. Far removed from the chaos of her everyday living environment, Tsin once told me with a sigh that "we Han" were meant to be out here, together with nature: here again,

FIGURE 7. Demolition surrealism in Tsin Village, Guangzhou.

representations of minorities as closer to nature are transferred onto representations of the true Han.

While Tsin found consolation in these Han Clothing Movement events, I observed a number of moments when her outspoken criticisms of the government, derived from her experiences in the village, produced notable discomfort among fellow Han Clothing enthusiasts. Some even spread conspiracy theories that she was a Falun Gong member who had been sent to shatter the happy harmony of the movement. Despite these doubts, she continued to participate and to believe strongly in the healing power of Han Clothing and the tradition that it represents. She told me on a number of occasions that she believed that some sort of external power, alien to true Chinese culture, had taken control of both government and private enterprise, and driven them to act in a manner that she could only describe as "crazy." There was thus a need, in her opinion, to return to real Chinese tradition, so that people might abandon the blind pursuit of ever-greater wealth at any cost, and might treat each other like people again. "We have five millennia of history, but when has anything like this ever happened in the past? Today, there are hundreds of thousands of people like us across the country, just trying to live peacefully in our homes, and they want to take our homes away and rob us." She continued, comparing the present situation to the past:

"There used to be morals and values and respect for one another. There used to be a heavenly way [*tian dao*]. Where is it now?"

Of course, in reality, the past was considerably more complicated than she portrayed, and is open to many interpretations and even abuses. While Tsin appropriated an ideal image of the true Chinese past in which such violence would not occur, the Tsin Village Enterprise Group and government were similarly imagining a past in which such abuses would be accepted without complaints by an obedient citizenry with supposedly traditional values of collectivism and respect for authority. Signs attached to one wall at the edge of the village in the fall of 2011 featured a puzzling image of a smiling Buddha with arms outstretched, alongside a cynical Confucianist slogan encouraging submission: "Sign the contract early and be relocated early. Make filiality a priority."

———

Returning to the macrolevel issues raised by Tsin's story, I am often asked during presentations of my research about the relationship between the Chinese state and the Han Clothing Movement. This, however, is a relationship that is difficult to decipher, as it is a relationship characterized by ambivalence on both sides. From the Maoist era through the reform era, the Chinese state has been clearly reliant upon the narrative of nationalism for legitimization, and has cultivated quite extreme nationalism through the educational system as well as the media system, in order to present itself as the nation's sole savior from predatory outsiders. Nationalism, however, is a profoundly affective ideology that can easily escape a central power's control, as demonstrated by the Han Clothing Movement: in contrast to mainstream Chinese nationalists who are dedicated to rationalizing each and every action of the "strong state" from any critique by a demonized "West," a binary relationship in which nationalists almost invariably stand with the government, Han Clothing Movement nationalists, through their ideal of a Han-centered nation unburdened of troublesome minorities, in fact directly oppose the central government's ethnic policy. The Han Clothing Movement is then one among many emerging signs that the nationalist culture that Beijing has fostered for legitimacy in recent decades could spin out of control, far beyond government intentions.

Yet perhaps on account of their reliance upon nationalism, the regime has shown no interest in cracking down on a large nationalist group, with the result that the Han Clothing Movement has grown into a nationwide social movement with branches in most major cities: a rarity in post–Falun Gong China. In private discussions with movement participants, issues of corruption, unaccountability, lack of transparency, and the arbitrary exercise of power were not topics from which most enthusiasts shied away, even in discussions with a meddling foreigner who may not "understand China." These criticisms become most strident when expressed through the conspiracy theory of Manchu control discussed in Chapter 5, in which the government is represented as an alien entity fixated upon genocide against the Han. Yet even among those most critical of the government, participants remain acutely aware of the limits of any type of social movement in China today, leaning in practice towards safety rather than confrontation with the state. This nationalist stalemate has even resulted in occasional rewards from the state, such as the opportunity for Han Clothing groups to participate in local state-sponsored tourism festivals, as described in Chapter 6, producing a puzzling partnership in which movement participants happily work with a government that they believe is actively oppressing their race, while the state temporarily gives official sanction to the movement's radical violation of official ethnic policy.

If the real relationship between the Han Clothing Movement and the Chinese state is difficult to decipher on account of the delicate dance between the two, movement participants' relationship to an ideal state is considerably clearer. Participants envision a pure Han race, and a corresponding fantasy of a pure Han power, stripped of the prevailing "barbarian" elements of state power. Herein, the acknowledgement of negative identity in the present is again tied to belief in an ideal identity in the past. The abstract notions of the "heavenly way" (*tian dao*), the "kingly way" (*wang dao*), and the "unity of heaven and humanity" (*tian ren he yi*) cited in Tsin's story, fantasies of a moment of unity between humanity, rulers, and the heavens, conveniently unconstrained by experiential realities, play a central role in this affirmation of Han identity and the ideal of a pure Han Chinese state. From the Yellow Emperor through the Song Dynasty, movement enthusiasts envision rulers who were at once larger than life yet also close to the people, realizing superhuman feats through dedication to common values: benevolence, filiality, and respect for the heavenly way.

It was only with the arrival of the Mongol Yuan Dynasty and later the Manchu Qing Dynasty, with their breakdown of the division between civilization and barbarism as racial outsiders, that this all-encompassing harmonious sphere uniting heaven and earth was shattered, transforming a political utopia into an everyday dystopia: a racialized fall from grace. Accordingly, in the often less than benevolent actions of the government today, movement participants see only the "savagery" of the Mongols and the Manchus. Again, counterevidence in the present, raising doubts about the pure Han state, is transformed to reaffirm belief in the fantastic identity of Han tradition and the transcendent path of the heavens on earth, just waiting to be recaptured.

MAKE THE HAN GREAT AGAIN

Susan D. Blum's provocative suggestion that in China "perhaps all but the highest-level cadres are subalterns" is reflected in the profiles above.[12] Of course, varying levels of subalterity exist both between and within groups. Movement participants are in many senses very fortunate, insofar as they were not born among the most oppressed in China today: Tibetans, Uyghurs, or Mongolians living under an increasingly unforgiving occupation. Yet this is little comfort for them. As is characteristic of the type of majoritarian nationalist politics that we have seen rising in countries around the world in recent years, they have come to believe that these "ethnic minorities" are the most privileged in Chinese society: they receive a few extra points on the college entrance exam, or have less stringent requirements under the family planning policy, or purportedly survive solely by right of the Han central government's misdirected generosity. In this binary relationship, the Han is envisioned as the oppressed victim of contemporary Chinese society.

Yet in other senses, movement participants are indeed not so fortunate, as illustrated by the profiles above. In the movement's imaginary framework of minority privilege and majority oppression, the former is undoubtedly false, while the latter still holds a curious kernel of truth in the dialectical relationship between the expectation and the experience of majority identity: one can enjoy relative privilege while still feeling and indeed being underprivileged. For although each of the participants described above is a member of the "national core," namely, the Han, an identity that affords them freedom from the discrimination and extreme oppression faced by some, they nevertheless remain strangers in what is assumed to be their own land. Han in this conventional, standard sense then means little more than being nonminority. It certainly does not mean being at the forefront of national and civilizational development, as those who are particularly invested in this identity believe it should.

A personal symbol whose symbolic significance extends far beyond the person, Han Clothing elevates the individual wearing it above his or her immediate surroundings, symbolically transcending the mundane realities of everyday life to be wrapped securely in mythical meaning, by making even the most mundane aspect of everyday life a symbolically rich and indeed fantastic extension of the self into the grandiose ideals of tradition and culture. Following Peter Berger's characterization of religion within society as "locat[ing] the individual's life in an all-embracing fabric of meanings that, by its very nature, transcends that life,"[13] so through the embrace of Han Clothing are individuals symbolically and seamlessly integrated into five millennia of transcendent tradition, no matter how remote such ideals might appear from their daily existence.

In response to the mundane, bland, and failed realities of the present profiled above, ethnicization adds ethnic characteristics, color, and dignity to one's self-image as not only "Han" but indeed, within movement narratives, the "great Han" combining minority-like ethnic fetishism and hyperconfident majority chauvinism. In response to the chaotic, uncertain, and anxiety-inducing experiences of the present, the exaltation of an eternal and magnificent Han tradition provides a sense of certainty and stability passed down from mythical ancestors to oneself, free from the concerns and fluctuations of the present. In response to the inevitable disappointments, injustices, and outrages of the present as experienced in the reality of contemporary China, an alternative vision of an as yet unrealized "real China" reassures one that this is not how life must be, and that there are other considerably more ideal possibilities. And in response to the fundamentally uncontrollable nature of everyday life, an alternative medium of control and indeed power is envisioned through which one can transcend the perpetual splitting of this world.

The meaning of Han Clothing symbolism is thus found at the intersection of social experience and personal desires: the movement allows participants in a diversity of situations to come together in imagining and enacting a transcendent existence elevated above their diverse yet commonly disenchanting worldly experiences, with the self as pure Han located conveniently at this ideal's center. A dual empowerment is thereby enacted in participants' imaginations, granting them mastery over the challenges of the world through the notion of tradition, while at the same time engaging in flattering representations of the self as a member of the purest and most civilized of nationalities, the Han. To invert Blum's formulation that reveals the conflicted source of this movement's desire, we find that there is nothing subaltern in the movement's real and great Han: only unrealized yet still essential power.

The primary value of fantastic Han-ness, then, is its production of an otherwise unattainable fantastic self, a process that I describe in more detail in the next chapter through an ethnography of primary movement activities. However, before we proceed, the personal origins of collective identities will be further analyzed through the curious example of one factional leader who has undergone what can only be described as a radical self-transformation through the legitimizing culturalized medium of Han Clothing.

BROTHER EMPEROR AND THE YELLOW EMPEROR©

Everyone in the Han Clothing Movement hates Brother Emperor. The feeling is virtually unanimous, despite my own impression that he is a perfectly fine, upstanding, albeit somewhat eccentric person. Brother Emperor is an unimposing, unkempt, yet curiously charismatic middle-aged man who leads one very unpopular wing of the Han Clothing Movement. I initially learned of Brother Emperor during my first discussion with Yan in Guangzhou. She had commented disparagingly that there are "all kinds of people" involved in Han Clothing nowadays, citing Brother Emperor as one example. Completely dismissing him as a lowlife and asserting that his faction's Han Clothing was made of low-grade polyester, she declared that if he and his group ever tried to set up shop in Guangzhou, she would call the police immediately to have him arrested. I was uncertain at the time as to how her animosity had reached these levels, but later found that such sentiments were common among Han Clothing Movement enthusiasts. Online, Brother Emperor was repeatedly referred to as "anti-Party and anti-socialist" (*fan Dang fan shehui zhuyi*), accused of running a cult, and mocked as a pervert for occasionally hosting Han Clothing underwear exhibitions with young female models.

The negative sentiments directed towards Brother Emperor, however, only made me ever more eager to meet him and hear his side of the story. I thus decided to contact him to see if he would be willing to meet. Unbeknown to me, my informal and very quickly composed note would soon be read by thousands of the country's Han Clothing enthusiasts with no filter. One early morning on vacation in Hong Kong, I was awakened by a text message from a Han Clothing activist in Guangzhou, written in English as follows: "Kevin, sorry to trouble you—could you please check your email as soon as possible? There are something [*sic*] very important I must tell you now." Having left my computer in Guangzhou to take a break from research and emails, I soon learned in a phone call with my informant that Brother Emperor had taken the liberty of posting my email on forums across the Han Clothing Internet sphere, celebrating me as a "foreign expert" who recognized his leading role in Han Clothing promotion. My friend in Guangzhou told me that the post was being hotly debated, and that she had been contacted by concerned movement participants because she was also affiliated with Sun Yat-sen University: my university affiliation in China, which was quite prominently displayed in the postings, along with my email address. The primary result of these posts was a deluge of emails telling me that Brother Emperor was a liar who ran a cult. I soon discovered that there exists a veritable mountain of websites criticizing Brother Emperor and exposing his "lies;" and of course, there was also an equally forceful barrage of online pro-Brother propaganda sent from my equally unexpected new friends allied with Brother Emperor. Considering that this was the most animated popular response that I received throughout the course of my research, my curiosity about the emotion surrounding Brother Emperor only grew, despite the fact that a few acquaintances reminded me ominously that "curiosity killed the cat."

Thus, against the unanimous advice of everyone with whom I had become acquainted and built trust in the preceding months, in the spring of 2011 I visited the "world headquarters" of Brother Emperor's faction, a tiny shop next to a bus stop, packed full of Han Clothing, mannequins, and *guqin*. Slogans stretched across the top of the headquarters' walls read "revitalizing the Han is the responsibility of each and every Han" and "Westernization is shameful, Han revitalization is glorious." Below these slogans, literally hundreds of images of people dressed in Han Clothing adorned all four walls of the space in an imposing collage. Although Brother Emperor told me that all of these photographs had been taken at events organized by his faction, I soon recognized quite a few photographs of acquaintances from Han Clothing groups in other cities who would have been very unhappy to learn that their visages were being used for promotional purposes here.

In an online profile, Brother Emperor characterizes himself as "the mightiest great thinker, author, strategist, and most important representative figure of the era of revitalization, and creator of the heavenly kingdom."

In person, he was no less enthusiastic about self-promotion. Before we had even sat down to begin our discussion, Brother Emperor eagerly asserted that he had been promoting Han Clothing since the early 1990s, a full decade before anyone else. He claimed that on February 2, 1991, or the 7900th year of the Xia calendar that his faction uses, he went to Cuihua Mountain, purportedly the home of the mythical figure Nüwa, creator of the world. Just as this site is imagined to have played a central role in the creation of the world and the growth of humanity and civilization, Brother Emperor emphasized that it would also eventually be recognized as a sacred location in the revitalization of Han civilization, Chinese civilization, and thus world civilization. The mountain had reportedly been covered in beautiful flowers in full bloom when Brother Emperor arrived dressed in full Han regalia. He proceeded to climb to the highest peak of the mountain, where he worshipped Nüwa. This moment of worship, he asserted, marked the establishment of his mystical, self-described "heavenly dynasty" (*tian chao*). This founding relationship with Nüwa is one explanation for Brother Emperor's idiosyncratic use of a Xia Calendar rendering 2017 as 7925, rather than the Yellow Emperor–based calendar used by other branches of the movement. Another possible explanation for this discrepancy would be the not-so-subtle symbolic capital accrued in reaching further back into history than any other calendar in the movement. The narcissism of this imaginary relationship with Nüwa, the mythical creator of the world, is thereby echoed in his self-produced calendar, which not so subtly includes a number of official holidays recognizing important moments in the life of Brother Emperor.

Brother Emperor's self-declared leading role in the Han Clothing Movement should come as no surprise to anyone who is aware of his declared genealogy. He told me that he is a direct descendant not only of Nüwa, but also of the Yellow Emperor. A booklet that he provided to me includes a detailed family tree tracing his descent through 309 generations from the former and 180 generations from the latter. Such a fantastic lineage has clearly been constructed as a sign of greatness, also demonstrated in the narrative of Brother Emperor's birth featured in the same pamphlet:

> There were many miraculous occurrences surrounding Brother Emperor's birth. His mother was bathing in a holy woman's pond in the Nanshan area. This pond connected directly to the sea. His mother rode a dragon to a holy palace at the bottom of the sea where she ate holy balls and began to feel pregnant. In her dreams she saw a phoenix carrying jade as well as a Kirin

carrying a holy book. Throughout her pregnancy, she felt as if she was surrounded at all times by dragons and phoenixes.

In this description of his sacred conception freed from the embarrassingly animalistic and equalizing act of procreation, Brother Emperor presents himself as a self-producing figure whose existence cannot be traced back to any mere mortal, reminiscent of the fantasies of radical autonomy and self-creation that Steven Sangren has analyzed in the figure of Nezha from *Fengshen Yanyi*.[14] His royal lineage and paranormal conception come together to produce what Brother Emperor described to me as a "heavy burden," referring to his self-pronounced personal responsibility to revitalize Han traditional culture. As much as cultural nationalism functioned as his "id," it also came to take on the shape of a superego, carrying a sacred and thus self-glorifying yet also very weighty mission.

At once bearing and enjoying this burden, in which he is heroically tasked from above with the mission of singlehandedly saving Chinese culture, Brother Emperor claims that he founded his branch of the Han Clothing Movement in 1993, and that he has since been at the forefront of movement activities. His main pieces of evidence supporting these assertions are two photographs, purportedly from 1993, showing him in traditional-style clothing. Upon closer inspection, these images appear to be the type of photographs frequently taken at tourist sites around China, wherein one can briefly rent "traditional style clothing" and have one's photograph taken for a small fee, and thus have no direct relationship with the purer sartorial and cultural vision promoted by the movement. However, now that the Han Clothing Movement has emerged as an idea promoting "traditional clothing," Brother Emperor presents these tourist photographs as evidence that he is a pioneer of the movement, having begun wearing Han Clothing a full decade before anyone else, claims which other movement participants openly mock as self-promotion that ironically cheapens the value of Han Clothing by confusing it with more worldly tourist photos.

From these imagined early beginnings, Brother Emperor constructs a similarly astounding history for his movement faction from the 1990s to the present. The group's first office was supposedly in Shanghai's Jinmao Tower, one of the most expensive office high-rises in the city and a highly unlikely location for an organization with no clear source of income. In 2008, he claims that he moved out of Jinmao Tower and established his headquarters in a scenic area of Beijing: his reasoning, he told me, was that Beijing is the political center of China, and that any movement to revitalize Chinese culture must thus begin from Beijing. Claiming that his headquarters are located at the "center of the world," he told me that he had introduced many senior Chinese leaders to Han Clothing. As a result, he claimed to have presented lectures on Han Clothing at the Forbidden City, the Bird's Nest Olympic Stadium, Tsinghua University, and even the Great Hall of the People. The veracity of any of these reported lectures is highly doubtful. Nevertheless, having imaginarily conquered Beijing, Brother Emperor told me he now aims to establish a Han Clothing store in every major city in China; then a store in every province; and eventually, he told me, a store in all two thousand-plus counties in China, followed by stores across the United States.

Employing a keen marketing sensibility towards these world-dominating goals, Brother Emperor selected a brand spokesman with whom all Han can easily identify: the Yellow Emperor. Brother Emperor not only brazenly uses the supposedly sacred image of the Yellow Emperor as a logo on his clothing, but also claims to have taken the unprecedentedly odd step of copyrighting this image. His faction's clothing tags feature a portrait of the Yellow Emperor fraternally juxtaposed with Brother Emperor's own image, with a caption reading, "the creator of Han national clothing: the founding father of the Chinese people, the Yellow Emperor." Showing me these tags, Brother Emperor bragged that he had total ownership over the image of the Yellow Emperor, the mythical progenitor and founding sovereign of the Chinese people.

Such bravado produced considerable outrage among movement participants. Yet Brother Emperor's self-exaltation has created a parallel personal self-reproducing psychic system, insofar as his critics' attacks only serve from his perspective to further reaffirm his declared leading role in the movement. Responding to my questions about the widespread dislike of his faction within Han Clothing circles, he responded that "when you are on top, there are always people who want to bring you down." Locating critiques of his faction within a flattering historical narrative, he recounted the past century of Chinese history as a history of precisely such ideological clashes against those on top, with increasingly disastrous consequences: from 1911 onwards, he told me, cultural conservatives clashed with reformers, Communists clashed with the Nationalists, everyone clashed with everyone else in the Cultural Revolution, and now, in the reform era, anyone will again do anything to drag others down so as to elevate themselves. In this vision of an all-out social war of all against all, he claimed that because he was the first person to promote Han Clothing, everyone wanted to clash with him, solely to make a name for themselves. And because, he claimed, his faction is the only Han Clothing organization to have hosted events in every province of China, smaller local organizations want to pick fights with him just to promote themselves. Any criticism, he alleged, was the product of jealousy that primarily reflects the current disastrous state of morals and personal character in China, a descent that begins from the Qing's elimination of Han Clothing. The only product of such "disgusting" tactics, he asserted, would be division. His loftier goal, he asserted, is to unite, like the Supreme Ultimate, with himself revealingly cast in this supreme role.

As our conversation drew to a close, Brother Emperor did not hesitate to apply his hyperbolic skills to praising me and my research. Describing me variably as a modern-day Marco Polo or Edgar Snow, he repeatedly emphasized the importance of my work with Han Clothing enthusiasts for promoting a true understanding of Chinese culture. As I left, he casually commented that I should share the results of my research with then-Secretary of State Hillary Clinton. When I responded that my dissertation would not likely take priority on Clinton's reading list, he said that I was underestimating myself.

Then, eager to avoid underestimating either one of us, he asked me to write a note and sign my name in his guest book. Certain that whatever I wrote would be shared on the group's site, I paused and expressed my own uncertainty as to what exactly I should write. Brother Emperor, without hesitation, suggested that I copy a section from one of his poems into the guest book, while he took a series of photographs. The poem, entitled "Go, China" (*Zhongguo, jia you*), read as follows:

> We need to wash away that century of humiliation and disasters,
> We must know that for 8,000 years we were always the highest, the greatest, the strongest,
> We were originally the center of the world and its master,
> When we are united in solidarity we will always be the greatest central power in the world.

. . .

That evening, as expected, images of a certain "renowned American anthropologist" visiting Brother Emperor were posted across a number of Han Clothing forums. And as expected, these images resulted in another series of emails from movement enthusiasts eager to reveal the dirty truth about Brother Emperor, and asking whether the photos were fakes produced through Photoshop. Many friends even claimed to be able to see the traces of Photoshopping, suggesting that there was no way that I could have actually gone forward with this visit. By this point, however, I was no longer surprised at the response, and had begun to develop a theory to explain why Brother Emperor was so widely detested by other branches of the Han Clothing Movement.

Granted, he was an eccentric individual who gave himself ridiculous titles, held quite a few untenable viewpoints, and never shied away from painting a very flattering portrayal of himself. These were the characteristics of his persona upon which his critics focused. Yet as we can see from the aforementioned analysis of personal dilemmas and redeeming self-representation through the Han Clothing Movement, these were not in any sense characteristics unique to Brother Emperor. Brother Emperor and his faction, in fact, are not in my analysis qualitatively different from any other branch of the Han Clothing Movement. Rather, the perceived differences are primarily quantitative: Brother Emperor took the self-glorification hidden within the movement's celebration of collective identity much further than others, with often embarrassing results. The primary source of animosity toward him is then the degree to which his completely unsubtle self-presentation as self-declared master of the universe made explicit processes of desire and exaltation that are otherwise implicit within the Han Clothing Movement, veiled comfortably under the self-legitimizing ideals of race, tradition, culture, and Chineseness. The act of distancing from him through criticism is then born from the discomfiting and anxiety-inducing recognition of similarity.[15]

In his daily life, Brother Emperor faces many of the same dilemmas as the movement participants described in the previous sections: the search for meaning, order, peace, control, dignity, and glory. His attempts to express, resolve, and surpass these issues through the type of self–re-creation provided by the Han Clothing Movement, however, have been uniquely fantastic, shattering the cover of tradition and culture that usually legitimizes the movement's cultural products. His self-naming as Brother Emperor, which sounds just as awkward in Chinese as in English, renders explicit the self-aggrandizing nature of movement participants' pseudoclassical pseudonyms. His meticulously detailed yet thoroughly unlikely genealogy, extending from Nüwa through the Yellow Emperor to himself, makes explicit the search for worth implicit within Han Clothing Movement portrayals of the Han race, the ancestors, and the self. His stated mission to revitalize Han culture makes explicit the search for meaning implicit within the Han Clothing Movement's goals of "revitalizing the Han." And his repeatedly displayed determination to be the first and the best in everything makes explicit the otherwise unspoken yet central component of self-interest and self-aggrandizement within the Han Clothing Movement.

Within the mainstream practices of the movement, the modes of personal desire analyzed in this chapter are carefully concealed through such legitimizing collective ideas as "Han-ness," "Chineseness," "tradition," "culture," or "essence." These labels provide a disinterested and naturalizing cover for the fantastic self-glorification in response to disappointing realities that had developed within the movement. By contrast, Brother Emperor's complete lack of subtlety and reliable overbearing in matters of self-presentation make the personally interested, self-glorifying operations of the movement all too apparent. The reason that Han Clothing Movement participants detest Brother Emperor, then, is that when they look at him, they see their desires, their solutions, and most importantly themselves, laid bare below a thoroughly discomfiting magnifying glass, with the naturalizing cover of tradition shockingly stripped away.

FOUR

Reenacting the Land of Rites
and Etiquette

BETWEEN THE VIRTUAL AND THE MATERIAL

> But certainly for the present age, which prefers the sign to the
> thing signified, the copy to the original, representation to reality,
> the appearance to the essence ... illusion only is sacred, truth
> profane. Nay, sacredness is held to be enhanced in proportion as
> truth decreases and illusion increases, so that the highest degree
> of illusion comes to be the highest degree of sacredness.
>
> —FEUERBACH, Preface to the second edition of
> *The Essence of Christianity*[1]

HAVING ESTABLISHED THE SIMULTANEOUS DILEMMA and appeal
of national identity as an always unrealized imaginary community caught
between image and reality, and having traced the location of the Han
Clothing Movement and its individual members within these tensions, I now
turn to a consideration of the objects, practices, and media through which
participants attempt to bridge these gaps. For the Han Clothing Movement
is not only a symptom of the dilemmas facing national being; at the same
time, it is an imaginary cure, suturing fundamental lacks in the experience
of nationhood. As described in the preceding chapters, Han Clothing
emerged first on the Internet as a virtual image of a traditional, utopian "land
of rites and etiquette" inverting the present and presented as China's lost
truth. This chapter examines three ways in which this always elusive truth is
fleetingly materialized and gradually incorporated into reality in the present
through the media of traditional clothing, ritual, and photography. Based in
a founding tension between the fantastic and the experiential, as well as
between the virtual and the material, the Han Clothing Movement combines the most "ancient" of apparel (Han Clothing) and practices (ritual)
with the most "modern" of technologies (digital photography) to extend a

96

FIGURE 8. Enthusiasts wearing Han Clothing, Zhengzhou.

sacred image of the nation across space and time. The combination of these three media (clothing, ritual, and photography) materializes and stabilizes the otherwise elusive grandeur of the Han, of China, and by extension of the self as a seemingly timeless reality, comfortingly misrepresenting a perpetually discordant process as a stable and eternal identity.

CLOTHING: MATERIALIZING THE GREAT HAN

In any examination of the objects and practices of the Han Clothing Movement, clothing must obviously be placed on center stage. Although there are many aspects to the movement, participants come together first and foremost for clothing, which is imagined to embody the fantasy identity first constructed online, carrying the very essence of Han-ness across time from the distant past to the present to one's own body in this present. An essential aspect of Han Clothing's power within the movement is its perceived symbolic depth: moving far beyond a banal understanding of apparel as covering or protection,[2] nearly every aspect of Han Clothing is imagined to represent a central component of Chinese culture. My notes from conversations with movement activists include countless, often unexpected details about the symbolism surrounding this apparel: the circularity of its sleeves refers to the compass, one of the great inventions of Chinese culture; the seam running down the back extends straight, all of the way from top to bottom, symbolizing by its unswerving nature the importance of moral rectitude (*zheng*); the bottom of the robe ends parallel to the ground below, symbolizing mutuality and balance, an essential concept in Chinese culture; the lack of buttons or such modern accouterments as zippers helps to ensure the natural flow of one's *qi*; the fact that the left side of the robe folds over the right side symbolizes the supremacy of *yang* over *yin*, or in a somewhat more esoteric explanation, of the mythical green dragon's victory over the white tiger; and the symmetry of the clothing's design as a whole signals the unity, stability, and harmony of society. In many cases, these symbolic associations appear highly unlikely and indeed fantastic: for example, if Han Clothing first emerged five millennia ago, long before the invention of the compass, then the roundness of its sleeves would not be symbolizing but rather predicting this discovery. Yet to overanalyze such historical inconsistencies would not only overlook the distinct possibility that Han Clothing's sleeves are round simply because sleeves are round, but also far more importantly overlook the allure of these "facts" far beyond their facticity. Doubts strip away meaning and are thus meaningless to Han Clothing enthusiasts: an informant once noted, revealingly, that the term for one type of male Han Clothing, *shenyi* (深衣), was homophonic with the term for deep meaning, *shenyi* (深意).

Han Clothing's plethora of meaning is buttressed by its fundamental materiality, a worldly extension of the virtual fantasies developed online. This materiality is manifested in two main senses: first, Han Clothing is imagined to have been passed down unchanged from the distant past, and second, it is immediately available here, in the present, to be possessed, held, and used.

Imagined as the first form of clothing in the world, Han Clothing was purportedly created by the Yellow Emperor, in his full culture-bearing capacities, roughly five millennia ago.[3] This first act of civilization, mythically concurrent with the establishment of homes and family life, provided protection to subjects as well as order to society, initiating the emperor's rule of "all under heaven." This clothing was then, according to movement mythologies, passed down through the generations and worn throughout the dynasties and their accompanying great historical moments until its suppression under the Qing. When Confucius developed his philosophical system that would in movement participants' minds produce an ideal society, Han Clothing was there. When the Qin Emperor founded the first unified Chinese state, Han Clothing was there. When the great inventions of paper, gunpowder, and the compass were discovered, Han Clothing was there. When Emperor Taizong reigned over the golden age of the Tang, Han Clothing was there. And when Zhu Yuanzhang led the victorious establishment of the Ming after the Yuan invasion, Han Clothing was there, just as it was when Koxinga gave all that he could to resist the murderous Qing. And after having been there at these moments, it is also here in the present, providing a link from these moments in the past to today. To believe that "Han Clothing" was created by and passed down from the Yellow Emperor is roughly equivalent to believing that something called "Western clothing" could be derived from Adam and Eve, and that "Western clothing" had been worn throughout the vicissitudes of history that followed. Nevertheless, such observations are again of far less import than the affective identifications with these mythical histories, collecting and transmitting the symbols of "Chinese culture" from the distant past to the present. According to movement mythologies, the sole remnants in the Yellow Emperor's tomb today are his Han Clothing: such permanence and stability is lacking in every aspect of real human existence, yet is imaginarily given concrete form in Han Clothing.

Such transcendent stability and indeed immortality is particularly resonant in an era of unpredictable and destabilizing change, as we see in China today, in which identity not only faces the usual existential challenge of its own impossibility but the further challenges of increasingly rapid sociocultural transformations. Anne Hollander has analyzed nonfashion or "traditional clothing" as linked to a fixed cosmology, representing an ideal of certainty to both its wearers and its beholders.[4] Insofar as such order and certainty is perceived as lacking, as seen in the previous chapter, Han Clothing is perceived as a solution to this lack, or an ideal vision of how things once were and how they might one day be again. As such, what Hollander calls "the trap of tradition" or "the prison of unquestioning wisdom" can also be experienced as an imaginary sphere of certainty, order, and thus comfort in an era of often overwhelming uncertainty. Contra the dynamism in sartorial culture recounted so evocatively in Finnane's recent history of fashion in China,[5] movement participants yearn for a static and unchanging vision of the Han and China: Han Clothing is thus in essence an antifashion, capable of overturning the disorderly rhythm of shifting styles and desires, which are homologous to the unpredictable shifts of contemporary society, to promote a lasting order embodied in the eternal figure of Han Clothing and the self covered therein. As one popular Han Clothing motto claims, "Han clothing on one's body brings a lifetime of peace" (*Hanfu zai shen, ping'an yisheng*).

Following Boris Groys's definition of "the new" as a revaluation of values that incorporates an aspect of the profane into the sacred,[6] it is then no surprise that movement participants deploy "the old" (nonfashion) to valorize and redistribute the sacred within today's profane experiential world. As the source of civilization itself, found at the origins of culture and carrying the symbols of the culture that followed, Han Clothing bears a striking resemblance to the sacred as analyzed by Maurice Godelier. In *The Enigma of the Gift*, Godelier defines the sacred as "a certain type of relationship that humans entertain with the origin of things,"[7] wherein the human origins of society are alienated to supernatural beings, such as the culture-bearing Yellow Emperor, thereby giving the social sphere embodied in these constructions a sacrosanct allure.[8] Culture, having been sacralized, is in turn embodied in sacred worldly objects that are presumed to represent these reigning supernatural powers. Han Clothing, as a symbol of culture descended from a mythical progenitor, bears these marks of the sacred, and so in turn does the movement's corresponding vision of the ideal Han society. Yet Godelier's subsequent analysis also reminds us how sacred objects, such as the *kwaimatnie*, bull-roarers, and flutes of the Baruya are never distributed equally.

The *kwaimatnie*, for example, are pairs of "oblong packet[s] wrapped in a strip of brown bark, which [are] again wrapped in an *ypmoulie*, the ceremonial headband worn by men, which is dyed red, the color of the Sun."[9] These objects, according to the Baruya, were given to their ancestors by the Sun, Moon, and spirits.[10] Although they then represent the origins of the Baruya as a whole, they are not distributed equally among the Baruya as a whole: they are solely the possession of men of *kwaimatnie*-owning lineages. These sacred items thereby, in Godelier's analysis, give these particular men symbolic power and set them apart from others in society as representatives of the divine, illusorily naturalizing their superiority.[11] Such unequal distributions of the sacred provide a novel angle for interpreting the social deployment of Han Clothing as self-representation, wherein those who don these garments come to perceive themselves as uniquely symbolically tied to the divine nature of Han-ness and tradition compared to their fellow compatriots: a traditionalist vanguard.

Han Clothing is precisely such a sacred object passed down from ancient times that one can not only hold but within which one literally wraps oneself as a symbolic representative of the often-cited trope of "five millennia of civilization." Han Clothing enthusiasts can have and hold this grandeur; one can rent it or one can buy it; one can wear it or one can tuck it away in one's closet for special occasions; one can distinguish oneself from those immediately surrounding oneself or one can post photos of oneself in Han Clothing online for others to see. Han Clothing as a materialization of a particular ideal of sacred Chineseness is there to be had, and one can literally do with it as one pleases. As a symbolically rich representative of Chinese culture purportedly derived from its origins, Han Clothing is then, in contrast to the usual shirts, slacks, jeans, and skirts donned by the average urban Han, an alternative form of symbolic capital in the present. Although Han Clothing enthusiasts, contradicting the fundamentalist narrative of all human history as class struggle imposed after 1949,[12] envision the past as a time of internal homogeneity, represented in the form of a single, standard ethnic uniform, they nevertheless as representatives of this imaginary unity in the present elevate themselves above their fellow Han as their sole authentic representatives.

One interviewee in Kunming recounted to me how when she wears Han Clothing she simply "feels different," allowing her to carry herself and behave differently. The ability of an object to change the way that one feels and one's sense of oneself represents the imaginary power of said object, materializing the imaginary as an intrinsic part of oneself: examples in more familiar contexts might include luxury brand items, Apple products, or organic and other eco-friendly merchandise that present a particular distinctive, elevated, and aestheticized image of their owner to viewers. Yet alongside this imaginary power, the existence of this object as simply an object means that one can own and thus control it, along with its attendant aura. The object emanates an imaginary power that extends far beyond it, yet at the material level this imaginary power is able to be held and thus fully possessed by its owner, who in turn objectifies him- or herself through this object as an embodiment of its ideal. The virtual and idealized images of Han-ness developed in Internet discussions and drawings are then transformed by Han Clothing into a stable, coherent, and possessable material unit, with a grand continuity established from the past into the present of which one is part: a symbolically rich envelope[13] that one can own and in which one can wrap and present oneself.

If clothing is "nonverbal communication,"[14] then Han Clothing transforms the self into a living story, materializing movement myths of Han-ness. The sign above the entrance to a popular Han Clothing store in Guangzhou reads "Han Clothing is, just like the Han language (Chinese language) and Han characters (Chinese characters), a central component of any Han's life." This is not only a statement of the value of Han Clothing, but also an articulation of a metaphorical relationship between these three aspects of "Han-ness" (*hanyu, hanzi, hanfu*). All are preformed structures or tools that come from outside of oneself, like the idea of the Han itself, yet become an intrinsic part of selfhood, and even the primary tools of the fantasy construction, self-presentation, and indeed the realization of the self. This external structure then comes to be interpreted as an inherent and indeed natural expression of oneself, as one who speaks Han language, reads Han characters, and now wears Han Clothing, and is thus fully and purely Han. Accordingly, although Han Clothing is worn on the exterior of the body, the message that it presents was frequently described by informants as "beauty from within emanating outwards (*you nei wang wai de mei*)": an external marker of a timeless internal essence.

Clothing is a symbolic medium, carrying cultural as well as personal images; yet its symbolic nature exists alongside its ordinary nature, meaning that messages expressed through clothing are naturalized as expressions of the intrinsic nature of the wearer. It is something of a truism to state that people who dress in a particular manner are generally perceived in that manner: the construction of an image of the self through clothing proceeds alongside a construction of this image as quite natural and unconstructed. These processes can work, however, in two ways. For example, when one attends a professional job interview either in the United States or in China, one generally wears a suit and tie to present a slightly more refined image of the self. Although all involved know that the interviewee does not wear a suit and tie all day every day, and that below this clothing he or she is just as naked as anyone else, the donning of this outfit often serves as a naturalized reflection of the minimal internal qualities necessary for one's recognition in such a setting. To arrive in a T-shirt and sandals would misrepresent the self, even if this is in fact how one usually dresses: this naturalized construction of identity via clothing is described most memorably in a satirical headline from *The Onion*: "Boss's clout evaporates after he's seen in shorts at company picnic."[15] Yet at the same time, in less formal situations where a T-shirt and sandals are appropriate, the interview outfit of a suit and tie can by contrast present an image of unseemly uptightness: this counterexample reminds us that even when the message conveyed by clothing is pejorative and thus unintended by the wearer, it is still often perceived by the viewer as a direct expression of the wearer's internal self despite its fundamentally mediated nature.

According to movement ideals, Han-ness proper should then be unproblematically communicated to all viewers through the medium of Han Clothing. Yet the naturalizing work of clothing means that while Han Clothing transforms the self into a living story, one can at the same time never be sure that the story told is the story that one wants to tell. Such naturalized miscommunication, I observed, is a common dilemma for movement participants. Ironically, considering the racial-nationalist origins of the Han Clothing Movement, movement enthusiasts walking the streets of China today are often misrecognized as "Japanese" or "Koreans." The alien nature of Han Clothing relative to its environment leads spectators to assume that its wearers are members of the quite diverse collection of non-Chinese within China singularly referred to as "foreigners" (*waiguoren*). Han Clothing, in fact, stood out so prominently on the streets of most cities that bystanders, rarely hesitant to grant me a stare or shout "Hello," barely took notice of me for an entire year while I walked the streets of China's cities with Han Clothing devotees. Instead, passersby would often laughingly shout "Konnichiwa" or "An-nyeong-ha-se-yo" or even exclaim "Japanese devils" (*Riben guizi*) toward the Han Clothing enthusiasts with me, based in the association of "traditional clothing" with such Asian neighbors. Such misrecognition, although annoying to clothing enthusiasts, is nevertheless repurposed for further self-flattery, as enthusiasts congratulate themselves on their deep grasp of Han tradition in contrast to their less informed compatriots, who after all mistake their proper national clothing for something foreign.

At other times, such popular misrecognition can have significantly more disturbing consequences. When the captain of a Chinese fishing boat was detained by the Japanese Coast Guard in September 2010 in the contested Senkaku Islands region, the now all-too-familiar scene of anti-Japanese protests (*fanri youxing*) emerged yet again in cities across China. One city rocked by these protests was Chengdu, which is also home to a large and fairly active contingent of Han Clothing enthusiasts. In an unfortunate collision of nationalisms, a young enthusiast wore Han Clothing one evening in October 2010 to dine at Diko's, an imitation of Kentucky Fried Chicken that

FIGURE 9. Photo-bombing Han Clothing enthusiasts, Lunar New Year Flower Market, Guangzhou.

localizes its product as "Chinese fried chicken." This movement participant unknowingly caught the attention of a crowd of anti-Japanese protestors who, failing to recognize Han Clothing as in any way "Han," presumed that this young lady was wearing a kimono and was thus Japanese, thereby transforming her in the odd logic of angry nationalism into a representative of Japan upon whom frustration about this incident could, and in this twisted logic should, be unleashed. Again, a message was clearly expressed, and presumed to be intrinsic to the wearer, but was certainly not the message intended. As angry youth surrounded the windows of the restaurant and chanted patriotic slogans, this Han Clothing enthusiast was reportedly left immensely perplexed as to what was happening. When she tried to leave the restaurant, however, she discovered to her shock as a proud Han that she was in fact the target of her compatriots' wrath. Refusing to listen to her explanation that she was wearing Han Clothing and not a kimono, the crowd forced her to kneel on the ground and take off her dress, under which she was wearing only a bra and panties. When she fled to the women's room inside Diko's, the crowd outside took the opportunity to burn her perceived "kimono" amid a rush of self-congratulatory cell-phone photography. A misinterpretation of Han Clothing's message led in this case to an ugly collision between two branches of Han nationalism.

Another frequent misinterpretation of Han Clothing sees this clothing style as a form of "cosplay," the popular cultural trend originating in Japan, in which usually young people dress as and take on the characteristics of their favorite characters from manga and anime programs. Comments from onlookers about "cosplay" and questions to enthusiasts about what characters they represent are a persistent irritant to Han Clothing devotees on the streets. The usual response from Han Clothing enthusiasts, "This is not cosplay at all, it's completely different," belies a certain anxiety, reminiscent of the aggressive self-differentiation by most movement enthusiasts from Brother Emperor, eagerly distinguishing Han Clothing from cosplay to defend against the potential recognition of their fundamental similarities. Enthusiasts suggest that whereas cosplay is simply a fad, Han Clothing is a lasting tradition; whereas cosplayers briefly take on imaginary avatars, Han Clothing enthusiasts realize their true identity and tradition. The preceding analyses, however, suggest the undeniable similarities between the two, namely, the taking on of a role or indeed an avatar greater than oneself as oneself. I was then not surprised to find in my research a certain degree of overlap between Han Clothing circles and cosplay circles in the Pearl River Delta: quite a few Han Clothing enthusiasts also displayed an interest in manga and cosplay, while some cosplay enthusiasts at expos or weekend gatherings would occasionally don Han Clothing. It is this similarity, or the fundamental equation of the two types of fantasy activity, that then produces the defensive reaction that the two activities are "completely different." Tellingly, less than fully dedicated participants in the Han Clothing Movement are often disparagingly labeled as "just doing cosplay."

Han Clothing thus, while suturing fundamental lacks in national experience through a materialization of the virtual idea of the "Great Han," continues to produce further identity dilemmas, naturalizing not only communications but also miscommunications of identity: this solution produces new dilemmas. Yet just as the solution to the problems posed by the inherently disappointing nationalist experience is to be found in further nationalism, so the solution to the problems posed by Han Clothing is to be found in Han Clothing: the broader promotion of knowledge about this national uniform will, in the minds of enthusiasts, resolve the problems of misrecognition discussed above, and thereby eventually lead to a sacred Han renaissance.

Yet this solution too has its limits, for Han Clothing's combination of sacredness and taken-for-granted-ness produces a far more irresolvable dilemma that has riled the movement from its inception: the tension between the sacred and the profane. The vast majority of movement participants wear their Han Clothing on special occasions, such as traditional festivals, rituals or other ceremonies, or at the least weekend gatherings with other movement participants, generally held in such aesthetically appropriate environments as temples, memorials, or parks. Yet the final goal of Han Clothing activities, as often stated, is to produce an imaginarily charmed society in which everyone wears Han Clothing. There thus remains a current within the movement that is dedicated to wearing Han Clothing on a daily basis: one on-site computer repairman, for example, was particularly proud of his habit, painstakingly documented in a mountain of photographs, of arriving at people's apartments to work on their computers in his Han Clothing, demonstrating an ideal vision of the simultaneous mastery of modernity and tradition, ethnicity and civilization, assumed to be unique to the Han; other movement participants also celebrate their determination to wear their Han Clothing on a daily basis to college or their office jobs. Such a deployment of Han Clothing seeks to distribute this apparel's sacredness throughout one's life and throughout society towards the goal of making both sacred as a whole; this is, after all, how the past is presumed to have been, a time in which everyone wore Han Clothing at all times, and in which society was characterized by etiquette, elegance, aesthetics, and social harmony.

This approach, while realizing the proliferation of the sacred and thus approximating fantasy, nevertheless runs the risk of making the sacred profane, or even cheapening the sacred by making it too widespread and thereby obliterating the fantasy around which the movement is structured. Brother Emperor, described in the previous chapter, repeatedly vacillated between describing all of his clothing as handmade and thus authentic in a traditional sense, or as mass-produced according to surging demand and thus popular in a seemingly more profane yet equally sacred mode: this is yet another tension to which there appears to be no clear solution. James Flugel proposes that clothing provides a medium to realize the "maximum of satisfaction in accordance with the reality principle,"[16] an assessment that applies with equal validity to Han Clothing and the unrelenting national identity reality principle that it attempts to overcome. For although one's image can be purified in Han Clothing, constructing an ideal heritage extending from the distant past into the present, one's surrounding environment nevertheless remains

FIGURE 10. The people of Panyu staring at Han Clothing enthusiasts.

unchanged and profoundly profane, as illustrated by the misconceptions and disappointments described above.

In the course of my research with Han Clothing enthusiasts, I repeatedly observed the often unintentionally comical ways in which the present broke through into ideal moments: inescapable "surrounding and observing" (*weiguan*) from curious bystanders, puzzled questions about enthusiasts' nationality, obnoxious photobombing and frequent sneaky attempts to pose in photographs with movement enthusiasts without asking their permission. Hence participants face a new problem: the greater the distribution of such sacred moments through the promotion of Han Clothing, the greater the risk that they will be spoiled, thereby failing to resolve the tension between the sacred idea and profane experience of China that originally generated this desire, and thus again reproducing this desire for the sacred as fantasy, along with the allure of its attendant cultural products.

This tension between the sacred and the profane is thus an expression of a far more fundamental point of concern for the Han Clothing Movement: the problem of the present. Movement narratives joyfully recount the grandeur of the Han people, extending from their mythic origins at the time of the Yellow

FIGURE 11. The people of Panyu staring at Han Clothing enthusiasts.

Emperor until the disgrace of Manchu colonization in the Qing Dynasty. These narratives, however, do not change the fact that movement participants live in the present; the sign described earlier reading "Han Clothing is, just like the Han language and Han characters, an integral part of every Han's life" is located directly above the entrance to a Han Clothing store in Guangzhou. It serves as a passageway, such that visitors are required to cross this symbolic boundary from the profane shopping mall with a Kentucky Fried Chicken located directly across the hall, to be reborn symbolically into this detached space of pure and sacred "Han-ness." Accordingly, the next section examines the inescapable location of the movement and its activities in the ambiguous present and the means by which attempts are made to distribute sacred and profane spaces in appropriate proportions therein.

RITUAL: COMING OF AGE IN SHENZHEN

The fundamental dilemma of the present could not have seemed more distant one spring afternoon in Shenzhen, a city that epitomizes the present and

FIGURE 12. Coming of age ceremony, Shenzhen.

all its problems as the pioneering capital of China's reform and opening policy. I was observing a teenage girl's coming-of-age ceremony (*chengren li*) marking the passage from childhood to adulthood in a traditional manner, during a celebration of the Shangsi Festival (*Shangsi jie*), the third day of the third month of the Lunar New Year. The master of ceremonies on this particular occasion displayed an unwavering propensity for speaking in Classical Chinese. Although this linguistic idiosyncrasy left the majority of spectators perplexed as to the content of his monologue, it added the allure of a seemingly pure tradition descended from time immemorial, a self-segregating mystification that I encountered repeatedly throughout my research. According to this master of ceremonies, when a young lady turned fifteen in premodern China, her parents would hold a coming-of-age ceremony. The pinning ceremony for women (*jili*), which was to be enacted that afternoon, was described as a "solemn ceremonial process" (*zhuangzhong yishi guocheng*) passed down from the ancestors. Yet the thundering declaration that the ceremony was now "officially starting" (*zhengshi kaishi*), a form of official-speak often associated with state meetings and events, belied the ways in which the past and the present are always intertwined in Han Clothing imaginings and practices.

Once the ceremony had begun, the initiate's parents entered first, and proceeded to take their seats onstage. Then the initiate (*jizhe*), dressed in elaborate and colorful Han Clothing that marked her as the center of attention, entered, bowed to her elders, and knelt upon a pillow. The host read aloud a passage in largely incomprehensible classical Chinese. Upon completion of this passage, the initiate's hair was combed, and a pin was inserted into her hair. She then went backstage to change into a new outfit, and when she emerged again, she bowed to her parents once more and returned to kneel on her pillow. Another indecipherable classical passage was read and another pin was inserted. This process was repeated one more time before the initiate knelt again upon a pillow and bowed deeply three times to the flag of the People's Republic of China, in a memorable anachronism for this traditionalist ritual that generated a few puzzled, awkward laughs from audience members. Despite such quirky moments, an air of solemnity reigned throughout the process.

As the ritual proceeded, the master of ceremonies explained the meanings behind each act, emphasizing in particular such meaning's omnipresence. For example, each time that a hairpin is added, the initiate's hair is held more tightly to her scalp, symbolizing increasing levels of "social responsibility" (*shehui zeren*). According to the MC's explanation, one can "run about" with one's hair in wild disarray as a child; yet adulthood requires a far greater degree of control and decorum. Hence, the repeated insertion of hairpins to the hair, bringing this unruly mass under control, is described as symbolizing the initiate's new role and responsibilities within society.[17] Each change of clothing is further described as making the initiate's attire increasingly "luxurious," thus emphasizing, alongside the pins, a proper balance between strength and beauty in the model woman, or what the master of ceremonies called "proper values" (*zhengque jiazhiguan*). Such proper values are again highlighted in the repeated acts of bowing to one's parents as well as, eventually, to the flag, both of which represent "knowing where you came from" and proper respect for one's elders.

Despite these symbolically deep explanations for each step in the ritual process, resembling the elaborate explanations of the various eternal symbolic elements within Han Clothing, the precise meaning of symbolic moments therein is again never as important as the simple presence of meaning as meaning itself. Although participants in the Han Clothing Movement viewed this moment as the revitalization of an essential ritual from traditional Chinese society, constitutive of both personal identity and the social order as a whole, what was enacted that afternoon was not so much a genuine traditional ritual as a drama of movement participants' relations to an imagined national past and the lived present through the legitimizing guise of tradition. The following analysis then intends, like the preceding analysis of Han Clothing, to question this practice's presentation as an "eternal tradition," and to instead interpret the social and personal motivations and rewards of this particular ritual representation of Han-ness: in the words of Seligman, Weller, Puett, and Simon in their *Ritual and Its Consequences*, what I witnessed that afternoon was the ritualized creation of "a subjunctive world in overt tension with the world of lived experience."[18]

A first prominent characteristic of this ritual is its segregated location, safely outside of the unpredictability of contemporary society. Victor Turner, drawing upon Arnold Van Gennep's analysis of rites of passage,[19] has highlighted separation or segregation from the outside world as a fundamental feature of the ritual process.[20] This separation is, however, particularly pronounced in Han Clothing Movement rituals, insofar as the ritual process is constructed in direct opposition to contemporary society and in hopes of, as I discuss below, the thorough reconstruction of society, producing a determinedly abstracting, insulating, and indeed immunizing tendency in ritual practice. These tendencies are most evident in the actual physical location of ritual: although the daily environment of the average Han Clothing Movement participant is the ever-bustling city, great efforts were made to locate ritual activities in the most serene and remote of spaces, such as mountaintops, riversides, or parks.

Yet beyond physical exteriority, an air of formality and traditionalism within the ritual space symbolically constructed this space as sacred and thus distant from the profane nature of modern society, emerging transcendent over a disappointing reality. In a world far too often devoid of meaning, absolute meaning is found in the mission of inscribing meaning in the world. Within a social environment that revolves around fast-paced living and *renao*, literally meaning "hot and noisy" but often translated as "lively," the solemn quiet that inevitably embraced the ritual environment was all the more striking: ritual participants moved slowly and carefully through the steps of the ritual process, while movement participants and the majority of outside viewers watched in intense silence. Within a linguistic environment that is thoroughly vernacularized, and in which the most imposing of languages is the formulaic and self-congratulatory voice of officialdom, the consistent use of Classical Chinese had a mystifying effect: the inability of most listeners to understand what was being said only made this at once natural yet also distant language all the more symbolically powerful.[21] In a world that can often seem meaningless and underwhelming, everything within the ritual space, from the arrangement of actors to the most minor of prescribed actions such as the insertion of a pin into the hair, is presumed to have deep symbolic and indeed almost magical meaning: this is not my own projection as an analyst seeking out symbolic meaning for me to interpret, but rather how participants explicitly talked about rituals, even in the process of their performance. And although, as discussed above, Han Clothing often seems completely out of place in most contemporary settings and provokes continual curious and even amused questioning from passersby, within this "as if" ritual space[22] with its solemn atmosphere, eloquent classical articulations, and presumably deep meaning, the elaborate designs of Han Clothing finally came to seem completely at home. Movement participants were thus in their element within the hermetically sealed ritual space, insofar as they were far removed from the social reality that both structures and denies their fantasies of Han identity.

This distance from everyday life leads us to consider a second characteristic of ritual: its imaginary power transcending this distance. Although the ritual space is located outside of and constructed in direct opposition to contemporary society, it is presumed to have an ordering effect upon society. A lengthy mystical-functionalist tradition in China extending from Confucius to the Qianlong Emperor[23] has celebrated a form of "magical thinking"[24] that imagines a metaphorical relationship between ritual space and society such that the proper enactment of rituals aids the ordering of the polity and indeed the world itself.[25] The system of ritual offerings in premodern China extended from the grand imperial altars all the way down to the village level, constructed around the assumption that "the logic of these ritual activities would appear to be the very logic organizing the social body and the rhythms of nature."[26] Even in a postmodern era, it should go without saying that such ritual efficacy is purely imaginary. Nevertheless, this long-standing school of thought has the advantage of historical distance working in its favor in the present: having read, as any student would, about the efficacy of rites and ritual in classical texts like *The Analects*, an overly romantic and mystified vision of the imperial past as a perfectly ritually ordered society in contrast to the profane and disordered present naturally emerges. Such a contrast could then, of course, be tautologically reaffirmed by the evident lack of traditional ritual in this profane, disordered, and experientially all-too-real social present, misrecognizing correlation between the two conditions for causation, and thereby transforming the imaginary vision of what "could be" into "once there was."[27]

Derived from this historical fascination with and exaltation of "*li*," as well as the mystical retroactive imaginings of a perfectly ordered society that it generates, traditional Chinese culture and society as a whole are envisioned in the present as having been uniquely saturated with ritual, and thus uniquely endowed with an all-encompassing meaning and order: a meaning and order that has since disintegrated and must now be revitalized. One informant from Wuhan shared with me his proposal for recapturing this imagined ritual glory: rather than a chicken in every pot and a car in every garage, he envisioned a ritual space in every park. Fascinated with the perceived ubiquity of ritual in imperial China and the parallel ubiquity of churches in American towns, he imagined a direct link between sacred ritual-religious activities and national power; after all, he mused, when ritual practice extended throughout Chinese society, China was a land of grandeur and wealth looked upon with envy the world over, a "middle kingdom" proper. Churches in the United States, he asserted, play an essential structural-functional role in communities across the country, producing solidarity and strength that extends throughout the polity, making America today a land of grandeur and wealth looked upon with envy the world over: again, this informant suggested that contemporary America was "more Chinese than China" (*bi women hai hua*), with real "Chineseness" being equal to "civilization," and that China had become considerably more barbarian (*yi*).[28] In seeking a resolution to this troubling situation, he drew upon a saying, "It is ritual that distinguishes people as people" (*ren zhi suoyi wei renzhe, liyi ye*);[29] accordingly, at the time of our meetings he was in the midst of drafting a proposal to be submitted to the National People's Congress recommending that a ritual altar be built in every public park across China. Such an initiative, he reasoned, could provide a space in which communities might gather together and develop a stronger feeling of togetherness, as well as a sacred space in which ancient rituals passed down from the ancestors could be performed, for the ritual enactment of a new political community.[30] The combination of greater communal solidarity and ritual efficacy was, in this informants' mind, central to bringing a new order to society, and making China "Chinese" again, such that the nation could again take on its proper role as a moral exemplar and teacher for other nations of the world. Such a functionalist ritual imaginary, located within the dynamics of national fantasy and the perceived "non-Chinese" nature of today's China, is an exemplary case of Edmund Leach's characterization of ritual as "mak[ing] explicit what is otherwise a fiction":[31] namely, the nationalist's ideal image of the nation, with the self located securely at its center.

This imagined efficacy is related to ritual's third characteristic: its imaginary production of a sense of control in opposition to the unpredictability and difficulties of the world beyond. From the earliest stages of the anthropological study of the ritual phenomenon, both Bronislaw Malinowski and A. R. Radcliffe-Brown noted the role of worldly anxiety in the creation of ritual and the resulting relief of anxiety in the ritual process.[32] Spatially, as noted above, the ritual space is a microsphere carefully insulated from the world beyond yet endowed with magical powers, creating an ideally controllable realm detached from the flows of unpredictability that dominate life. Yet this sense of control and predictability is further symbolically supported by the fact that the actions performed within this space are even further removed from any hint of unpredictability: simplicity, repetition, and invariance are the main characteristics of ritual action,[33] allowing for the realization of what Jonathan Smith has called "ritualized perfection."[34] This is apparent in the example of the coming-of-age ceremony described above, which revolved solely around the repeated insertion of pins into an initiate's hair: the type of activity that in profane settings seems highly unlikely to draw a captivated audience.

Despite the simplicity and banality of these actions within a nonritual setting, Bruce Kapferer shows in his analysis of the Suniyama ritual in Sri Lanka that such acts are nevertheless endowed within the ritual space with meanings that are anything but simple and banal. The enactment of "activities integral to the routine activities of the lived-in life world" is tightly prescribed and precisely ordered in the ritual space,[35] based in the belief that their completion, removed from the indeterminacies of the real world, will have substantive real-world effects through an otherworldly agency that extends far beyond the immediate ritual space. They are enacted slowly and with careful attention to detail,[36] as was made painfully apparent that afternoon in Shenzhen, to ensure the proper steps and the presumed proper effects. These predetermined, intricately prescribed, repetitious, and simple actions functioning within a virtual model of the world that is at once located within but at the same time safely segregated from this real world furnish a sense of control and power that is otherwise lacking in a world in which getting anything at all done, much less anything existentially significant, is reliably far from simple.

As Victor Turner has memorably observed, ritual renders "the structurally inferior as the morally and ritually superior," transforming "secular weakness" into "sacred power,"[37] constructing a new world that overcomes the inevitable disappointments of the everyday world outside.[38] Cut off from this external world and its uncertainties and complications, yet imagined to have profound effects upon this external world; at once simple and repetitive, yet also deeply meaningful and powerful, ritual activities endow their enactors with agency far beyond that which they enjoy in their daily lives. The profiles in the previous chapter highlighted the ways in which the burdens and enormity of life continually bore down upon movement participants, often leaving them unable to attain their ideals no matter how they tried; ritual action completely inverts this situation by endowing even the smallest and simplest of actions, such as bowing or inserting a pin into one's hair, with a profound meaning and far-reaching effects. The ritual space then provides a microcosmic realm for the acting out of an elusive fantasy of extreme personal agency in relation to society:[39] whereas Han Clothing materializes the virtual fantasies of Han-ness developed online, with mixed results on account of the profane social environment, the ritual space allows one to act out these fantasies of identity and power in the material world, in an empowering sacred war by other means against profane reality.

Contemporary social alienation, a long-standing tradition idealizing ritual's efficacy, and personal desires for control and power (in an uncontrollable world in which it is easy and indeed logical to feel powerless) are then essential to the rise of ritual as a central activity of the Han Clothing Movement. Parallels between imaginings of ritual and imaginings of Han Clothing are instructive: both are constructed in opposition to mainstream modes of contemporary existence; both promise an otherwise elusive order through intricate attention to detail and a particularly rich symbolic depth; both are presumed to be capable of changing the course of contemporary China, and both place the self firmly at the center of these symbolically rich and practically powerful media, exercising control through the material possession of clothing as eternal culture or the imaginarily practical action of ritual as agency. The control provided by each stabilizes otherwise irresolvable aspects of existence, from the fleeting nature of one's sense of identity to the uncertainty of the current social order and of one's position and path therein. Most importantly and fundamentally, however, both imaginarily express direct relationships to the sacred. Han Clothing imagines this direct relationship extending from the mythic origins of humanity towards the present; yet as noted in the previous section, even after recapturing this symbolically sacred materiality in the present, the current social environment continues to pose dilemmas that make the sacred appear remote or even foreign. Ritual responds by producing an insulated yet hypermeaningful virtual sphere in which the fantasies of Han Clothing can be acted out in the present, finally managing to locate oneself, however fleetingly, within the sacred image of the "land of rites and etiquette."

RITUAL: MY BIG SACRED HAN WEDDING

Reflecting this search for control and power in a fundamentally uncontrollable world, the primary ritual activities promoted by the Han Clothing Movement revealingly revolve around life-changing and usually uncertain moments in an individual's life: such rites of passage as the entrance into adulthood, the entry into marriage, and the birth of children. *Chengren* or the entrance into adulthood, for example, is one of the central focuses of movement ritual activities, as well as arguably one of the more difficult and socially charged passages in one's life experience: one might say, at least, that it is perceived as such at the time, raising questions of self-assertion, independence, sexuality, and relations to one's family and society as a whole. The profiles in the previous chapter illustrated the centrality of these very issues in movement participants' lives: from difficulties in finding a stable career and a reliable source of income, to continued reliance upon and cohabitation with parents, difficulties in finding and keeping a partner, and general challenges in asserting independence as an "adult" proper, whatever this might mean in the current socioeconomic context. Faced with these issues, there is no single solution; nevertheless, movement participants find it quite pleasant to imagine that there may be one. Thoroughly taming the inherent complexity of this real-world process through the considerably more straightforward and brief ritual process, one begins as a nonadult and emerges soon thereafter as an adult. The imagining of traditional Chinese society as a society saturated with ritual that proceeded in step with the rhythms of the universe then not only envisions a well-organized social order, but also corresponding individual life courses immersed in a similarly logical order, conveniently marked by solemn and symbolically deep rituals guiding and even enacting a smooth and utterly painless transition from one life stage to the next.

Logic, order, and solemnity are by contrast not exactly the first words that come to mind when describing such transitional moments nowadays. During my time living and working in Shanghai, one of my close friends went through a marriage process that can be characterized as typical of contemporary urban life. The first step after the always anxiety-inducing proposal was a day-long couple's photo session, in which the couple's costumes appeared to have been infected with some sort of sartorial multiple personality disorder, ranging from a quite conventional white tuxedo and puffy white bridal dress to a gaudy men's outfit resembling generals' clothing from the Napoleonic era accompanied by an elaborately bejeweled Cinderella-like dress.

When the wedding day arrived, the proceedings were anything but solemn. With guests seated at circular tables in a hotel conference room, the bride and groom were accompanied onto the stage at the front of the room by a spotlight, blaring music, special effects fog, and some mild pyrotechnics, leading me to wonder whether I was at a wedding or a rock concert. The gaudily dressed host, dedicated to creating and maintaining a "hot and noisy" (*renao*) environment, would have been more in his element at a Las Vegas revue than a solemn wedding ceremony: he only took a break from his unrelenting commentary booming over the room's sound system to accompany the bride and groom to various guests' tables for round upon round of toasts of high-proof liquor. Particular emphasis was placed upon the bride and groom crossing arms and completing a "bottoms up" (*ganbei*) cheer to represent their intertwinement: the pungent *baijiu* liquor used for these incessant toasts ensured that the bride, groom, and even the guests could not help but stumble as they departed at the end of the evening. Along the way, a few of us proceeded to the bride and groom's room for the rowdy practice known as "practical jokes in the nuptial chamber" (*nao dongfang*) in which, among other dirty jokes, the bride moves a boiled egg up the right pants leg of the groom, around his crotch, and down his left pants leg using only her mouth. At the end of the night, the couple lay under their bed sheets and gradually disrobed before their departing audience, tossing their clothing items out one by one. If it wasn't for all of the *baijiu*, it would have indeed been a very awkward and shamefully memorable evening.

"That type of a wedding ceremony, that's a barbarian [*huren*] ceremony. We Han don't decorate ourselves or our wedding chambers so gaudily [*hua*]. We don't have all of that noise. And we never force people into toasts [*mianqiang quanjiu*] or make dirty jokes. We Han didn't do these types of things until the barbarians came in the Yuan and the Qing," claimed one informant, voicing his disenchantment with the state of the modern Chinese wedding. And as a long-standing bachelor, he has good reason to be disenchanted. As illustrated in the previous chapter, the process of finding a marriage partner in today's China has become increasingly complex, with factors of money, status, looks, personality, location, property, and countless other considerations bearing down upon young couples. Furthermore, once these initial obstacles have been overcome, the challenge of staying married has also grown, with rapid increases in recent years in extramarital affairs, divorces, and increasingly contentious financial disputes. Although one should be skeptical of any narrative of decline from an idealized past that is home to the immaculate family that served as a blissful safe haven from the corruption of the outside world, these real social trends nevertheless produce an impression of the increasingly rapid disintegration of the family structure, conventionally portrayed as the core of Chinese culture itself. And again based in the imaginary relationship between ritual and broader society, the unruly state of the contemporary wedding reflects the unruly state of contemporary marriage culture; the disorderly wedding is a metaphor for a disorderly matrimonial culture. And Han Clothing Movement enthusiasts again have a solution.

An authentic "Han" wedding as promoted in recent years by movement enthusiasts is a far more serious affair than the standard contemporary wedding, endowed with solemnity and meaning from start to finish. Upon entering, the bride and groom proceed to either side of a jade basin, bow to one another, and use the crystal-clear water within the basin to wash their hands and faces, purifying themselves for their new married life together. They then proceed to eat from the same plate and to drink in unison; yet rather than rejoicing in a spirited "bottoms up" downing their drinks with arms interlocked, they exchange glasses with one another, slowly and solemnly drinking together. The bride and groom then proceed to lock their hands together tightly, symbolizing their unity, before proceeding to a final step in which each has a piece of hair cut from his or her head, and the two pieces of hair are tied together to again represent their intertwinement and inseparability: this time binding initiates' hair to one another's. Each movement is accompanied by detailed narration by a considerably more subdued host than one would find at a standard wedding, along with frequent quotations from the Chinese classics explaining in the most complex and mystical of manners the ancient origins and deep meanings of each stage of the ritual.

From preritual purification to interlocking hands, hair, and glasses, and from a solemn atmosphere to slow sips of wine, this ceremonial arrangement provides layer upon layer of meaning and solemnity, producing a vision of marriage far closer to a sacred ideal than the boisterous and disorderly "modern" wedding ceremony of the average urban resident. In a similar situation of social change and uncertainty, John Gillis's study of the popular search for supposedly lost family values in America in the 1990s cites the rapid consecration and proliferation of ritualized "family time," embodied in family dinners, bedtime, and such repeated celebrations as birthdays and anniversaries, which "turn all our events into ritual and image, all history into myth, in order to give ourselves some of the sense of permanence and connection that modern time denies us."[40] The isolated, easily controllable, yet symbolically sacred space of ritual at once provides a refuge from and a presumably efficacious site of defense against perceived social disintegration: the purportedly ancient Han rituals of marriage and other important life moments are granted recuperative powers in their ability not only to temporarily capture idealized images of past practice in experiential space in the uncertain present in ways that simply donning Han Clothing cannot, but also to imaginarily revitalize the fundamental institutions of society through a return to stabilizing roots.

Such imagined ordering effects from ritual within a chaotic world were articulated most memorably by an interviewee who drew my attention to the word for a traditional Chinese festival, *jie*. While *jie* is generally understood as simply meaning a holiday or festival, as in Labor Day (*Wu Yi Laodong Jie*) or the Spring Festival (*Chun Jie*), this informant argued that *jie* does not refer to "holidays" in the "Western" sense of the word, but rather means "a joint" or "a section" (as in the term *guanjie*, referring to bodily joints). Unearthing a deeper meaning, he argued that *jie* are in fact unstable or crisis-prone moments in the calendar divined by wise ancestors, and thus thresholds through which we must all inevitably pass on a regular basis, with China's lunar calendar placing such a *jie* in every month, on a day corresponding to the number of the month: the second day of the second month (offerings to the earth god), the third day of the third month (anniversary of the High Emperor of the Dark Heaven), continuing in this manner through the year.[41]

The ritualized practices associated with these particular moments are then designed to assist this passage, immunizing the individual against each crisis: the world is thus again envisioned as fundamentally imbalanced, alongside complementary magical visions of ritualized practices righting this imbalance. For example, on the fifth day of the fifth month of the year, widely known as the Dragon Boat Festival, this informant claimed that one is highly prone to develop stomach ailments; in order to prevent such problems, the tradition of eating wrapped glutinous rice (*zongzi*) was developed. This, he argued, is the true meaning of "passing a holiday" (*guo jieri*); it is a time that must be passed, and communal ritualized action, extending from the imperial palace to the households of the average Zhou, helps to ensure their smooth passage. "This is the wisdom of our ancestors," he said with a smile. But the problem, he noted, is that nowadays glutinous rice is just as likely to produce stomach ailments as to prevent them.

These two adjacent statements succinctly capture the central contradiction facing movement participants: the tension of perceived eternal wisdom and eternal experiential disorder. Again, a tautology intertwines ritual and society in these imaginings: rituals are perceived as having played a central role in ordering society in the past; the perceived lack of order in contemporary society can then be attributed to the corresponding lack of ritual; as such, the revitalization of ritual would revitalize society and social order. In contrast to the inherently disorderly world in which we live, it is pleasant to envision a world ordered by ritual; and in opposition to the disorder and uncertainties of life, who could resist the image of a thoroughly ordered life whose progression is marked by a series of grand rituals, at once guiding and celebrating one's smooth progression through life? As Han Clothing traces an imagined tradition of glory from the origins of humankind through to its re-creation in the present, the enactment of these purportedly ancient Han rituals then claims to provide a technique and a space in which this glory can be realized in the present. Yet as with the discussion of Han Clothing in the previous section, this imaginary ordering never lives up to its intended results. Han Clothing itself is an abstraction from the reality of lived society, and ritual adds yet another layer to this abstraction by creating an imaginary virtual space fleetingly removed from external realities, and an all-powerful set of techniques seemingly removed from the realities of the world. Nevertheless, these external realities always eventually find their way in: as Seligman, Weller, Puett, and Simon note in their discussion of the relationship between ritual ordering and the disorderly outside world, ritual itself "means neverending work."[42]

This perpetual incompleteness of ritual's world construction, leading to its compulsive repetition, was apparent in one of my earliest interactions with movement devotees in Guangzhou, when we gathered together for a Song-style tea ceremony. Roughly twenty enthusiasts, dressed in Han Clothing in the still sweltering heat of Guangzhou in September, gathered in the apartment of a local professor to drink tea the way that it was once done by the ancestors. As we gathered around a table to watch the professor mix the finely ground tea in a bowl with water, he informed us of the magical properties of teas past: tea in ancient China contained seven times the nutrients of tea today, and water was considerably cleaner and thus produced a purer taste. Yet after continually building our expectations for this little personal taste of the real, lost China, just as the tea was almost ready to be shared in solemn, expectant sips, the ears of all present suddenly rang with the deafening buzz of a drill; the clamor was so powerful that we could not hear one another speak, and almost instinctively raised our hands, previously solemnly folded together politely at waist level, to our aching ears. The professor held the bowl of tea in his hands, completely still and unblinking, waiting for the drilling sound to cease; when it finally came to a sudden halt after an unbearably lengthy span of time, our host explained that the university was installing an elevator in the adjacent apartment building, and expressed his regrets about the noise.

Quite a significant amount of drilling was completed that day. Having spent more than half of the past decade living in apartment buildings in China, I had become accustomed to the never-ending sounds of apartment renovations, but the noise that day was unlike any that I had ever heard. And this cacophony seemed to arise spontaneously at the most solemn and thus the most inconvenient of moments; after that first sound-shock, the ambiance of the tea ceremony never quite recovered, interrupted repeatedly in the most jarring of manners. The memory of this impertinently obnoxious drill and its interruptions of the atmosphere that morning remained with me throughout the course of fieldwork, a reminder of the seemingly inescapable intrusion of imperfect reality into the fleeting ideal images and moments around which the Han Clothing Movement constructs itself. Yet I was soon to encounter a quite unexceptional yet also highly telling discovery, revealing the next level of pleasurable alienation towards the imaginary ideal of the real China: not even a trace of these auditory intrusions was apparent in the photographs taken that September day.

PHOTOGRAPHY: THE CAMERA OBSCURA OF
NATIONAL FANTASY

One February morning I made the lengthy trek from the southern edge of Guangzhou to its northernmost point, the foot of Baiyun Mountain. I had been invited by a few local Han Clothing enthusiasts to view a cherry blossom display marking the beginning of spring: precisely the type of leisurely activity in intimate contact with one's natural surroundings that movement participants assumed their ancestors experienced on a daily basis. An air of quiet solemnity reigned as we sat at the entrance to Baiyun Mountain, but there was no ritual nor any other particularly sacred procedure underway; rather, the ladies of the group were painstakingly completing their hair and makeup. Although I arrived nearly half an hour late for our bright and early 8:00 A.M. Saturday morning gathering, I had learned that the inevitable make-up process was a reliable safety buffer for late arrivals. The process continued for another twenty minutes after I had arrived, as the men of the group shuffled about, occasionally striking up conversations and occasionally providing advice and reassurance on hair and make-up to their female compatriots. When all was finally in place, we made our way into the cherry blossom exhibition, glanced at a few cherry blossom trees and the shockingly massive sea of people that had already gathered by 9:00 A.M., and began work on what I discovered to be the true objective of this visit: taking pictures.

Much like the willed isolation and resulting solemnity of the ritual space as an enactment of Han-ness, proper photographs of Han Clothing could not be taken just anywhere, especially in the standard urban living environment of the average movement participant. My acquaintance in Tsin Village, for example, was fond of having her photograph taken in Han Clothing, but she never wanted such photographs to be taken in Tsin Village. The beauty, stability, and grandeur in the ideal image of Han-ness had to be captured not only in the clothing and figures embodied in the photograph, but also in the background. Baiyun Mountain provided the perfect backdrop: it was a natural setting, at once beautiful and imposing, with a green mountain extending to the skies above, and colorful cherry blossoms all around. As such, beyond all of the talk about nature, cherry blossoms, and traditional culture, the very modern technology of digital photography was to be the focus of the day. One fellow Han Clothing enthusiast had clearly been invited on account of his high-tech digital camera with an almost humorously long zoom lens; he was the designated cameraman, occasionally shouting out commands to the

FIGURE 13. Enthusiasts posing for photographs, Baiyun Mountain, Guangzhou.

subjects of photographs like a high-profile fashion photographer. I had clearly been invited on account of my digital camera, as well as my repeatedly demonstrated willingness to take pictures as ordered, making me the reliable backup photographer, ensuring that no magic moment would be lost. We began with a few simple poses next to cherry blossoms, the results of which participants found satisfactory. These successful first photographs seemed to have created a certain momentum, leading us on that long day to all types of increasingly complex poses: standing on a hillside, overlooking the expansive countryside below as if it were one's own domain; standing on tiny rocks in the middle of a creek, presenting an image of balance and serenity despite the all too real possibility of falling in and ruining one's outfit for later photographs; standing gallantly on top of a rock formation in the middle of the park, looking down solemnly towards one's photographers, elevated above all others. Each pose seemed to combine an ideal image of dignified heroism and classical serenity, draped in five millennia of history: precisely the ego ideal that movement enthusiasts aimed to create.

The day at Baiyun Mountain literally lasted from eight o'clock in the morning past six in the evening, and we had no food besides some instant noodles purchased at a stand along the way. We also never in fact had a moment to pause and take in the natural scenes around us except as potential backdrops to yet another photograph. Nevertheless, what we did have was a group of well-dressed and made-up Han Clothing enthusiasts armed with digital cameras, producing pleasant imaginary memories of a day that in fact never was. I left with over three hundred new virtual images on my camera's memory card, which I proceeded to spend endless hours distributing to participants online in the following days. The results were aesthetically pleasing, and as such quite pleasing to the participants. Yet beyond simply the result, the entire day itself was analytically fascinating, in that the suggestion that we "look at cherry blossoms," a seemingly traditional, contemplative, and dignified activity, was in fact primarily a pretext to ensure that we could all look back at ourselves in traditional, contemplative, dignified, and thoroughly abstracted poses for years to come, with or without cherry blossoms.

Although this visit to Baiyun Mountain was distinctive in terms of the sheer and unrelenting intensity of photography, it was nevertheless not an exception. No matter the event, photography served as an essential part of Han Clothing gatherings: an unspoken Han national tradition. Taking pictures was, alongside clothing and ritual, another central concern of devotees, and as I discuss below, these three aspects of the movement complement each other. Needless to say, photography was not an act in which the Han ancestors engaged. Yet beyond predictable anachronistic irony, which quickly grows analytically uninteresting on account of its pervasiveness, the integration of one of the most modern of technologies into this traditionalist movement further reaffirms the fact that despite the obsessive discussion of the power of tradition, the Han Clothing Movement is in fact a movement firmly based in and responding to present conditions, which photography finally allows participants to transcend, in search of an ego ideal, which photography as a stabilized virtual image finally allows participants to simulate.

PHOTOGRAPHY: THE REALITY OF THE IMAGE

One can't possess reality, one can possess images.

—SUSAN SONTAG, *On Photography*[43]

Han Clothing forums are literally plastered with images of participants dressed in Han Clothing; every devotee that I met had his or her collection of Han Clothing portraits; and every gathering of the movement that I attended had its designated photographer for the day. Nevertheless, in contrast to the promotion of clothing and ritual, photography is a rarely spoken aspect of group activities. The unspoken and even repressed nature of photography within the movement suggests that, like the widely disparaged activities of Brother Emperor or the policing of cosplay comparisons, this practice lays bare a fundamental truth about movement activities that participants would prefer to leave unexamined.

The fundamental tension traced through the drama of Han-ness examined in this and preceding chapters has been the disconnect between the ideals of "China" or "the Han" and their everyday experiential realities. Whereas these ideal images hover far above experience as promises of the grandeur of one's community, they simultaneously present challenges as fundamental lacks seemingly perpetually incapable of realization, caught between the virtual and material: although Han Clothing, as a concrete material link passed down from the ancestors through five millennia, would seemingly stabilize the ideal image of Han-ness, this outfit remained fundamentally unable to resolve fundamental problems of the experiential living environment in which enthusiasts found themselves continually hounded by pollution, crowding, questions, stares, and mockery. Ritual, as a mystified practice passed down from the ancestors over five millennia, seemed to create a safely quarantined virtual space, segregated from the real world, such that fantasies of the revitalized Han and the self therein could be realized. Yet the continued intrusion of the external environment, the reality from which the Han Clothing Movement strives to escape, remained persistent in the form of unimpressed audiences, befuddled policemen, and untimely drills. Within this seemingly unending drama between virtual ideals and material existence, photography injects an idealizing transcendent materiality into the formula as a perfect solution: photography is, like Han Clothing, stable and material, and, like ritual, capable of simultaneously framing and idealizing, continuing the logic of the previous two components of the movement to their logical conclusion in a frozen objectification of fantasy able to be kept and viewed repeatedly over time.

The idealizing and transcendental function can be seen in the fact that every photograph is involved in a careful process of framing and preparation,[44] while nevertheless maintaining the image of transparent and unfiltered truth. Examining the usual process involved in a taking a picture, one typically first locates oneself in front of some appropriate backdrop, and then proceeds to pose and smile, while the photographer adjusts the frame to ensure that the image is centered and generally appealing, without any unexpected or unflattering additions. The majority of components in this formula were all addressed above, from make-up to backdrops to poses. Yet the framing process reminds us that an important detail of a photograph is not only what it includes, but also what it excludes: few things in everyday self-representation are more unsettling than a well-posed photograph against a pleasant backdrop that nevertheless includes a directionless bystander wandering by, or even worse a photo-bombing bystander who consciously disturbs the otherwise pleasing image through the addition of humorous facial expressions or the extension of certain fingers. Such intrusions distract from the center of attention and detract from the aura of the image. Yet while actively avoided in the process of taking a picture, such disturbances are seemingly naturally absent from the final photographic product, ideally presenting a coherent and naturalized image.

Although this framing tendency has been part of the photographic process from its inception, the recent advent of the digital camera further enhances this tendency by allowing for rapid shots capturing one moment after another, the immediate review of photographs so as to avoid surprises, as well as a nearly infinite space for storage compared to the traditional 24- or 36-exposure rolls of film still used just a few short years ago. This newfound versatility allows subjects dissatisfied with first, second, or tenth attempts to ritually retake their shots until they achieve the precise effects that they are seeking: a process that occupied large spans of time during movement gatherings. Even if intrusions or distractions are present in real life, as they inevitably are, there is then not the slightest trace of these realities in a carefully framed photographic image.

As one might expect from the persistent intrusions into movement events narrated in previous sections, our day on Baiyun Mountain included many such disturbances: not only were there seas of people amid the cherry blossoms, detracting from the natural aura and giving the exhibition the feel of a crowded downtown city block, but Han Clothing, as always, attracted a massive crowd of curious onlookers staring, following, asking questions ("Are you here to film a television series?" "When does your performance begin?"), posing in front of, and even demanding particular poses from participants ("Move a little to the right—yeah, that's good"). At one point, our presence had generated such a massive crowd that we were enclosed on all sides by fascinated photographers.

Left with no choice, we climbed a steep hill on the edge of the cherry blossom exhibition to find some breathing room, and, of course, take some pictures of our own without interference from the throngs of onlookers below. While the majority of the crowd stayed at the bottom of the hill, still eagerly snapping photos, a few dedicated photographers decided to follow us uphill. To our amusement, one fellow with large Jiang Zemin–style glasses and a particularly high waistband grabbed my arm on the hillside and shouted "Hello! Picture?!?" in broken English. Slightly confused, I smiled and looked towards my acquaintances in Han Clothing, who glanced at him with a similarly perplexed look. Failing to note the awkwardness of the situation, this photographer lifted his camera, took two photos of my confused companions, and yelled to them, again in English, "Very good! Thank you!" before proceeding to shake my hand extremely vigorously. He then wandered back down the hill, as we wandered further up the increasingly steep hill, off the beaten track, to escape these growing and unpredictable crowds.

Thanks to the diligent avoidance efforts of my acquaintances and the reliable framing effects of the photograph, not a single trace of these distractions was in any way apparent in our photographic retrospective. Each entry in this collection of images managed to portray carefully staged moments of isolation, unity with nature, and grandeur as an "actually existing situation."[45] In contrast to the crowds and the chaos, we found Han Clothing devotees standing gracefully in the midst of a gently flowing stream, gallantly atop boulders, or triumphantly casting their glances over the countryside below. Each image thus presents a "neat slice of time"[46] removed from its always far less neat environmental surroundings.

Previous sociological studies of photography have tellingly noted its role in the integration of the family unit.[47] Family photographs are generally taken at moments of solidarity and happiness, such as family festivities or vacations, ensuring that they capture pleasant memories. Afterwards, no matter the arguments or other tensions that plague family life, the decision to pull out a photo album and view it together, reviewing these idealized moments, then brings about another moment of otherwise elusive integration and peace.[48] This insight into the social structuring function of photography is relevant to the role of photography in the Han Clothing Movement's goals of identity construction. For movement photographs are similarly taken at moments and in settings that are carefully constructed in order to realize, finally, an otherwise elusive Han-ness: enacting a solemn ritual passed down through the millennia, pensively sipping a cup of tea, completing a calligraphic inscription of traditional poetry, or simply standing serenely in the midst of a creek, comfortable in the embrace of nature. These are poses and moments that enact the imagined and otherwise elusive essence of Han selfhood, while remaining through framing and objectification immune to the environmental disruptions that have plagued other attempts to "return to the eras of Han and Tang." As such, they build upon the systemic logic of clothing and ritual discussed above, continuing these integrating efforts towards their final yet always seemingly unattainable conclusion: the ideal image of the Han, produced in response to the challenges and discontents of the material world, and realized in a final act of abstraction from the reality of this material world in the virtually objectified form of the photograph, in which it is presented as a transparent material reality.

This idealized image of Han-ness can only be achieved fully through photography because this medium combines abstraction from the material world with a fundamentally stabilizing materiality: whereas images are prepared, posed, framed, and edited, thereby enacting a certain seclusion like the ritual space, they are nevertheless generally understood as transparent and self-evident reflections of reality, like clothing's presumed direct reflection of the truth of its wearer. When one sees a photograph of something, even a photograph of something that one has not seen with one's own eyes, the photograph is presumed to "furnish evidence" of the object or event captured therein, on account of this medium's fundamentally "innocent" and thus "accurate" relationship to visual reality.[49] The seeming veracity and objectivity of the photograph[50] is expressed most memorably in Roland Barthes's observation that, in a photograph, the pipe is really just a pipe,[51] thereby realizing via photography the otherwise elusive status of Identity.[52] Similarly, the photography of the Han Clothing Movement hides the painstaking efforts involved in the production of this image, such that the Great Han is finally truly and simply the Great Han, true Identity for all to see: the carefully constructed image of "Han-ness" in the path of the much-cited five millennia of tradition is finally made manifest in its full grandeur, sacredness, and seemingly unconstructed reality.

Yet the photograph not only facilitates the construction of an imaginary world that is made to appear transparently real; it furthermore extends this emblematic moment seamlessly across time toward true eternity. The abstraction that removes the image from the unpredictability and disorder of the surrounding world in which it would otherwise be lost is supplemented by the material stability of the virtual image, which further abstracts this moment from the passage of time, in which it would otherwise pass and perhaps be forgotten. Reflecting upon this fundamentally mystifying and thus mesmerizing relationship between the photograph, life, and the passage of time, Susan Sontag incisively observes that "[l]ife is not about significant details, illuminated in a flash, fixed forever. Photographs are."[53] On a similar albeit unexpected note, André Bazin begins his study of the ontology of the photographic image with a detailed discussion of Egyptian practices of embalming the dead. Through this revealing juxtaposition, Bazin brings to light what he calls the "mummifying" effects of photographic images, capturing moments and freeing them from the passage of time and the constraints of space that otherwise govern them, while nevertheless appearing completely natural.[54] Photography thus enables its users to beautify and to eternalize, two of the central concerns of the Han Clothing Movement, producing an idealized and illusorily stable alienated self-image in response to the gray and perpetually uncertain and unstable world in which they live.

These contributions to image construction, in the end, are why photography plays such a central role in Han Clothing activities, and stands out as such a cherished possession of Han Clothing devotees, a very "modern" companion to their "traditional" clothing. For the photograph's virtual integration and stabilization of the idealized image then finally realizes the integration and stabilization of the self, the original source and subject of Han troubles, within this image. Pierre Bourdieu notes that throughout history, the ability to own a portrait of oneself has been an extremely rare privilege: only the wealthiest of individuals could procure such a portrait, and even then this labor-intensive undertaking could only be an image of one particular moment in time.[55] The invention and proliferation of photographic technology over the past two centuries has drastically altered this situation, making the portrait vastly more available, and even placing this possibility directly in the hands of individuals in the form of the camera or increasingly the camera-phone without, however, greatly devaluing a carefully framed portrait's distinction. Such portraits have proliferated throughout Chinese society over the past few decades, making everything from baby portraits to wedding portraits to family portraits to selfies into core contributions to individuals' perspectives upon themselves and understandings of their life course, and constructing an image of the self seemingly just as sacred as the portraits that hover over ancestral shrines.

Bonnie Adrian has noted in her study of wedding photography in Taiwan that one is often hard pressed to recognize individuals in these photographic portraits, as people are so unlike their everyday selves that the "portraits might as well be paintings."[56] Yet this, in the end, is precisely the point. The tendency of the photograph to transform the photographed into a work of art[57] distanced from its reality, as well as presenting a seemingly objective certificate of presence[58] as reality finally allows for a self-projection that overcomes the fundamental gap in existence, caught between the grandeur of identity fantasy and the banalities and discontents of everyday existence. The integration of this ideal image is finally achieved by careful editing and abstraction from such material realities, capturing this virtual abstraction as a fundamental reality and materially stabilizing it over time in the form of a photograph, with the self located in the center as a permanent representative of the equally permanent grandeur of the Han. From the sketches first uploaded and viewed on computer screens in the aftermath of APEC, claiming to show "true Han Clothing," to the carefully framed and posed images of movement participants in their Han Clothing now also viewed on computer screens, the Han Clothing Movement makes a lengthy and circuitous journey from a virtual world imagined in opposition to the present towards a materialized image transcending and replacing the present. It is then precisely through its elusively stabilized imago "making men and their circumstances appear upside-down"[59] that the omnipresent camera obscura of the Han Clothing Movement becomes a camera lucida of national fantasy, producing and stabilizing an ideal image in an always less than ideal world.

FIVE

The Manchu in the Mirror

Society is made of those whom it comprises. If the latter would fully admit their dependence on man-made conditions, they would somehow have to blame themselves, would have to recognize not only their impotence but also that they are the cause of this impotence and would have to take responsibilities which today are extremely hard to take. This may be one of the reasons why they like so much to project their dependence upon something else, be it a conspiracy of Wall Street bankers or the constellation of the stars.

—THEODOR ADORNO, *The Stars Down to Earth*[1]

THE IDEAL IMAGES OF HAN-NESS and Chineseness sought in the Han Clothing Movement face endless worldly obstacles, and can only be realized as identity ever so briefly through a process of ever-increasing levels of abstraction from subjects' actual living environment: passing from Han Clothing's sacredness in a profane world, through the segregated and thus transcendent ritual space, to the objectified and carefully framed image of photography. The profound elusiveness of this ideal, this true Han-ness unable to be realized in a Han-dominated society, founded in yet also violating the grounding assumption of identity, begs for some type of explanation. And during a dinner with Han Clothing devotees in Guangzhou early in my fieldwork, the movement's preferred explanation for this perpetual gap in identity, the absence of the "real China" in the real China, first came to my attention. Alongside promoting clothing, etiquette, ritual, and traditional education, another important yet not commonly cited aspect of the movement's activities, I learned, is the production of conspiracy theories about "the Manchus," a largely Sinicized minority group whose ancestors were once the rulers of the Qing Dynasty.

Discussing clothing styles with movement enthusiasts over dinner, our discussion turned to a comparison between Han Clothing and the *qipao* (or *cheongsam*) and *magua* (or *tangzhuang*). These clothing styles have in recent decades been at the forefront of representing traditional Chinese clothing in venues as diverse as the 2001 Asia-Pacific Economic Cooperation meeting in Shanghai, where world leaders donned the *magua* for the standard APEC photo-op in "local attire," to fashion shows and high-end clothing stores, where the *qipao* has reemerged as a popular sartorial embodiment of the idea of Chinese tradition in the present.[2] Angrily contesting the dominance of these styles, informants went to great lengths to explicate their foreign and thus inferior origins. The *ma* in *magua*, they noted, refers to horses, animals that represented Manchu identity in the Qing Dynasty through the ethnic marker of horsemanship.[3] "Look around," one acquaintance asked, "do you see us Han riding around on horses? What use is a horse jacket (*magua*) to us?" The *magua* then was a Manchu imposition masquerading as representing China. The same, I learned, was true of the *qipao*: the *qi* in *qipao,* another noted, refers to "banners," a term designating soldiers of the Qing Dynasty and their families, recognized as "the principal institution which unified the Manchu people and defined Manchu identity" in the Qing era.[4] My acquaintances were clearly unimpressed: "These are savage clothing styles, for primitive Manchu people who ride around on horses," they continued as I listened in initial utter perplexity. "You see, that's why the slit on the *qipao*'s leg stretches so high. Nowadays, it's only good for hookers (*jinü*) and sluts (*sao B*) who love to expose themselves (*zouguang*)." "Putting their goods on display," another enthusiast added, with a laugh.

The vehement feelings displayed towards these two not so apparently detestable clothing styles were at first surprising. Yet just as movement participants insist that Han Clothing is a symbol of an essential Chinese culture in need of revitalization, so they insist that the dominance of the *qipao* and *magua* in sartorial representations of China is a symbol of a far more insidious reality that has proceeded largely unnoticed by the majority of their compatriots: the Manchu race's determined efforts to control clothing, food, culture, education, finance, politics, and even military power in the reform era in order to eliminate the Han race and destroy China. This unexpected turn in the conversation that evening then suddenly opened onto a deluge of bizarre conspiratorial accusations against the Manchus: a full century after the downfall of the Qing Dynasty, Manchus are supposedly dedicated to beautifying and thereby eventually revitalizing the Qing Dynasty against the Han; they have already infiltrated all levels of the state apparatus, and particularly dominate the cultural and educational bureaucracies; they love to kill Han babies through their one-child policy; and their greatest enemy, which they are dedicated to eliminating, is none other than the Han Clothing Movement and its vision of a true Han China.

My initial suspicion that these sentiments might be the focus of only one wing of the movement were set aside as I heard similar narratives repeated almost word for word by other movement participants. And my suspicion that these obsessions might be derived from the local history of anti-Qing fervor in Guangdong Province was similarly overturned as anti-Manchu vitriol literally followed me through every city that I visited over the course of my research. Throughout my research interactions, there was a reliable turning point in the dialogue with local groups, after establishing a certain degree of rapport, in which the topic of conversation would suddenly turn to "the Manchus," and I would listen amid mixed emotions of curiosity and perplexity to the wide array of Manchu-centered conspiracy theories circulating throughout the movement, such that my field notes eventually became a virtual encyclopedia of quite untenable beliefs about the secret power of these sly savages.

Based in the dilemma of the elusiveness of Han-ness analyzed in the preceding chapters, this chapter examines these theories and other similar conspiracy theories, both within the Han Clothing Movement and beyond, so as to explain the seduction, when faced with the very real challenges of the world, of a fundamentally unreal theory of this world and its challenges. The roots of this seduction, I argue, are found in the relationship between conspiracy thinking and identity thinking, and particularly in conspiracy theory's narrative resolution of the dilemmas of identity analyzed in previous chapters: conspiracy and identity here emerge as two sides of the same coin, insofar as conspiracy theory can only be based in identity, and, correspondingly, only the externalizing and explanatory functions of conspiracy theory can finally fulfill the elusive ideal of identity.

THE PERMANENT XINHAI REVOLUTION

I begin this analysis of conspiracy and identity with a relatively succinct summary of the beliefs surrounding Manchus within the Han Clothing Movement, with commentary and analysis reserved for later.[5] The goal in this section is to provide an overview of "the facts" as they stand with regard to the average movement enthusiast's vision of "the Manchus." There is an abundance of such "facts," for as Richard Hofstadter has demonstrated in his study of the paranoid style in American politics, conspiracy theories are structured around the careful accumulation of seeming proof towards a narrative "full of rich and proliferating detail."[6] Despite the transparently ludicrous nature of many of these ideas, in order to understand the power and appeal of these conspiracy theories as a whole, it is necessary to present them within their "emic" context.[7]

In the beginning, according to devotees of the Han Clothing Movement, there was the distinction between Chinese and barbarians. Although often idealized as a form of universalizing culturalism devoid of ethnoracial implications, the distinction between Chinese and barbarians in fact lacked any such distinction between culture and biology: the two were viewed as overlapping, essentially biologizing or racializing culture, such that those dwelling outside of Chinese culture were viewed as innately "distant savages hovering on the edge of bestiality."[8] The distinction between Chinese and barbarians, which Han Clothing enthusiasts believe maintained the purity of their race and thus civilization, was first historically weakened by the Mongol Yuan Dynasty (1271–1368 C.E.), which is portrayed, in contrast to prevailing state ideologies of the Yuan's natural Chineseness,[9] as a barbarian invasion of civilization proper. The distinction between Chinese and barbarians then collapsed completely with the subsequent fall of the Ming and the rise of the Manchu-controlled Qing Dynasty (1644–1911 C.E.), described as an "external power" (*waiguo shili*) in a curious appropriation of paranoid official rhetoric against Beijing's official doctrine of national unity. Citing Mencius, who famously remarked that "I have heard of men using the doctrines of our great land to change barbarians, but I have never heard of any being changed by barbarians,"[10] movement participants see a dark transition with the arrival of the Qing: rather than barbarians adopting Chinese ways as a step towards civilization, Han Clothing Movement enthusiasts see the Qing as the beginning of Chinese adopting barbarian ways, and thus the end of a once pure Chinese culture.[11] This tragic transformation is embodied within movement narratives in the historically accurate image of the queue reshaping the Chinese body, as well as in a historically inaccurate but commonly cited tall tale of the Qing eliminating "Han Clothing" by force.[12]

Han Clothing Movement narratives furthermore portray the Qing as not only culturally imperialist and barbarian but indeed as a genocidal force, intent upon exterminating the Han race: a goal that purportedly remains at the center of Manchu motivations to this day. Fascinatingly, evidence for this claim is found in a widely shared document entitled "Policies to Eliminate the Han" (*Miehan zhengce*), which claims to reveal Manchu plans during the Qing Dynasty to massacre the Han as a whole. Divided into sections dedicated to methods for eliminating various groups within the Han (peasants and merchants, students, scholar officials, soldiers, women, and monks), a brief excerpt is sufficient to capture this pamphlet's overall tone:

> We are a nomadic people. Three hundred years ago, heaven guided us through the pass. The Chongzhen Emperor lost his realm, and the bandit Wu Sangui betrayed his ancestors and surrendered to us . . . Any Han people who rebelled would be killed. And any who surrendered would be played like a fool. We drained their wealth as an offering to ourselves, and we muddled their brains to enhance our power . . . If the Han dare to think of opposing the Manchus, how could we then not choose to eliminate them? We have been their emperors for three centuries. Our ancestors refrained from eliminating them out of mercy. But now, some glowing embers can be seen in these long-dead ashes of the Han . . . It will be easier to eliminate them once and for all while many of them still have yet to awaken and their oppositional power is not yet strong.[13]

As this excerpt undoubtedly suggests to the discerning reader, these "Policies to Eliminate the Han" are not in fact actual policies drafted or implemented by the Qing imperial house. Rather, according to a recent paper by Kong Xiangji and Murata Yujiro,[14] these supposed policies are a forgery drafted in the early part of the twentieth century by anti-Manchu activists based in Japan, and later smuggled into China. Claiming that the document was discovered by a well-placed Han official in the palaces of Beijing, the publication and distribution of these forged policies in the late Qing functioned as agitprop intended to foment popular antagonism towards and rebellion against the Manchu Qing Dynasty. The online resurgence of this obvious forgery a century later as proof of the Manchus' long-standing genocidal intentions provides this peculiar pamphlet with an even more curious afterlife, playing a role of repeated reinvention within these paranoid theories similar to another infamous and equally versatile forgery, the supposed "Protocols of the Elders of Zion," in twentieth and twenty-first century anti-Semitism.[15]

Han Clothing Movement participants consider the true Xinhai Revolution of 1911 to have been an anti-Manchu rather than an anti-imperial revolution, framed within the longstanding racial war through which they interpret history and current affairs. Yet whereas the Xinhai Revolution is generally understood to have ended the Qing Dynasty and thus Manchu power, movement narratives portray this revolution as only a first strike against Manchu domination and violence in a struggle that continues to this day. Within this worldview, vitriolic anti-Manchu sentiment from the 1911 revolution[16] combines with Maoist revolutionary terminology to produce a "permanent Xinhai Revolution."

First, 1911 was a political Xinhai Revolution, recapturing political power from the genocidal Manchu ruling class. Yet the failure to achieve their objective of destroying the Han during the Qing only made the Manchus ever more determined, and they returned a devastating blow with the rise of the Beiyang Clique, sabotaging the Republic's political institutions and national unity, followed by the emergence of Manchukuo with Emperor Pu Yi as head of state, collaborating with the Japanese in their common goal of destroying China. Then, 1945 and 1949 were military Xinhai Revolutions, insofar as they successfully eliminated the remaining military power of the Manchus, which is presumed to have been the primary source of instability in the Republican era. The Chinese Communist Party in the Maoist era, according to movement portrayals, is cast not as a revolutionary party nor a communist party, but rather as a clandestine anti-Manchu party, determined to eradicate remaining Manchu power structures. Following this logic, the period from 1966 through 1976, usually known as the Great Proletarian Cultural Revolution, was in fact a Cultural Xinhai Revolution targeting insidious Manchu culture.

Through this Manchu-centered conspiratorial framework, despite their deep attachment to the idea of traditional culture, movement enthusiasts are still able to idealize the Maoist era: I was told by a number of movement enthusiasts that by the time the campaign against the "four olds" began, true Chinese culture had after all already been destroyed centuries before by the Qing, and that the culture upon which the Cultural Revolution declared war was in fact an oppressive, alien Manchu culture in need of elimination in order to revitalize true Chinese culture. The death of "Manchu lackey" Lao She in 1966, for example, is cited as a cause for celebration and a sign that the permanent Xinhai Revolution was finally rooting out the last remaining vestiges of the Manchu power base once and for all. Mao's warped implementation of permanent revolution was then just the final stage in a righteous permanent Xinhai Revolution.

Despite the continual political, military, and cultural victories over Manchu power extending from 1911 to 1976, movement narratives unanimously envision the post-Mao era as a period of reactionary and far-reaching Manchu restoration. One commonly cited history reads:

FIGURE 14. Han Clothing enthusiasts commemorate the 99th anniversary of the anti-Manchu revolution at Guangzhou's Tomb of the 72 Martyrs.

The Manchu cabal, with the overwhelming support of international anti-China forces, has grown increasingly dedicated and unrelenting in its attempts to split the motherland in recent decades. It has teamed up with the Taiwan Solidarity Union, the East Turkestan Islamic Movement, Tibetan and Mongolian independence movements, and Falun Gong, forming a conglomerate dedicated to destroying our motherland once and for all. The capitalist roaders in power rely upon the old hereditary aristocracy of the Manchu bannermen to survive and continue their traitorous selling out of the country. And this Manchu aristocracy relies upon these capitalist roaders in power in order to realize their aspirations of splitting the nation and returning to power.[17]

As this excerpt demonstrates, movement conspiracy theories portray resurgent Manchu power as a veritable ideological state apparatus in the reform era, extending through the fields of politics, economics, and culture, each of which will be discussed in turn below.

Just as Henry Ford in his conspiratorial anti-Semitic classic *The International Jew* provided a detailed list of the institutions and industries controlled by "the Jew," Han Clothing Movement participants have gone to great lengths to document the infiltration of all levels of contemporary Chinese society by "the Manchu." And just as Ford claimed that "the single description which will include a larger percentage of Jews than members of any other race is this: he is in business,"[18] so movement participants assert that the single description that will include a larger percentage of Manchus than members of any other race is this: he is in government. Most are found in family planning institutions, which are imagined to be the power bases of the resurgent Manchu conspirators. Yet the imagined Manchu presence extends far beyond this field: former State Council Spokesman Yuan Mu, supposedly a descendant of a *Hanjun* bannerman,[19] is often cited as one of the most prominent examples of clandestine Manchus at the pinnacle of state power, along with former Beijing mayor Chen Xitong and other figures in the state-cultural apparatus. Precisely on account of the self-affirming and self-reproducing logic of conspiracy theory,[20] regardless of whether a politician is actually Manchu or not (and the majority indeed self-identify as Han), their official description as Han is interpreted only as a way of covering up their nefarious Manchu deeds, thus reaffirming the conspiracy even in its denial.[21] Manchu infiltration of the People's Liberation Army is furthermore proven by the unfounded yet popular rumor that China's first aircraft carrier, the Liaoning, was originally supposed to be named after Shi Lang, a Han "traitor" who commanded Qing fleets in the 1600s. At the same time, today's rampant corruption and reliable lack of state accountability are furthermore attributed to the Manchu infiltration of all branches of government and the innate Manchu tendency towards despotism, imagined to have been imported into China during the Qing, polluting a once pure and benevolent political system based in the unity of heaven and humankind.

The Manchu infiltration is so severe, in fact, that movement narratives assert that the "three northeastern provinces" (a term derived from Qing-era terminology that refers to the traditional Manchu homeland in contemporary Jilin, Liaoning, and Heilongjiang), are able to operate virtually autonomously thanks to their guardians in high places. The reported quantity of "autonomous regions" (*zizhi qu*), "autonomous counties" (*zizhi xian*), and "autonomous villages" (*zizhi cun*) in these provinces leads movement participants to assume that the Manchus have already achieved initial success in their goal of shattering China's unity. Of course, such a conclusion can only be based in a far too literal interpretation of the word "autonomy" from a majority perspective, which is read, in fact, far more literally than any similarly concerned member of a minority nationality familiar with actual realities could ever consider plausible.

Corresponding to their perceived ever-expanding role in government, Manchus are furthermore imagined to be central to the functioning of the economy in contemporary China. Again, similar to anti-Semitic portrayals of the "the Jews" as controlling international business and finance, Manchus are presumed to secretly pull the strings of the economy, and to use this control solely to their advantage: or, in other words, they are imagined to magically exercise control over that which is in fact completely uncontrollable.[22] As such, the state-owned enterprise layoffs of the 1990s are imagined to be the product of Manchu policy to impoverish the Han, as are the unpredictable yet frequent fluctuations in China's stock exchanges: purportedly blatant examples of the Manchus' unrelenting yet well-disguised pursuit of self-interest and control over all matters. Other economic troubles, such as sky-high real estate prices, are attributed to Manchus in government and in business (the two are deemed inseparable) hiding their ill-gotten gains safely in the inflationary real estate market: a potentially perceptive analysis of the current state of runaway real estate inflation, muddled by a deceptive ethnic spin. And in the culinary industry, such companies as the Qiao Jiangnan Group, which runs a chain of Sichuanese restaurants across the country, are accused of being sly fronts for Manchu power. Beyond raising money for the reestablishment of the Qing, these restaurants are furthermore accused of serving well-disguised non-Manchu food cooked in gutter oil (*digouyou*) and other poisonous additives, so as to render unsuspecting Han customers infertile and shorten their life spans, making the Han willing consumers of their own destruction.

Beyond politics and economics, Manchu influence is furthermore imagined to have had a profound effect upon contemporary culture. Throughout my research, most disconcerting trends in contemporary Chinese culture were attributed directly to Manchu influence: the crass materialism and ostentatious displays of wealth characteristic of the nouveau riche (*baofahu*) are traced back to the Qing, whose rulers, having made the transition from remote barbarians to imperial elites, are viewed as the first bad-mannered nouveau riche; coarse practices such as spitting, relieving oneself in public, cheating others, rudeness, loudness and rowdiness, forcing others to drink in overzealous toasts, shrill Mandarin unsuited to reading classical Tang poems, and other such "savagery" is attributed solely to the influence of a barbarian Manchu culture upon a once pristine Han culture in which such things simply did not happen; fear of authority, picking on the weak, and state repression and state-sponsored massacres are again attributed to a savage Manchu political culture characterized foremost by violence, as seen in the ten-day massacre in Yangzhou in 1645, and literary inquisition (*wenzi yu*), as seen in the historical suppression of anti-Manchu writing during the Qing.

And just as Ford argued that "the Jews" controlled the modern press toward the realization of world domination,[23] so these theories argue that Manchus control the operations of the Chinese media toward their goal of revitalizing the Qing and destroying the Han. Manchus are presumed to have a stranglehold on the reform-era Ministry of Culture and the Propaganda Department, two institutions whose opaqueness and overwhelming power make them particularly ripe for such conspiracy theorization. The popularity of programs like "Lecture Room" (*Baijia jiangtan*) which repackage dynastic history to indirectly push culturalized state-friendly arguments about the present, is interpreted as a symbol of Manchu control of television due to such programs' frequent romanticized discussions of the Qing. And the Qing-era costume dramas that have long been a staple of prime time television, derisively called "queue shows" (*bianzixi*) by movement participants,[24] are read as ominous signs of Manchu dominance and beautification of their lost dynasty. A movement enthusiast in Chengdu told me that "the Manchus control the Propaganda Department, and they use this position to promote their rule and the restoration of the Qing. How else could you explain all of these endless movies about the so-called benevolent rule of Kangxi and Qianlong?" Such an interpretation is a clear example of the tendency within conspiracy theories to read deeper and more ominous meanings than is reasonable into pieces of fiction and entertainment,[25] similar to the idea touted by Jerry Falwell in the late 1990s that the Teletubbies were a medium for gay propaganda.[26] Revealingly, a number of people told me throughout my research that the supposedly pro-Han miniseries *Great Emperor Wu of the Han Dynasty (Han Wu da di)* and *Great Han Empire (Da Han di guo)* had been banned by Manchus in the cultural bureaucracy because they violated the state's anti-Han policy, despite the fact that these shows were by my observation still broadcast all too frequently. Rumors also circulated throughout my research that middle schools across the country were on the verge of announcing compulsory courses in Manchu culture for all students. Meanwhile, Bernardo Bertolucci's award-winning 1987 film *The Last Emperor* was considered a sign of the internationalization of the Qing restoration project due to its perceived romanticization of Manchu rule and, in later sections of the film, its demonization of Han state power and the Han anti-Manchu activists usually known as Red Guards.

These examples are just a very brief sampling of the quite elaborate and far-reaching theories that the movement promotes. There is not sufficient room here to fully document every detail of this conspiratorial framework for viewing the world, and that is precisely the point. These examples, ranging from politics to economics to culture to everything in between, are meant to provide an introduction to the world constructed through these conspiracy theories. We might call this image unrealistic, or even dark. Yet what stands out most about this description, I argue, is its constructed completeness, combining what Kathleen Stewart has described as "tiny details and big structures of feeling."[27] The Manchu conspiracy theory promoted by members of the Han Clothing Movement does not simply explain a few random phenomena in China today. It is a comprehensive, all-encompassing narrative covering and explaining all major issues in contemporary society from politics to economics to culture, inscribed within a unifying narrative of barbaric Manchu oppression and heroic Han resistance. This completeness is the final destination sought by the Han Clothing Movement's identity project, a process traced in the preceding chapters. Yet this completeness can only be finally and fully achieved via conspiracy theory, which serves like photography, in this case like a photographic negative, to stabilize their image of Han-ness: a necessary supplement to the perpetual failure of the exaltation of identity in practice.

A STRUCTURAL READING OF CONSPIRACY AND IDENTITY

Conspiracy theories existing on the margins of society have entered mainstream scholarship in recent decades, generating thought-provoking discussions about the proliferation and power of these culturally infectious ideas.[28] Yet no single interpretation seems capable of explaining the sheer vitality and power of conspiracy theory as a genre. Seeking to understand this power through the example of the Manchu conspiracy theories described above, I propose that conspiracy's appeal is a product of its intertwinement with, and affirmation of, an otherwise untenable ideal of identity, the core concern of the Han Clothing Movement. Considering the structure of conspiracy theories, I see two primary processes in their representation of the world that reveal their relationship with identity and thus the source of their appeal: (1) a clear, founding division between "us" and "them," followed by (2) an all-encompassing explanation of the world according to this distinction.

First, a conspiracy theory divides the world into two groups, "us" and "them," with clearly defined characteristics on each side: generally, positive characteristics are attributed to "us," and negative or conniving characteristics are attributed to "them." In the case of the Manchu conspiracy theories examined here, the primary distinction is "Han" and "Manchu," the former oppressed yet heroic, the latter powerful yet inhumanly cruel. In the case of the majority of Chinese nationalist conspiracy theories,[29] the primary distinction is between "China" and "the West" or "Japan." In the case of the best-known global conspiracy theory of the world domination of "the Jews," the primary distinction is between "us" (whoever is articulating the theory) and "the Jews." And in the case of Marxism as a "conspiracy theory of society,"[30] the primary distinction lies between "the proletariat" and "the capitalists"[31] or in its Maoist variant "the people" and "non-people."[32] In each of these representations, the world is coded into easily intelligible (and thus overly simplistic) binaries, with clearly defined characteristics attributed to each side. Such a process of division and attribution along boundaries is, notably, also a founding process in identification. Within this first step in conspiracy theory, then, conspiracy relies upon identity for its formation along the distinction of "us" and "them."

In the second step in its formation, however, conspiracy theory proceeds to affirm identity in a manner that the structure of identity itself, founded upon a perpetually elusive lack, cannot achieve. Despite the seemingly unifying bonds of identity, reality never quite matches the ideal, and identificatory commonalities do not necessarily produce benevolence, or even for that matter amity. Yet this is not the case in conspiracy theory, wherein the line between "us" and "them" provides an always clear and inviolable distinction. For after dividing the world into "us" and "them," conspiracy theories proceed to explain everything in the world according to this distinction, thereby perpetually affirming and thus reproducing this framework, such that all actions can be predicted based solely in identity, providing an elusive sense of certainty and thus control. The distinction of us and them produced in any conspiracy theory is then envisioned not as simply one factor among others, but is rather imagined to be the sole reason: the reason that can explain anything and everything, thereby comfortingly mapping the entire world in accordance with its founding identificatory distinction.

As illustrated in the preceding examples, the Manchu cabal provides an explanation for matters large and small, pressing and distant, from spitting to state violence, from the fall of the imperial household to contemporary macroeconomic concerns, and from tedious television miniseries to the cancer of corruption. Identity as an idealized image as promoted within the Han Clothing Movement fails to incorporate and explain such phenomena itself, insofar as the current Han-dominated society fails to accord with their ideals of Han culture. And this is where the all-encompassing binaries of conspiracy theory step in: by locating a single external source to these problems, not only is the overwhelming complexity of experience reassuringly simplified, but the singular cause of these issues is found comfortably outside of one's identity label, in "them." A stabilizing name is given to the incomprehensible and the unnamable, similar to Siegel's analysis of the process of "naming the witch" in East Java.[33] Conspiracy theory is then not only therapeutic,[34] but indeed fundamentally redemptive of an otherwise elusive stable sense of self. Explanation through the distinction between Han and Manchu autopoeitically reproduces this distinction of Han and Manchu along lines of good and bad, using its output as its input[35] and thus achieving the maintenance of a unified and ideal image of "us," the Han, through the maintenance of a corresponding unified and negative image of "them," the Manchus. As much as conspiracy thinking relies on the binaries of identity thinking, the binaries of identity thinking rely on conspiracy thinking for their perpetuation. Unattainable in actual practice as a result of its untenable idealization and the emptiness of lived experience, identity can then only be realized via conspiracy theory's production of a stable, simplified, fulfilling and fully encompassing vision of the world, redeeming and indeed rescuing a very particular and stable vision of "us" through the figure of "them." The permanent Xinhai Revolution described in the previous section is then a metaphor for the perpetual struggle against the disappointments of reality, towards the resuscitation of a practically untenable yet affectively fulfilling vision of identity.

But within this relationship between us and them, why have the Manchus in this particular case been placed in the role of "them"? Why has the struggle to redeem an imagined Han identity been envisioned as a "Xinhai Revolution"? In my analysis, two primary components of Manchu-ness make the Manchu an ideal subject for the reconstruction of Han identity. First, unlike discussions of aliens, the New World Order, the Illuminati, or "the Jews," the fact that the Manchu-dominated Qing Dynasty actually existed and reigned over China for three centuries provides a crucial foundation lacking in most conspiracy theories. Such actually existing facts, however, provide an illusory foundation for far more unrealistic conclusions. Illustrating the redemptive and ideal-identificatory function of such conspiracy theory, through this anti-Manchu worldview, the reform-era historical trope of the century of humiliation is able to be conspiratorially and damningly transferred onto the shoulders of the Manchu, whose barbarian theft of the mandate of heaven explains the disarray and disintegration of the idealized "unity of heaven and man" that followed in the nineteenth and twentieth century. "If you hand the mandate of heaven over to a bunch of barbarians," one participant told me, "what do you expect to happen?" The source of the downfall of the imperial order and the ideal society over which it ruled is then not to be found in any defects within this sociopolitical order, and should not be a cause for reflection or reform. The imperial order is thereby redeemed as the pinnacle of Han culture, in need of restoration as the sole political order suited for China: precisely the traditionalist political argument made by many Han Clothing Movement enthusiasts, and a conclusion that could only be reached via conspiracy theory.[36] The Manchu thus plays the role of the devil of national identiodicy, explaining away as the product of Manchu malfeasance all within the real China that fails to correspond to the idea of "the real China."

Beyond the power of the Manchus in the past, the second core component of Manchu-ness contributing to the viability of this conspiracy theory is the Manchu's fundamentally indiscernible nature in the present. As is widely recognized, the Manchu population of China today is small and largely Sinicized. As a friend of Manchu descent in Guangzhou commented during a lively and memorable discussion of my research on these conspiracy theories: "We Manchus have been completely Sinicized/Han-ified [i.e., *Hanhua*] over the past century. We don't have any land, nor any customs, nor any distinguishing features. Our language is almost dead. So how can these people claim that we run all of China? Fuck, does it look like I run this country?" From a rational perspective, such Hanification and the resulting nondistinct nature of the Manchu would indicate the Manchu's lack of power in the present, a lack of power that was all too apparent to my friend in his lengthy hiatus between jobs. Yet from another considerably more conspiratorial perspective, this largely nondistinct yet essentially foreign nature means that the Manchu can be found anywhere and everywhere, and can thus be used to explain anything and everything as an unrecognized outsider intervening in China's internal affairs, which would have otherwise been charmingly free from problems "since time immemorial." It is then precisely because the Manchu people have been thoroughly Sinicized and have neither strongly distinguishing features, nor customs, nor language in the present that they can be imagined as the omnipotent and omnipresent cabal secretly running the country and destroying its culture. And as noted above, the denial of any figure's perceived Manchu belonging is deemed to be part of the conspiracy and thus an affirmation of this figure's Manchu nature. Therefore, just as the lack of distinct ethnic characteristics provides a blank canvas to construct a fantasy vision of the Han towards which movement participants aspire, so the corresponding lack of distinct ethnic characteristics in the modern Manchu provides a blank canvas to embellish the imaginary enemy and discover them wherever necessary, thereby exercising complete explanatory control over an otherwise inexplicable and often quite disappointing world.

The all-encompassing nature of conspiracy theory realizes a perpetually self-reaffirming sense of idealized Han identity and community that is not only reliably lost in the everyday underwhelming experience of Han-ness, but that indeed cannot be attained by any other means. The image produced by the sum total of conspiracy theories within the movement is of a hypermobilized Manchu monolith engaged in constant and unending war with the Han. As a result, a coherent and unified "Han-ness" lacking in everyday experience, wherein "the Han" is experientially divided not only into ideals and reality but also equally importantly into rulers and ruled, rich and poor, local and outsider, or Northerner and Southerner, and beyond,[37] is rediscovered in united opposition to the crimes of the ruthlessly unified and predatory Manchus. Envisioning an extensive Manchu conspiracy to oppress and even eliminate their race, the Han is thereby reenvisioned not as the core creator of the less than perfect current state of affairs, but rather as the chosen yet downtrodden victim of a cruel external conspiracy, successfully employing the paranoid theme of persecution central to conspiracy theory as a genre[38] towards particularly narcissistic ends. By constructing a vision of the world in which the inequalities, discontents, and disturbances of daily life are solely the products of Manchu malfeasance, these theories again allow movement participants to imagine a world free from these disturbances, premised upon the removal of the Manchus from their imaginary positions of power and the subsequent realization of true Han-ness. Conspiracy theories, in their negative portrayals of contemporary realities, are thus based in the belief that a positive alternative is possible, and even the natural order of things: these fundamentally untenable and unrealistic theories of negative realities provide refuge for positive ideals and imaginaries that are otherwise unattainable.

Each step in conspiracy theory, from division and externalization, to the reassuring unity of explanation, to the resuscitation of otherwise untenable ideals of identity, can be seen in the most elaborately detailed articulation of the Han Clothing Movement's Manchu narrative: the idea that the Chinese state's controversial one-child policy was planned and executed solely by clandestine Manchus dedicated to the final elimination of the Han. This example, undoubtedly the most commonly cited and emotionally charged conspiracy theory among movement participants, is uniquely revealing not only in its portrayal of the Manchu, but also in its portrayal of the relationship between the government and the governed. For amid all of these perplexing and fundamentally unreal Manchu narratives, we can find a grain of truth providing the foundation for a theoretical reexamination of the experience of identificatory political power itself.

REPRODUCING HAN-NESS

Han Clothing Movement participants unanimously trace the reform-era resurgence of Manchu power to a moment in 1979 when Tian Xueyuan, a supposed descendant of Manchu bannermen (who in reality identifies as Han), was named the director of the Population Research Institute at the Chinese Academy of Social Sciences. Soon after taking this position, Tian became the architect of the country's highly controversial one-child policy, which mandated until late 2015 that urban residents have only one child. Similar to the theories surrounding the Kafka-esque Propaganda Department mentioned above, one can easily understand why this particular policy has emerged as a focus of conspiracy theories: after all, no phenomenon could be more amenable to conspiracy theorization than a state policy that intervenes in the most intimate of reproductive processes and the very origins of life itself. Yet beyond the ripeness of this phenomenon for conspiratorial thinking, the most fascinating aspect of these conspiracy theories is the story that they tell about movement participants' views of China today through the metaphor of the one-child policy: enthusiasts see the policy as representative of the barbarian fall of contemporary society and the oppressed, subaltern fate of the Han majority therein, at the mercy of a dominant and brutal Manchu minority whose sole purpose in life, more than a century after the fall of the Qing, remains the elimination of the Han from this earth.

In Manchu conspiracy theory narratives, the one-child policy is characterized as an exclusively Han one-child policy. Indeed, there was an exception to the one-child rule for minority nationalities in rural areas, but movement participants greatly exaggerate this exception as evidence of Manchu collusion in the drafting of this policy, while overlooking the fact that a high proportion of China's Manchu population in fact lives in urban areas and would thus not be exempt from these regulations. Revealing the centrality of affect over logic in the production and reproduction of conspiracy theory, I was asked by many Han Clothing devotees during my research, "Does this [the one-child policy] seem like something that a race would do to its own people?" This question gives voice to the fundamentally alien feeling of this policy, which in turn serves as evidence of its supposed alien origins: the entire family planning bureaucracy and its rationalized yet thoroughly irrational means of attaining its goals are read as persecution of one race by another. Reminiscent of Hofstadter's observation that the paranoid mentality is far more coherent than the real world,[39] such an explanation indeed seems far more rational and is undoubtedly more comforting than the identity-shattering fact that a largely Han state (also part of "us") arbitrarily imposed this policy upon a largely Han populace.

By associating the Manchus primarily with the one-child policy, rather than, for example, something more benign such as taxation or the slow handling of paperwork, the imagined Manchus in power are proven not to be regular bureaucrats, but indeed bloodthirsty madmen and madwomen, descendants of the genocidal Qing. Then, on account of his intrinsically evil Manchu nature, Tian's intention clearly is not to control population growth, nor to balance the population with available resources, nor whatever other paternalistic, scientistic excuses have been put forward to rationalize the one-child policy, but rather to oversee the complete elimination of the Han race and the destruction of superior Han culture. Tian is accused of having formed a secretive think tank with a group of fellow Manchus, for the sole purpose of researching and implementing programs to eliminate the Han, continuing and bringing to fruition the goals first expressed a century earlier in the "Policies to Eliminate the Han." Among the purported members of this think tank are Ma Xu, director of the Reproductive and Genetic Center of the National Research Institute for Family Planning, as well as Li Bin, former minister of the State Population and Family Planning Commission, and currently the chairperson of the National Health and Family Planning Commission.

Movement participants portray Li Bin as a bloodthirsty baby killer, even "crueler than the Japanese," in a widely distributed post that juxtaposes Li's image with a horrifying photograph of Shaanxi mother Feng Jianmei. Feng is a young woman who was forced to abort her child seven months into her pregnancy in 2012 because she could not afford the fine for a second child. Yet after the procedure, Feng took the dramatic step of graphically photographing herself in bed alongside her blood-covered, deceased 30-week fetus. The post juxtaposing these two images labels Feng as a "helpless Han mother" (*wuzhu de hanzu muqin*) and reads:

> *Manchu Tartary Family Planning Official and Child-Killing*
> *Beast Li Bin Specializes in Killing Han Babies*
>
> Minister of the State Family Planning and Population Commission and leader of the entire family planning enterprise Li Bin is a Manchu-Tartary descendant of Li Guoxiong. Li Guoxiong was a lackey of Manchukuo who "led the wolf right into the house" by collaborating with the Japanese Imperial Army in occupying Northeast China, wasting the human resources, material resources, and fiscal resources of the region and enslaving its people, even collaborating with the invading imperial army in slaughtering Chinese soldiers.
>
> Li Bin loves living by a double standard, using her power to manufacture false population statistics so as to deceive the Chinese people and the entire world. This Manchu-Tartary baby-killing beast has in the name of "family planning" stripped the Han race of its equal rights to reproduction and conspired to eliminate the Han so as to Tartar-ize China. She aims to overthrow China to reassert her control of all under heaven, revealing that her inhuman and rapacious designs remain as strong as ever.

Li Bin here is the epitome of the bloodthirsty Manchu, juxtaposed graphically within this representation with the most innocent of her victims, who had not yet even been polluted by this world before falling victim to its cruelty. Such representations externalize this experientially incomprehensible policy onto an other, while drawing upon the negative historical connotations surrounding the Manchu, identifying Li Bin as only the latest in a long line of China-hating savages, so as to present the scapegoat as nothing less than a fundamental existential threat, requiring Han unity. The one-child policy is thereby removed from its seemingly rational aspirations and inserted into an alternative historical narrative of resisting the foreign invader: this image juxtaposing a baby and its murderer then serves as a rallying cry for Han unity, consolidating and even exaggerating a sense of "us" through an exaggerated sense of a completely foreign "them," thereby making the otherwise unclear category of "Han-ness," which the movement aims to promote, present and real in an unprecedented and immediate way.

And finally, on account of this supposedly evil genocidal power, the Han as a whole is portrayed as oppressed and fundamentally endangered, expressing the disappointments of reality through the metaphor of an insidious racial oppression. Within the context of a society largely produced and dominated by people who self-identify as "Han" yet far removed from movement expectations, this portrayal of the oppression of the Han serves to explain the reliable evasiveness of the movement's ideals, or the inescapable gap between Han identity as presented by the movement and the realities of everyday experience in contemporary China. Revealing this logic of a pure society being overrun by minorities, one scientistic yet thoroughly unrealistic graph on a Han Clothing website, frequently cited by movement participants, claims to demonstrate the demographic outcomes of the one-child policy, tracing the population growth of the five core nationalities (i.e., Han, Zhuang, Hui, Manchu, and Uighur) alongside China's "ten Muslim nationalities" from 1990 to the year 2290. The results show conclusively that the Han population will dip below minority levels around 2140 and will eventually disappear by 2290, tellingly dropping below even the Manchu population. No actual statistical basis or other form of explanation is provided for this highly unlikely demographic shift. Rather, imaginary evidence is structured around an already discovered conclusion, affirming the identificatory sentiments of both the author and the viewers of the graph. Such portrayals cast the Han as the victim of a cruel society controlled by others, irrationally dedicated to the Han's destruction, in a narrative that is very similar to the American far right's portrayals of the "war on Christmas"[40] or a white minority under siege.[41] Unity of identity, unable to be reached by any other means, is finally achieved through a complex, imaginary network of conspiratorial victimization and corresponding heroic resistance: the negative conspiracy theory of Manchu genocide in fact belies a positive conspiracy theory of pure and ideal Han identity.

"Does this seem like something that a race would do to its own people?" The belief that forcible family planning could only be a Manchu imposition to destroy the Han and that its implementation has been "crueler than the Japanese" is revealing, in that it brings to light the commonly assumed yet underanalyzed link between political legitimacy and identity.[42] Generally speaking, the worthiness of a particular political power is presumed to be tied to its provenance: a state power derived from one's own nation or ethnic group is often presumed to be inherently good and naturally benevolent when compared to a power coming from the outside, which would be inherently cruel and naturally abusive. And although it is true that an external occupying power may often be cruel and abusive, there is no corresponding guarantee that an internal power will be inherently kind. There are, after all, countless counterexamples in the history of governance. Yet this vision of native politics remains a pleasant myth of identity that we repeatedly tell ourselves despite its being equally repeatedly disproven, and which Han Clothing Movement participants apparently go to great lengths to rationalize, diligently tracing the "foreign" sources of an all-too-real government that is all too unpleasant yet also all too internal, at once sharing an identity yet at the same time violating this same identity, all while rationalizing its violations through identity mythologies and the corresponding specter of menacing "foreign powers."

The flip side of the stranger king allegory that gives voice in the anthropological literature to the fundamentally external nature of political power[43] is the myth of the native ruler who is fundamentally one with his domain by right of identity, a power all one's own: a myth that can only be kept alive by perpetually representing the crimes and disappointments of internal rulers in reality as external impositions. This tension within experience then leads to the unending paranoid search for leaders behind the curtains who are not "our type," so as to reaffirm the purity of "our type" (i.e., reaffirming the unity of identity) against the challenges and disappointments of reality. Other examples beyond the figure of the Manchu in contemporary China include the argument that the world and thus China are run by the Rothschilds,[44] the Freemasons,[45] "neoliberalism," and even, most curiously, Japan and the United States. Similar accusations from a certain dogmatic French philosopher have, in typically hyperbolic fashion, labeled Nicholas Sarkozy's politics as "transcendental Petainism," equally curiously accusing the former French president of collaboration with "the Yankee model,"[46] rendered for full dramatic (or in Badiou's terminology, "militant") effect in the metaphor of collaboration with a no-longer-present Nazi invader.[47]

And although conspiracies often envision the United States as the conspirator behind the scenes clandestinely running the world, many similar yet inverted conspiracy theories have emerged in recent years within the United States itself. White power groups transform whites into a persecuted minority through their imaginings that the United States is run by either "the Jews" or foreign and domestic conspirators within a "new world order."[48] Former president Barack (Hussein!) Obama is imagined variously as a "Muslim" and/or "foreigner" beholden to presumably colonizing "Kenyan" values (in the words of Newt Gingrich), while also being beholden to an "anti-colonial worldview" (in the words of Newt Gingrich, from the same sentence).[49] The confused combination of "anticolonialism" and presumed "foreign" colonization in Gingrich's thoughts is symptomatic of the contradictions within which we find ourselves whenever we try to think through the relationship between the assumptions of identity and the realities of political power.

Nowhere are these contradictions more apparent than in the academic discourses of postcolonialism and antiorientalism, promising modes of analysis that are nevertheless far too often manifested as conspiratorial witch-hunts with more sophisticated theoretical vocabulary. Both have become implicated in a fantasy of identity and a correspondingly far too simplistic and academically politically correct binary of oppressor and oppressed, the identity boundaries of which are often not so clear in practice. Allen Chun has made a related point in his recent paper "Toward a Postcolonial Critique of the State in Singapore," in which he insightfully pushes postcolonial theory beyond its comfortable affirmation of "subaltern" identity toward a framework for analyzing institutions in general.[50] Chun observes that the "poverty of the postcolonial" is to be found precisely in its most vulgar (and arguably most common) sense: as an affirmative statement of identity alone.[51] Derived from Said's myopic presentation of Orientalist activity as developing solely upon one axis, namely, the East-West binary, the academic hunt for "Orientalism" and "colonialism" serves only to reproduce and reinforce the imaginary East-West difference that serves as its founding distinction, comfortingly mapping the entire world in accordance with this distinction in a manner identical to a conspiracy theory,[52] while at the same time simply transferring from one side of the binary to the other the simplistic portrayals which it claims to oppose. Within this rhetorical circuit sharing the structures of conspiracy theory, and immunized against critique by its self-congratulating moralizing claims, conventional postcolonialism serves as a theoretically elaborate conspiratorial celebration of identity.

A potential solution to this conundrum, however, can be found in Chun's suggestion to take identity out of postcolonial analysis. More specifically, this means that postcolonial theory's application must not be limited solely to overtly colonial/postcolonial societies, but should rather "be regarded as a critical framework for any theory or institution" that "rel[ies] on similar genres of cultural representation, discursive authority, identity formations and knowledge functions"[53] toward practices of "unacceptable, intolerable, and insupportable domination."[54] Chun proceeds in his article to demonstrate such an expansion and reapplication of postcolonial theory through an analysis of the superficially noncolonial yet culturally and politically stifling state in Singapore.

A similar line of analysis might be proposed for interpreting the one-child policy and its enactor, the state in China. For in human history, what better example of colonization might we find than a state's intrusion into and monitoring of the reproductive capabilities of its populace? In the handbook of traditional anticolonial analysis, *Orientalism*, Edward Said writes that the divisions of "West" and "East," or of "us" and "them," are "generalities whose use historically and actually has been to press the importance of the distinction between some men and some other men, usually towards not especially admirable ends."[55] Yet the resulting overemphasis upon the distinction of "West" and "East" in Said and his followers' analyses primarily serves to affirm and reproduce an equally rigid and stifling binary identity,[56] while failing to subject to critique far more socially relevant distinctions, such as ruler and ruled: a distinction also employed "usually towards not especially admirable ends," particularly when the power of the state can be illusorily legitimized through the binding force of collective identity in contrast to "outsiders."

The nation as a fantasy-driven affective identificatory system contributes greatly to the contradictory human relationship to political power, insofar as an internal yet perpetually external power serves, on the one hand, as the primary enactor of the fantasies of the nation on a massive scale, as well as, on the other hand, as the primary enactor of injustices and catastrophes on an equally grand scale. This same political entity that produces fleeting moments of pride through its exercise of power, such as the 2008 Olympics, can also produce considerably more durable moments of confusion, discomfort, anger, and dismay through its exercise of power: arbitrary decision-making and controls, censorship, forcible family planning, and various other limits, humiliations, and shames. If Orientalism "is knowledge of the Orient that places things Oriental in class, court, prison, or manual for scrutiny, judgment, discipline, or governing,"[57] then the first and last Orientalists have been none other than "Oriental" rulers, whose simultaneous distinction from and unity with the ruled illusorily justifies in advance their actions. The one-child policy that Han Clothing Movement enthusiasts struggle to comprehend through an externalizing myth similarly relies upon the collection of data, and the placement of a subject under scrutiny, judgment, discipline, and governing towards the rationalization of "unacceptable, intolerable, and insupportable domination."[58]

Thus, to frame the question of political power in terms of "insiders" and "outsiders" as both this conspiracy theory and conventional anticolonialism does is a reflexive affirmation of collective identity that completely ignores actual social dynamics, thereby illusorily rationalizing situations internal to "the East" or "China" wherein a state apparatus is able to monitor and control intimate reproductive processes while at the same time being represented as a liberator and the sole line of defense against supposedly predatory and imperialist "foreign invaders." It is then no surprise that the founding distinction of identity that rationalizes this behavior in the first place as "internal affairs" (*neizheng*) must be reaffirmed through the externalization of the actions that it falsely rationalizes, as can be seen in the reflexive critique of critique as invariably "Orientalist," as well as in the theory of the Manchu as a menacing colonizer.

The imaginary figure of the evil Manchu is then in fact the core of a similarly imaginary pure Han identity, sustained through conspiracy thinking. The Manchu is portrayed as the sole source of evil in Han Clothing Movement narratives, so as to externalize the violence practiced by the modern Chinese state and thereby provide a basis in the popular imagination for what might be called a positive conspiracy theory: the belief in natural unity and camaraderie within identity, and the utopian political belief that there must be "good people" within the state bureaucracy who will make everything "right" in the end. A fulfilling ideal of untarnished Han-ness lost in the corruption of the real world is redeemed through the imaginary figure of the evil Manchu engaging in perpetual acts of sabotage against what should otherwise be a perfect polity and society. This negative conspiracy theory of the all-powerful Manchu cabal then primarily serves to maintain a fulfilling positive conspiracy theory of a Han society and a Han state, which would solely by right of their pure Han identity alone be benevolent and perfect. So long as such externalizing images of foreign invaders continue to play a central role in the construction of Chinese and Han identity, explaining away a discomfiting reality while at the same time concealing the fundamental conflicts of that reality,[59] the native stranger king as an internalized external power will continue to have free reign to reproduce the many discomfiting aspects of this reality. Illustrating the politically futile nature of this imaginary identity politics, the next section examines a moment in which a group of Han Clothing activists actively organized to confront, once and for all, their Manchu enemy.

One Friday evening in the fall of 2010, I received a text message from a friend in the local Guangzhou Han Clothing organization, telling me to meet him and a few other Han Clothing enthusiasts at 8:00 A.M. the next morning on the edge of town. He would not respond directly to my inquiries about what would happen the next day, only cryptically assuring me that I had to see it for myself. When I emerged from the metro station the next morning and found my companions, I noted immediately that everyone appeared to be in particularly high spirits. Finally breaking their silence to tell me the plan for the day, I was immediately fascinated: we were confronting a Manchu lackey and converting him to the cause of Han Clothing.

I soon learned that a local designer had developed an exhibition in his gallery featuring "traditional" Chinese clothes. Archaeologically speaking, because the Qing Dynasty is historically the closest dynasty and thus the most likely to have clothing remnants to display, and politically speaking, because official narratives dogmatically emphasize the completely unproblematic "Chineseness" of the Qing Dynasty, it should not have been a surprise that all of the outfits featured in this exhibition were from the Qing era. It is also, however, not a surprise that these outfits were viewed as foreign "Manchu clothing" in the eyes of Han Clothing activists, and thus as a sign of creeping Manchu hegemony. Encouraged by a leading figure in the local Han Clothing Movement who had learned of this exhibition in a professional setting, two members of the local association had clandestinely visited the gallery over the past week, staking out the situation. Their conclusion was unanimous: "He is promoting *Manfu* [Manchurian clothing], and fighting *Hanfu* [Han Clothing]." We seemed to have tracked down one cog in the expansive Manchu machinery of Han oppression, and were about to confront him: perhaps in the hope of catching him slightly off guard, a meeting had been arranged for 9:00 A.M. on a Saturday morning.

Prior to our arrival at the studio, participants had envisioned a burly, wicked Manchu behind the scenes of the exhibition, determined to slander the Han through the promotion of Manchu clothing toward his final goal of Han extermination. "He's part of the plan, he has to be," was a refrain repeated many times that morning. In contrast to this image of the evil other, participants agreed to emphasize a "civilized" (*wenming*) approach that would show their difference from such savagery, "speaking some reason" (*jiang daoli*) in hopes that this curator might change his wicked ways, and recognize the one and only true path for China: Han Clothing and a corresponding Han-dominated culture. Toward this goal, I was informed that only the better educated and more understanding members of the local Han Clothing association were notified of this event, in order to ensure that the argument would be presented clearly and reasonably. Although everyone in the movement promoted the Han ideal, some participants were "no good" for this type of activity. As for myself, in addition to serving as a witness to this epic showdown, I was clearly also invited to serve as symbolic "international support."

Upon arriving at the studio, the Manchu whom we were to meet immediately deployed his deceptive ways. His assistant told us that he had not yet arrived for our 9:00 A.M. discussion, an understandable tardiness on a Saturday morning that could nevertheless be interpreted in a sinister manner by right of his imagined scheming Manchu nature. As we wandered through the exhibition, glancing at a quite expansive collection of Qing Dynasty textiles and modern reproductions, movement participants became convinced that our host was insincere in his agreement to meet and was stalling for time. The conspiracy theories grew with each minute that the meeting was delayed, until everyone was convinced that he was already in his studio, and might even be planning something. Who could know? These paranoid theories continued to unfold at a rapid pace until the moment that our host arrived, at which point they promptly ground to a halt. For rather than facing down a scheming Manchu, we instead stood face to face with a noticeably hung-over and somewhat flamboyant Cantonese-speaking clothes designer who was certainly not looking for a fight this early in the morning.

The meeting, conducted on sofas in a sunny corner of the curator's expansive studio, began with each Han Clothing advocate making a short presentation, explaining Han Clothing. No matter whether Han Clothing really has five millennia of history or is an invented tradition, the movement itself, over the past decade, has developed a quite "traditional" way of presenting Han Clothing, which was repeated once again that morning. The outlines of this portrayal should already be familiar to readers: the Han and their clothing have existed for five millennia, since the time of the Yellow Emperor. Han Clothing was erased by the barbaric Qing. The outfit of the Tang is not from the Tang, and *magua* and *qipao* are not Chinese clothing. As we made our way gradually through these talking points, the designer suddenly leaned forward and politely interrupted this monologue with a few words that no one was expecting: "I just want to say that I absolutely detest the brutality of the Manchu Qing government and completely support Han Clothing."

I strongly suspect that our dreaded Manchu opponent had conducted research on the movement before our meeting, as he came across as even more adamant in his outrage against "the Manchus" than many Han Clothing activists. Less than twenty minutes into our conversation, we found ourselves collectively reflecting upon the cruelty of the well-known Qing massacres in Yangzhou and Jiading: with the newly added historical detail that the true origins of these massacres was the determination to erase Han Clothing and thereby destroy the Han spirit. Our former enemy nodded eagerly in agreement, "It's horrible." And thus, an activist interjected, once Han Clothing is revitalized, the Han's spirit will be brought back to life. Our former enemy could not have agreed more strongly, "I would be happy to work with you on that."

We remained in this designer's studio until later in the afternoon, missing lunch because we were so absorbed in the discussion of ancient clothing, debating the role of hats in premodern society, and awkwardly perusing an unusually large collection of traditional erotic art that our former Manchu opponent had collected over the years and was for some reason eager to share with us. Before we knew it, we were all the best of friends, and this once clandestine cog in the Manchu machine of oppression eagerly agreed to work with the local Han Clothing association to produce a promotional film to be released before the Chinese New Year. Everyone agreed that far too few people knew about Han Clothing, and that it was necessary to expose more fellow Han to their national clothing, so that they might recognize its full beauty and glory. And most importantly, everyone agreed that they could work together toward this goal.

From this case of mistaken opposition, a new alliance had been built and an opportunity had been created to promote Han Clothing more widely. These should not have been disappointing results, to say the least. But as we sat down for a very late *yumcha* lunch, the atmosphere among participants was considerably more subdued than the excitement of confrontation that I had witnessed earlier in the morning: the eagerness of the pure Han confronting the purely evil Manchu. Reflecting upon our lengthy meeting, one advocate observed that Han Clothing enthusiasts often have good intentions but also far too often make the mistake of opposition when dealing with others. Today's encounter, he added, was another example of this trend. Rather than an occasional mistake, however, this opposition is in my analysis central to the movement and its affirmation of identity, particularly in light of the notably subdued atmosphere at lunch that afternoon. For when one has an enemy whom one can oppose and who can serve as an explanation for and denunciation of the world as it is, all seems clear and certain. This group had fastidiously prepared to face the feared Manchu: the supposed source of all that is wrong in contemporary China. But then, suddenly, the all-encompassing theory of the Manchu cabal that reinforces Han identity encountered a real-world exception that could not be explained within its framework, and everything suddenly seemed considerably less exciting. Over lunch, bureaucratic arguments were already emerging about how to proceed with the promotional video. Who would be responsible for the various tasks involved in this process? Unenthusiastically, a few people volunteered. Yet by the time that the Chinese New Year arrived, the video was not produced: disorganization, debate, and disagreement among participants eventually led to the total collapse of this unexpected united front, which provided a great promotional opportunity but also greatly complicated worldviews.

Early in my research, a scholar once asked whether my work with Han Clothing enthusiasts was intended to study the "power of civil society," a misinterpretation that nevertheless provided useful ground for reflection. Indeed, considering for the sake of analysis this movement's place within a potential civil society, we might note that Han Clothing is among the largest officially tolerated (or at least officially ignored) nationwide social movements in reform-era China, with branches in most cities: such ambitious social movements are usually the victims of state crackdowns before even having a chance to make their voices heard. Yet if the conspiracy theories reviewed in this chapter are one direction in which civil society is proceeding, while other possibilities are actively suppressed by the authorities, this could only be cause for pessimism. Conspiracy theories such as those peddled by Han Clothing activists are not in any sense exceptional: quite similar examples can be seen in Song Qiang, Zhang Xiaobo et al.'s *China Can Say No* and *Unhappy China*,[60] wherein "them" equals the United States, Japan, Taiwan; or Song Hongbing's bestselling *Currency War* series,[61] wherein "them" equals the Rothschilds; or pro-state scholar He Xin's eccentric latest work *Who Runs the World?*[62] wherein "them" equals the Freemasons; or Larry Lang Xianping's nationalist-pessimistic critique of the state of the Chinese economy,[63] wherein them equals "foreigners" manipulating the economy; or the reflections of such New Leftists as Kong Qingdong and Sima Nan, which combine Marxist-Maoist rhetoric with nationalist-fascist paranoia to condemn the United States, Japan, Taiwan, Hong Kong, and of course, most obsessively, their traitorous "running dogs" within China.[64] Such conspiracy theories have proliferated rapidly throughout Chinese society over the past two decades, and the reliable similarity among these mutually conflicting examples indicates the appeal of conspiracy thinking for explaining that which otherwise simply cannot be explained: the otherness of the self.

Each of these modes of description comfortingly provides a framework to understand and interpret the world through the distinction between us and them, removing "us" from responsibility for the present while placing all of the blame upon "them," namely, those who run the world and are thus solely responsible for its shortcomings. By opposition, "we" emerge unscathed as victims in the present and potential saviors for the future, at which point "China" will variously "say no," become happy, resist the Rothschilds and the Freemasons, realize economic independence, finally root out the traitors, or of course establish a truly "Han" and thus truly "Chinese" form of governance and society. The shift from elusive identity to an explanatory, all-encompassing, and externalizing conspiracy theory achieves the transformation of a fundamentally imaginary and perpetually disjointed community into a thoroughly documented and perpetually self-reaffirming community: this mode of identity thinking, escaping the perpetual discordance central to its experiential reality via conspiracy thinking, thereby perpetually reproduces identity itself. These theories are thus richly therapeutic for their believers,[65] insofar as their paranoid structure allows for the stabilization and attainment of an otherwise lost and perpetually elusive sense of completeness in the present. Yet for all of their emotional redemption, these ideas remain in the end thoroughly impoverished frameworks for interpretation and action, mystifying the very real challenges of the world and re-presenting them through a seemingly all-encompassing and empowering but fundamentally delusional and thus disempowering narrative. For all of its romantic, empowering associations in academic work, the exercise of "agency" can be thoroughly disempowering in practice.

Much like the self-reproducing paradox of the fantasy of national identity, these conspiracy theories serve at once as symptoms of sociopolitical dilemmas and as fleeting sources of therapy. Yet in the end, the real source of the perpetuation of injustices is precisely the identificatory investment in the idea of "the Han" and "China" that these conspiracy theories rationalize and thus perpetuate, thereby ensuring one point of consistency in an always rapidly changing and uncertain world: the continued appeal of both identity thinking and conspiracy thinking, each sustaining the other.

SIX

Producing Purity

Nationalism is our form of incest, is our idolatry, is our insanity.
— ERICH FROMM, *The Sane Society*[1]

THE HAN CLOTHING MOVEMENT is a collection of individuals seeking the elusive realization of a transcendent and whole ideal of identity that they call Han. Yet within this search for wholeness and the overcoming of all divisions, there remains one internal division that participants maintain as essential, and indeed as eternal as Han-ness: the division of gender. Amid Han Clothing's unity as Han, clear gender distinctions are made such that there are carefully differentiated types of Han Clothing for men, and other types for women: men wear *shenyi*, *zhiduo*, or *xuanduan*, while women wear *ruqun*, *aoqun*, and *da'ao*. Even Han Clothing styles suitable for both male and female devotees, such as the *zhiju* or *quju*, are clearly distinguished in terms of color and designs, with darker and more solemn colors for men, alongside brighter and often floral designs for women. And for those who might miss these clues, stores clearly divide clothing styles as suitable for either "men" (*nanzhuang*) or "women" (*nüzhuang*).

Nationalism is primarily a masculinized ideology.[2] In a movement that places such an emphasis upon a singular and eternal unity, the perceived importance of this gender distinction in history belies its role, and particularly the role of the "traditional lady," as the assumed cornerstone of a proper, male-dominated, traditional Han-ness and Chineseness today. In this process, a backward-looking and essentially misogynist view of gender is given a veneer of false legitimacy through the notion of "tradition" and the possessive will of nationalism. The resulting limiting vision of femininity clearly has appeal to male participants, insofar as it imagines submissive and loyal women who "belong" to Han men purely by right of their being born in China. Yet this smothering vision of womanhood is also in many cases embraced by women participants who, by casting themselves in the role of the "traditional woman," renounce freedom of choice for national-traditionalist cultural capital on a reliably perplexing marriage market.

In the following analyses, I first review the ways in which "culture" and "nation," two of the core concepts of the Han Clothing Movement, produce a highly restrictive and regressive vision of gender relations. I then proceed to examine these trends in action at a so-called ladies' academy in contemporary urban China affiliated with the Han Clothing Movement. Finally, in light of the preceding analyses, I critique the limiting and normative nature of the movement as a whole, in contrast to its unrealized potential, as a self-organized social group concerned with the dilemma of the present, to promote a novel openness in contemporary China.

MEN OF ACTION, WOMEN OF RESTRAINT

The images of men and women on the following two pages embody the ideal images of masculinity and femininity within Han Clothing imaginaries. One can see commonalities in their clothing styles denoting their common Hanness. Yet upon closer inspection, one is able to see that men's styles typically feature darker and presumably more "masculine" colors, while women's styles lean towards notably brighter hues and far more elaborate designs. Following this distinction, the bodily comportments of the people in the two images are also revealing. The man stands in a determined and assertive pose, atop a massive rock. By contrast, the woman is considerably more restrained, demonstrating a certain demure bearing, hiding behind a fan. This fan itself, in its act of covering her face, is also revealing. Men in the movement would at times carry outwardly directed accessories, such as an imitation sword, arrows, drums, or other implements, suggesting a more active and even aggressive posture in relation to the world. Women, by contrast, possessed no such accessories, often keeping their hands folded in front of their chests, or even hidden within their sleeves. At the most, a woman may have a fan behind which she could hide coyly. These two images are representative of the standard male and female poses in photographic portraits within the movement, revealing the logic of gendered differentiation internal to "the Great Han," envisioning men of action, and women of restraint. It is only through this binary division, according to movement participants, that the whole can be complete and indeed great.

Activists have repeatedly insisted that Han Clothing is primarily an external medium for representing deeper and more fundamental matters of

FIGURE 15. Gendered enactments of Han-ness, Guangzhou.

culture, tradition, and Chineseness. The same is perceived to be true for gender relations. Just as Han Clothing expresses a constructed vision of glory as an internal Han essence, these divisions in clothing and accompanying poses represent socially constructed gender distinctions as a natural and eternal division, dehistoricizing its historical production.[3] In the case of men, these portrayals reflect a complex combination of valiant heroism and superior civilization that is nothing short of spectacular. In the case of women, these portrayals embody a reserved and docile nature frequently rendered in the stock phrase: "beauty that emanates outward from within" (*you nei wang wai de mei*), suggesting a natural feminine "beauty" characterized by internal restraint and coyness that is reflected on the outside. Thus, just as Han

FIGURE 16. Gendered enactments of Han-ness, Guangzhou.

Clothing reflects the intrinsic Han-ness of the Han, so these distinctions in clothing and bearing between Han men and women are assumed to reflect intrinsic differences between the two sexes.

Nevertheless, as this Han essence has purportedly been lost in the modern era, so this supposedly natural distinction between the sexes has been lost as well. The crisis of modern Han-ness is intertwined in movement imaginings with a perceived crisis of modern Han women, who are considered essential to the continuation of tradition,[4] yet who are also seen as actively abandoning tradition in the present. Discussions with male Han Clothing enthusiasts over the course of my research reliably characterized contemporary Han women in the age of reform and opening as far too "open." In the monologue recounted at the start of this book contrasting China's past and present, women were accused of dressing improperly, with "private" parts of their bodies hanging out for all to see, like "Westerners." This forwardness in dress naturally reflected deeper issues, such as a corresponding forwardness in domestic affairs and material concerns which participants viewed as incompatible with proper womanhood: modern women were described as too "overpowering" (*qiangshi*) (a criticism that would not be directed to a man),[5] betraying standard gender roles, and solely concerned with such material matters as apartments, cars, and luxury items, thereby forgetting their "traditional values."

Such forwardness is further imagined to correspond to an inelegant eagerness in sexual matters: after all, calls for "purity" in a gendered context inevitably lead to a focus upon feminine sexuality.[6] One movement participant, a self-declared virgin in his late twenties, displayed a determined virginity complex,[7] repeatedly bemoaning the lack of "pure" women in China today. He recounted to me on multiple occasions his tragic encounters with the opposite sex, whom he characterized as invariably "polluted" and susceptible to seduction by "black devils." Yet beyond one sexually frustrated informants' hang-ups, this fascination with purity was a theme repeatedly raised by both men and women within the movement. Another participant, after a few drinks, would inevitably begin enquiring about my own sexual experiences like an investigator at a crime scene, failing to hide his anger as he possessively asked precisely how many of "our Chinese women" (*women Zhongguo guniang*) I had known during my time in China. My discussions with male Han Clothing enthusiasts thus suggested that the ideal image of Han femininity embodied in the coy image above was a rare sight, as was the case with all ideal images, to be replaced by inelegant, unreserved, coarse, immoral, and even traitorous modern women who were neither "true Han" nor even "true women."

Reflecting this dilemma, in the winter of 2011, I had dinner at the home of Tang, a single man with a fairly successful career who viewed himself as a "true Han" and thus a real man: similar to Bourdieu's observation of the equivalence between "manliness" and "Kabylness" (*thakbaylith*),[8] both "true Han" and "good guy" are rendered in Chinese as a *haohan*, or "good Han." The only area in which Tang considered himself a failure was in relations between the sexes. Yet he was predictably adamant that this failure was not his fault, but rather the fault of today's women. Tang told me, in an inversion of the ideal of beauty emanating outwards from inside, that modern women "strive to make themselves beautiful on the outside, to cover up what's inside."

Opening his laptop, he showed me a series of images of the "modern" woman. In these meme-like images, a woman was first shown on the left in a fairly unflattering picture, purportedly au naturel, and then again on the right, in a considerably more flattering portrayal, with make-up. Certain inconsistencies within the photos, such as the shape of the individuals' faces, a trait that cannot be changed easily with cosmetics, suggest that these are not in fact images of the same people, but rather images comparing two different people who are made up and dressed to look similar, to provide viewers with a seemingly true photographic representation of their deepest misogynistic suspicions of women's inherent deceptiveness.

The real issue here is not the veracity of these images, but rather the source of their appeal and resonance with certain male viewers, who assume that they lay bare, in yet another example of conspiracy, a suspected dirty secret: the idea of women as double agents, using a false exterior beauty to entice and even seduce men while covering over a deeper ugliness. For at the same time that these male viewers desire the women pictured as potential objects, they also, as spurned potential suitors, hate these same women for the rejections that they experience in daily life. The most comforting outcome of this ambivalence[9] is the self-affirming conclusion that the beauty that both lures and rejects oneself is fundamentally false, or an illusion: removing the make-up of the alluring good Han reveals a scheming Manchu-like fox spirit in disguise. In contrast to the imagining of the traditional woman whose "beauty emanates outward from within," an imagining that lives on despite its illusory nature, these images claim to reveal an illusory outward beauty that covers over a deeper truth of internal decay in the modern woman.

Yet much as the widely bemoaned realities of the present were not representative of the real China, which could only be found in the past, so the reality of the true Chinese woman, according to Tang, could be rediscovered in the imagined traditional woman, who embodied this unity of internal and external beauty. Tang told me that the "real" Chinese women of the past, against the real women of the present, had no need for cosmetics: their beauty had a deeper internal moral foundation that emanated outwards for all to see. Tang claimed that this internal beauty was based in a commitment to the three obediences (*san cong*). According to this framework, early in her life, a woman will obey her father; later in life, she will obey her husband; and finally in widowhood, she will obey her son. Tang's explanation of the notion of *cong*, generally translated as "obedience," rendered this concept as a combination in his words of the three concepts of obedience (*fucong*), reliance (*yikao*), and focus (*jituo*). In his view, obedience (*fucong*) was embodied in both thoughts and actions, with a woman following the guidance of a series of leading men in the course of her life. Reliance (*yikao*) was an economic matter, in so far as the traditional woman would always have a central male figure to rely upon for the resources that she needed throughout the course of her life. And focus (*jituo*) was a spiritual matter, a matter of dedication to a particular man and his family. The benefit of this internal obedience, reliance, and focus, according to Tang, was that women would show beauty from the inside out based in these guiding principles, which could then be appreciated and enjoyed by the male figures in each stage of her life. Accordingly, she would be rewarded with guaranteed security and stability in each stage, extending from birth in relation to a father through death in relation to her own son: a happiness unknown by what he referred to, in a moment of anger, as today's "so-called equal, so-called democratic, so-called independent, and so-called strong women." A woman's real strength, Tang believed, was to be found in obedience.

There remained hope for revitalization of this ideal image, in Tang's opinion, through a return to what he called "traditional" ways and values.[10] Another evening, Tang shared with me a new Chinese-language website that had generated a substantial amount of discussion on Han Clothing forums: the Rare Treasure of Chastity website (*Yapin zhencao wang*),[11] dedicated to promoting chastity among the next generation of Chinese youth. It was founded by Tu Shiyou, a 38-year-old woman from Hubei Province who openly claimed to have saved her virginity for marriage. Tu's reserve with regards to matters of sexual exploration, however, stood in stark contrast to her unreserved self-promotion: publicizing online the results of a hymen inspection conducted at Wuhan's Tongji Hospital as her official "virgin certification," she openly called herself a "Chastity Goddess" (*Zhencao nüshen*), and tasked herself with nothing less than saving the next generation from the creeping dangers of a supposedly "Westernized" sexuality. She was thus essentially a female version of Brother Emperor, with the sole difference that her focus was sexual rather than sartorial conservatism. As a result of her outlandish self-portrayal, captured in her self-description as a "Chastity Goddess," the response to Tu's efforts in popular culture had largely consisted of outright mockery. Yet her articulation of such traditional values had caught the attention of the Han Clothing Movement and my acquaintance Tang. This Tu Shiyou, he told me, is a real Chinese woman, recapturing the longstanding and outstanding moral tradition of the Chinese people that needed to be recaptured amid the uncertainties, instability, and immorality of society today. This, he declared, is real beauty.

The gap between imagining and experience developed in the analyses thus far is clearly also relevant in Tang's case: while some men in the West may imagine an "obedient" "Oriental" and thus "feminine" woman as a solution to their own insecurities, others in this "Orient" are similarly imagining a vision of the "traditional" "Oriental" woman as a response to their failed experiences in the present. Constructed in an imagined binary between East and West and around moralizing requirements of obedience, chastity, and reliance that do not extend to their male counterparts, this vision of the "real Chinese woman" is less a practical framework for behavior in contemporary life than a misogynistic fantasy. Revealingly, in these constructions, no one is more certain about the characteristics of a "real" woman than men, such that the narcissistic reconstruction and objectification of the self towards one's ideal image in movement participation develops alongside a corresponding misogynistic reconstruction of "women" towards one's ideal image as objects capable of control and indeed possession.

Furthermore, as is often the case in the Han Clothing Movement, this retrogressive fantasy is articulated through the metaphors of "culture" and "tradition," providing an exterior (or even, one might say, cosmetic) appearance of innateness and righteousness that is otherwise lacking, appropriating culture as a conservative defense against what should be universal values.[12] If beauty in the past emanated from the inside out, and if cosmetics serve as an external disguise for the internal decay of the modern woman, the notion of traditional culture as deployed in these Han Clothing Movement narratives of femininity is then the forceful insertion of an externally defined and highly limiting vision of traditional beauty into the interior of contemporary individuals as their proper essence, to which they must conform or risk being judged in violation of their proper selfhood. Just as much as the idea of culture is a collection of ideas and practices, it is also an idea in and of itself circulating within the cultural world and fully capable of being used and even abused:[13] as a fantasy, or as an illusorily self-legitimizing edict, or, in this case, as both, constructing a misogynistic fantasy of womanhood as the natural state of gender relations from time immemorial that must be recaptured.

Richard Handler's analyses of nationalism as "possessive individualism"[14] are relevant to this point, insofar as in addition to "having" a nation and "having" a culture (as well as in turn being possessed by the idea of that nation and culture), a male nationalist further envisions himself as possessing a certain natural right over the women within his territory as enactors and reproducers of his fantasy of national culture. The origins and repercussions of this dominant possession are examined in more depth in the next section.

THE NATIONALIST TRAFFIC IN WOMEN

During my research, a particularly belligerent post from a movement participant whom I had met a few times at activities in Guangzhou began circulating on Han Clothing sites. Entitled "Single Men[15] of China Unite, Stop Foreigners and Black People from Stealing Chinese Women!" the post attempts to explain some Chinese men's admittedly difficult single status through the cunning of "foreigners" and the corresponding corruption of Chinese women. Finally, building upon his analysis, the author further proposes some fairly disturbing "solutions" to these issues.

The article begins:

> November 11 is Single's Day [*Guanggun Jie*]. Getting down to the bottom of it, the primary reason that many of us are single is that there are more men than women here in China. And why is this so? The main reason is that family planning has produced a gender imbalance in our country. But there is also another reason: because foreigners [*yang ren*] and black people [*hei ren*] are stealing China's female resources [*Zhongguo de nüxing ziyuan*] in large numbers.[16]

We might pause for a moment to note that women are characterized here not as human beings, which would include the character for "people" (*ren*) extended here even to presumably subhuman "foreigners" and "blacks," but rather as "resources" (*ziyuan*). This is a term generally reserved for natural resources possessed by a nation, such as oil, coal, forests, or water, suggesting that in the author's view, women are items to be possessed, used, and of course never shared.

From an anthropological perspective, the notion of women as "resources" evokes Claude Lévi-Strauss's thesis in *The Elementary Structures of Kinship* that the origins of culture itself can be traced back to the "exchange" of women.[17] Lévi-Strauss argues that this exchange through exogamy forms peaceful alliances between men that serve, like communication between people, as the foundation of culture. However, just as the world appears to be naturally divided into languages that construct mutually unintelligible communities of communication in the romanticized ideal of the mother tongue, this movement-promoted post similarly presumes that the world is divided into national communities that demarcate the natural limits of exogamy. Thus, while exchange would serve as the foundation of culture as a universal, the limit upon the exchange of such national "resources" beyond national-cum-racial borders, enforcing a form of nationally legitimized exogamous incest, would serve as the foundation for singular national cultures; and although Lévi-Strauss found similarities between the exchange of wives and the exchange of words, women in this framework are to be treated as "state secrets," to be kept within the confines of the nation-state for reasons that never require further explanation or justification.[18]

Providing evidence of the importance of these "resources," and by extension the broader significance of the author's concerns beyond his own sexual frustrations, the article claims:

> In Latin America, the majority of citizens are of mixed Indian-European[19] descent. How did all of this mixing happen? Theoretically, there are two possibilities: a white man and an Indian [*Yindi'an*] woman could have children, or an Indian man and a white woman could have children. But only one of these possibilities actually happened in reality: all of the current residents of Latin America are descendants of mating between white men and Indian women. There are almost no cases at all of descent from the pairing of white women and Indian men. As a result, the Y chromosome of the Indian race is about to disappear from this earth! Why? Because white women look upon Indian men as inferior monkeys, and are completely unwilling to get in bed with them! But did you know? The Indians are brothers of us yellow people! And they are about to be made extinct by the white people! Even if the X chromosome passed on by Indian women is able to continue to exist in this world, their genetics have already been completely changed by those white people! Now, if we Chinese are not able to be revitalized, the fate of the Indians today is the fate of the Chinese tomorrow! The Y chromosome of our Chinese race will be erased from this earth by white people!

The "resourceful" essence of women is articulated here in the bluntest of terms, with clearly defined gender roles required in order to ensure the survival of the nation. It is also presented in the starkest miscomprehensions of biology. Genetically, unique nationalities are presumed to have unique chromosomes: a highly doubtful premise, to say the least. This is not, however, a random ill-considered idea held by one isolated individual scrawling incoherent manifestoes on the Internet. The idea that there is a biological basis for Han-ness as Chineseness is in fact a commonly held belief in the modern era, expressed through metaphors of blood, biological markers, and DNA.[20] Most memorably, during a conversation with Han Clothing enthusiasts in Guangzhou about the purity of the Han race, a friendly acquaintance claimed that all Han have three unique chromosomes that have been passed down from the era of the "Three Sovereigns" (Fuxi, Nüwa, and the Farmer God) to the present, with each chromosome representing one of these mythical figures. Appealing for my confirmation of his quirky theory as an "educated" "Westerner," I simply responded that I did not know much about genetics.

This imagined purity, embodied in the idea of eternal national DNA carrying the traces of mythological superheroes, relies upon the national "resource" of the woman for its perpetuation, despite the fact that, reflecting the patrilineal logic central to Chinese culture for millennia, the woman remains within this portrayal physiologically unable to contribute substantively to this purity. Continuing his discourse on the existence of DNA from the Three Sovereigns, my acquaintance asserted that, when analyzing (the predetermined conclusion of) the purity of the Han race, one had to admit that of course some "mixing" had occurred throughout the millennia, particularly because the Han as civilizers had long interacted with and come to absorb other less advanced races in the process of history, described in Chapter 2 as the "snowball theory" of the Han.[21] But on the one hand because of the mental mapping of men as active and women as passive, with sex thereby being interpreted as an act of masculine domination and possession of a woman,[22] and on the other hand because of the mental mapping of civilization and barbarism envisioning other races as "inferior," my informant was adamant that such historical pairings could only be manifested as Han men marrying women of other races. Han women, as members of a superior race, would never marry "out" to other nationalities in traditional Chinese culture. The revealing assumptions behind the idea that civilizational-racial dominance equals male sexual dominance were then further reflected in his assertion that "male chromosomes" are stronger than "female chromosomes," thereby conveniently guaranteeing the purity of the Han within this imaginary arrangement. Any pollution from other races' women would be erased from the Han DNA chain within three generations in this framework, my acquaintance argued, thanks to the contributions of men and the power of their genes. Of course, this is a pseudoscientific and not entirely coherent reincarnation of the longstanding paternalistic exclusion of women from kinship in Chinese reproductive politics, rendering women as "outsiders" (*wai*) who were once invisible on ancestral tablets[23] and are now invisible in the composition of imaginary national DNA. Just as the end product of this masculinist theory's previous incarnation was a pure patriline, so the end product of this elaborate yet biologically misinformed theory is the fairly predictable and clearly desired result of Han national purity: the conclusion towards which the argument is constructed.

Returning to the excerpt above, its equally unreal imaginings of biology envision a similarly dominant role for men in reproduction. In a slight variation, the author creates the idea of "national chromosomes" to assert that the act of a male of one race, possessing his race's XY chromosomes, reproducing with a female of another race, possessing only her race's XX chromosomes, would thereby permanently replace the Y chromosome of the female's race with the Y chromosome of the male's race. All males following from this pairing would then only have the Y chromosome of the "other race." This was perfectly acceptable when, as many Han Clothing Movement participants imagine, the Han was a "snowball" that would attract women of other backgrounds and incorporate them into an unassailably dominant Han patriline unable to be polluted by their female input. Yet this system of exchange had been inverted in the present, threatening not only the longstanding purity of the Han race but also its continued existence.[24] Rather than being the race that imported women, the Han had become, like the "Indians" described above, a race that primarily exported women to be enjoyed by "foreigners" and "black people," and was thus losing precious resources and witnessing growing threats to survival.

The author continues to describe the purportedly bastardized results of this trend:

> There is a well-known fact recognized by Chinese the world over. A child produced from the pairing of a Chinese man and a foreign woman will generally identify as Chinese, will speak Chinese well, and will be recognized within the Chinese community as a mixed-blood child. But a child produced from the pairing of a Chinese woman and a foreign man will not generally identify as Chinese, will speak horrible Chinese, and will be viewed as a mutt within the Chinese community.

The products of these rapidly growing foreign man–Chinese woman pairings will then be less than fully Chinese. And as a result, according to this author's logic of patrilineal projection, the only possible outcome of this deficit in shared female resources will be the subjugation and eventual extinction of the Han. Just as the Han of the past is presumed to have once assimilated other less exemplary nationalities who are now lost in the annals of history, following the Manchu transformation of pure Chinese society, a similar fate of assimilation and disappearance now purportedly awaits the Han of today.

Because women reproduce not only the population of the nation but also its boundaries,[25] borders here are imagined not only as lines on maps, but also as boundaries surrounding individuals and their bodies, making even the most "private" of parts a matter of national concern and an object of policing around which reinforced walls must be built. Employing colorful metaphors to characterize such "sexual colonization" as a "grave threat to our national security," the author continues:

> Throughout history, in the wars between tribes, nationalities, and nations, the victor has been able to eliminate all of the men on the opposing side, and then make their women into sex slaves and tools of reproduction. There is a line from Cai Wenji's "Poem of Sorrow and Anger" to describe this war-like situation: "decapitated male heads hang along the side of the forward marching horses, while the women are carried behind." The foreigners and blacks of today are not coming on horses. Instead, they are marching forward with their reproductive organs sticking straight out to conquer China. And indeed, there are no decapitated heads dangling from the side of their sexual organs. But each and every time that one more Chinese woman is conquered by a foreigner or a black man, this means that there will be one more single Chinese man without descendants!

Sexual activity here is neither love nor passion nor even consensual enjoyment. Typical of the emotionally gratifying misrepresentations of nationalist thought, relations between people are alienated through the determinant prism of national identity and the masculinist vision of possession. Channeling the animalistic urges of sexuality into nationalist gratification, sex and reproduction become national holy war by other means, resulting in either the capture or surrender of women, and the resulting growth or depletion of the population of pure Han descendants.[26] Comparable to similar operations throughout the Han Clothing Movement, the author's very personal sexual anxieties and frustrations, projected onto the figure of "foreigners" and "black people," are thereby sublimated into seemingly far more lofty concerns of fundamental national survival and granted an otherwise unattainable legitimacy and urgency.

The author concludes by reporting that he has "raised this matter with the relevant departments numerous times, alerting them that this phenomenon is a threat to national security," but that those in power refuse to take concrete steps to protect the nation. Forced to take matters into his own hands, the author envisions a far-reaching alliance of collective action to protect his precious national resources:

> If you are a representative to the National People's Congress, please revise the Marriage Law of the People's Republic of China as soon as possible to forbid Chinese women from marrying foreign men. Also, do not grant Chinese citizenship to bastards born of the combination of foreign men and Chinese women. We cannot allow the descendants of foreign men to occupy our educational resources . . .

> If you work in public security, please learn from the police in Russia. If you see a foreigner, check their passports. Also go to schools where foreign instructors are teaching and check their passports in front of their students, to let everyone know that China is not heaven on earth for these foreigners!

> If you are a taxi driver, please refuse to accept foreign men or black men accompanied by Chinese women in your cab. There are already some taxi drivers in Guangzhou who have started doing this.

> If you own a store, please refuse to sell items to foreign men or black men accompanied by Chinese women.

> If you own a restaurant, please refuse to seat foreign men or black men accompanied by Chinese women.

This concluding call for action embodies the Han Clothing Movement's vision of a nation united in solidarity, a phenomenon that can feel all too rare amid the chaotic hustle and conflicts of contemporary urban life. And considering the overall tone of the article, this would seem at first to be a nation united in opposition to the growing encroachments of the foreign male, again a mode of resisting an invasive sexual imperialism. Yet one might note that in the many discriminatory proposals proposed in the name of protecting the nation, there remain two victims: the "foreign man" and the Chinese woman.

This vision of a nation united is thus a nation united against its own women and their free will, a masculinist nation united in a desire to imperialistically declare its possession and control of women's bodies. Just as the distinction of man and woman reemerges amid the celebrated unity of the

Han, so this distinction again reemerges amid the distinction between Chinese and foreigner. Beyond the anger vividly expressed towards male outsiders in this rhetoric of national unity in sexual warfare, the true target of this author's diatribe remains the women of China, women towards whom he shows a marked degree of ambivalence. Freud aptly characterized ambivalence as a complex combination of desire and hatred,[27] a combination that leads to both conscious and unconscious conflicts and unpredictable emotional swings: phenomena that are all too easily apparent in the preceding passages. On the one hand, women are clearly objects of aggressive desire whom the author aims to possess, and believes that he has the power to possess. On the other hand, however, they are active agents of their own desire whom the author is unable to possess. On the one hand, the author clearly "values" women as objects of desire and as guarantors of the purity of the national line. On the other hand, he fundamentally denies any substantive contribution by women in this national reproductive process, labeling them primarily as containers carrying the pure national DNA of their male counterparts, to be used by men as they please. Conflicted and unable to realize his desires, the author appropriates the idea of the nation and its resources as a means to legitimize and strive towards his fantasy, eliminating his ambivalence towards women through a declaration of ownership, and as a result realizing through pure reproduction a correspondingly pure and ideal nation.

Thus, just as the idea of culture can be used to insert an idealized and "traditional" fantasy of femininity into contemporary women, who are thereby judged according to their conformity to this ideal, so the idea of the nation can be used to falsely stake a claim upon the nation's women as one's own, thereby leaving women to be judged by their male counterparts and presumed owners as to whether they are pure or improper, and whether they are fully contributing, or not, to the sacred mission of national reproduction. Within this national-sexual framework, women are to be rhetorically "cherished" and "valued" as essential to the process of national reproduction; yet it is also precisely on account of their cherished role in the process of national reproduction that they are to be denied fundamental agency and choices.[28] It is because they are so valuable that they are unable to be free. They thus become, as the post's author stated, resources: objects that can be possessed, overseen, and used by their male compatriots, while also being prevented from transgressing the arbitrary and thus all-too-fragile boundaries of nationhood. In the following section, I analyze my experiences at a traditionalist training ground for producing such "pure" Han women, conforming to a male fantasy, realizing themselves through the restrictions of race and national mission, and thereby earning themselves the lofty title of "ladies" in neotraditionalist circles.

> When the dominated apply to what dominates them schemes that are the product of domination, or, to put it another way, when their thoughts and perceptions are structured in accordance with the very structures of the relation of domination that is imposed on them, their acts of cognition are, inevitably, acts of recognition, submission.
>
> —PIERRE BOURDIEU, *Masculine Domination*[29]

After nearly nine months interacting with members of the Han Clothing Movement and listening to the sorts of xenophobic ideas and quirky conspiracy theories described in the preceding chapters, I planned to take a short break by visiting a so-called traditional "ladies' academy" twelve hours away by train. Although affiliated with the Han Clothing Movement and involved in the promotion of Han Clothing, this ladies' academy appeared at first glance considerably more mainstream, or at least somewhat less extreme than the groups with whom I had been spending the majority of my time. Established in the middle of the past decade, this academy has been celebrated in local media as the first women-only traditional educational institution since 1949, and has even been featured in a profile on China Central Television. The teachers at the academy also claim that they have been covered in stories by the Associated Press and the *Yomiuri Daily*, although I was unable to find evidence to substantiate these claims. Regardless, the academy has succeeded in drawing students from the nearby metropolitan area as well as from all over the country, toward the stated mission of recreating its students in the image of the pure and traditional woman: the "lady." To achieve this goal, students at the academy immerse themselves in the often-cited "five millennia of tradition" through a rigorous daily schedule consisting of reading the classics, including the Ming-era *Classic for Girls*; memorizing poetry; learning etiquette, painting, sewing, and the rules of tea ceremony; playing the *guqin*, a traditional Chinese musical instrument; and, as I noted during my visit, learning to cook traditional Chinese dishes for their teachers at lunch and dinner. A typical schedule, occupying a student's entire waking day, is summarized below:

6:00	Wake up
7:00	Breakfast
8:00	*Tao Te Ching* study
9:00	Etiquette
10:00	*Guqin*
11:00	Lunch
1:00	*Guqin*
2:30	*Tao Te Ching*
3:30	Etiquette
5:00	Dinner
6:00–8:00	Study
9:30	Bedtime

Approaching the ladies' academy on the first day of my visit, I made my way through a winding network of alleys: the humid spring air was dense with the pungent odors of street food and motorbike exhaust fumes, and the narrow alleyways were overflowing with a chaotic mix of pedestrians, bikes, and motorcycles speeding by, ringing bells and honking horns, and ever-so-narrowly missing one another at the very last moment. Eventually reaching my destination, I found myself standing before a massive, traditional style door closed tightly, as if to shut out the chaotic world beyond. My diligent efforts at knocking on this imposing entryway failed to generate any response, and it was only after I made a phone call to the interior of the academy that a student came to the front to unlatch the heavy door. Bowing and silently gesturing for me to follow her inside as the door closed behind me, I was led through one layer of the courtyard to another to yet another, with each layer seeming to serve as a defense against the city outside, whose clamor ever-so-gradually faded into the distance. Crossing a wooden bridge over a small pond with fish, and then through a set of elaborately carved wooden doors, I arrived at the core of this ladies' academy, where I found three men dressed in Han Clothing sitting in silence around a table drinking tea. Lanterns hung from the ceiling and an image of Confucius was placed prominently at the center of the north wall, while a rare and almost eerie silence lingered in this remote room in the heart of this bustling city. Before even introducing themselves, they were quick to ask me about my views on contemporary China, and to inform me that the China that I was visiting, the China outside, was not in fact the "real China." I had heard this many times before. Yet this time, my interlocutors reassured me, the real China was to be found "in here."

It soon became apparent that perhaps my twelve-hour train ride had not brought me quite as far as I had assumed. Although this theory of the fundamental unreality of modern society is unanimously promoted throughout the traditionalist groups with whom I conducted research, each wing has a different scapegoat to blame. Han Clothing enthusiasts, as described in the previous chapter, reserve the majority of their wrath for "the Manchus," while many traditional education enthusiasts show a strong dislike for the New Culture Movement and modern "intellectuals" in general, as I discuss in this book's conclusion. Having become fascinated with Manchu conspiracy theories, I asked the head teacher at the ladies' academy during my stay what he thought of this idea of Manchu hegemony. He spared no words in describing these ideas as "ludicrous," and asserted that only "a bunch of idiots" could believe in such theories. At this ladies' academy, the all-male teachers had instead found a new source for all that was wrong with contemporary China: none other than their target students, Chinese women.

In our discussions, the teachers asserted that Chinese civilization had been based from the beginning of time on the delicate balance between *yin* and *yang*, which they read as equivalent to a balance between male and female: here, their portrayal of society mirrored Bourdieu's study of gendered representations in Kabyle society, wherein the entire cosmos is comfortingly structured in a series of oppositions that endlessly reflect the male-female binary.[30] In a familiar pattern, a past moment of perfection was posited, in which there was a flawless and complete balance between *yin* and *yang*, male and female, and outside and inside in society, in relation to which the present can only be a downfall. This balance between *yin* and *yang*, stabilizing society, had reportedly been lost in the past two centuries. When I asked what they meant by this "loss of balance," the main teacher leaned forward and said quite directly, "Nowadays in China, men aren't like men, and women aren't like women." Society, he told me, is backwards: it makes people unlike themselves, making the ugly beautiful and the beautiful ugly. And his goal in this academy was to make things right again, so that beauty can again be recognized as beauty.

Taking a few steps back to premodern history to understand this "beauty," one teacher proudly told me that pre-1911 China was the most free and democratic society that ever existed. It was, he claimed, a society based on balance, or a certain harmony between the heavens, the earth, and the people. Everyone had a clear place or ranking within society, and as a result, society ran smoothly. This is of course a retroactive idealization benefiting from distance: in the now idealized Ming Dynasty (1368–1644 C.E.), scholars were already concerned about the degradation of culture and particularly of women.[31] Nevertheless, this idealized and unitary past seemed very real to him, standing proudly against the discord of the present. A core factor in this social machine's supposedly seamless operation was the clearly designated role of women in traditional society; or rather, to be more precise, outside of society. Citing one version of the myth of Nüwa and Fuxi, the creators of the world according to Chinese mythology, he argued that there had been unchanging gender differences from the very beginning of time: while Fu Xi reigned as the first of the renowned three sovereigns, Nüwa was primarily a creator, or a mother, as nature had intended, producing a naturalized division of labor between the sexes from the very origins of humanity. This is how things had been, and how they should be again, he emphasized, transforming gender as a process of historical construction into a natural and ideally unchanging phenomenon.[32]

Providing further "historical evidence," he pointed to the Han Clothing that he was wearing, in which the right side of the robe is placed on the inside, while the left side of the robe crosses over on top. He told me that the right side represents the feminine while the left side represents the masculine (*nan zuo nü you*). His Han Clothing, purportedly emerging at the beginning of civilization and existing unchanged into the present, thus symbolically carried a fundamental truth, representing the proper relations between the sexes: *yang* as male is meant to be on the outside, while *yin* as female is meant to be on the inside. Or in other, more direct words, he told me, women are supposed to be at home, a site of purity,[33] whose innocence is maintained in the modern world precisely through its imagined separation from the outside world.[34] This is how society had been arranged according to "heaven," and how it must therefore be arranged again.

The historical downfall of this state of proper gender harmony and perfect societal balance was attributed to the infiltration of what one teacher called the "Western idea of gender equality" in the twentieth century. "You Westerners only have a little over two centuries of history," he dismissively declared, "so what makes you think that you have found the only correct model for the entire world?" This rhetorical turn, rationalizing fundamentally anachronistic gender ideologies through the affirmative ideals of tradition and nation, deserves closer analysis. The teachers had expressed their thoughts, which can only be accurately characterized as sexist, in the mystical language of *yin* and *yang*, citing as well the supposed division of labor between the mythical figures Nüwa and Fuxi, and thereby presenting their prejudices as part of a "tradition" extending from the beginning of time to the present.[35] This deployment of tradition conveniently abstracts the ideas at hand from the type of actual experiential human relations that might reveal them for what they are, and thereby naturalizes, eternalizes, and legitimizes the fundamentally experientially illegitimate.

Beyond this traditionalist abstraction, however, this rationalization of sexism was further buttressed through the deployment of nationalist sentiment: by using the phrase "the Western idea of gender equality," the teachers created an all-too-appealing (and all-too-common) binary relationship of inversion and opposition between an imagined China and an imagined West that presents the ideal of equality between the sexes (and other rights-based values) as a non-Chinese idea and hence as unnatural in and even corrupting of an otherwise pure cultural sphere: appealing to the idea of collective identity in order to rationalize subjugation, gender equality is rendered as national inequality or cultural imperialism that must be resisted. The dignity of nearly half of the nation's population can thereby be suppressed for the imaginary dignity of "the nation" as a whole, such that in the name of identity, people come to argue for and embrace subjugation not only of their fellow citizens but even in many cases of themselves: similar processes are apparent in the nationalist rejection of human rights as a "Western conspiracy" meant to "weaken China" and prevent its "rise." And while I acknowledge that indeed neither women's rights nor human rights were ever a prominent component of Chinese traditional culture, we should also note that such rights have not been a prominent component of any premodern culture, and remain solely a point of aspiration for most today; cultures nevertheless change, thankfully. Yet by expressing their ideas through the metaphor of an eternal national tradition, viewing culture as a stable object to be maintained rather than a living process, such openness to change is renounced, and sexism is illusorily made to appear not as sexism, but as a "natural" and "correct" viewpoint in need of protection from the cruel depredations of a predatory outside world.

In contrast to traditional society, in which everyone had and knew their "proper role," the teachers characterized contemporary society as having lost all balance between *yin* and *yang*. The modern rupture of this imagined unadulterated sphere of traditional culture and its comforting boundaries[36] was metaphorically expressed by one teacher through an allegory of the city walls located a few blocks away from the academy. He told me that in the early 1950s, during the period typically referred to as "Liberation," the walls of the city were destroyed, leaving only narrow streams as the barrier between the city and its surroundings. The academy's founder ascribed a certain historical immunizing role to these city walls, asserting that since their destruction, all sorts of "poison" (*du*) had been entering the city day after day, for decades on end. The streams that surround the edge of the city, while unable to block the entry of such poisons, nevertheless hinder their exit, such that these poisons linger and build up within the urban surroundings. The result, the academy's teachers informed me, is a thoroughly imbalanced and overly feminine-dominated (*yin*) environment in which the natural balance between *yin* and *yang* has been lost and feminine *yin* poison pollutes the air upon which everyone must rely to survive.

Conveniently, however, within such an environment polluted by *yin* poison, even social issues conventionally attributed to men could thereby be attributed to women. For example, one day during discussion, a teacher asked me: why do you think that men in China nowadays go out to dinner every night with colleagues, forcing each other to drink, and then go to nightclubs or barbershops or saunas? Answering his own question before I could, he told me that these phenomena exist because women "are not at home anymore." Even when a woman is physically at home, he claimed, her heart is not there (*xin bu zai jiali*), rendering this idealized pure site as impure. The result, he asserted, is that men nowadays are similarly not at home. This was not an issue in traditional China, he assured me, where everyone knew their proper place. An essay composed by a teacher and distributed as a handout at the academy read: "Taking a look at women nowadays, all that is on their minds is freedom, liberation, independence, and taking charge. They have long ago lost their genuine selves . . . the hegemony of the Western barbarians' ideas of 'freedom,' 'democracy,' and 'human rights' has erased our natural ways and made the harmony of the past lost forever!" Such an invocation of tradition is a complex rhetorical switch, in that the author raises certain social issues in contemporary China that are often related to men, such as binge drinking, infidelity, or the sex industry, but claims to find the fundamental problem solely in women, whose deviation from longstanding traditional and thus correct models of being had threatened the stability of society as a whole.

Yet for all of its seeming complexity, this was a rhetorical move with which I would come to be quite familiar during my stay at the academy. Producing a similarly imaginative analysis of the milk powder scandal of 2008, this same teacher traced the source of this crisis not to immoral business practices wherein poisonous chemicals could be placed in milk powders in order to ensure profits, producing kidney stones in innocent and unknowing infants. Rather, to my surprise, the source of this crisis was to be found, in his interpretation, in women. In traditional China, he told me, a woman would stay at home and feed her baby with milk from her breast. But now, he claimed, women go out to work, or their hearts simply are not "at home," and babies are left with nothing but milk powder and an *ayi* domestic helper. Thus, if women were doing what they were "supposed" to do according to tradition, namely, overseeing the domestic sphere that is their responsibility as representatives of the domestic *yin*, there would have been no milk powder scandal.

Another teacher at the academy pursued a similar line of argument in his analysis of materialism in society, attributing the perverse power of money within contemporary society to "money-worshipping women" (*baijin nü*). Here, this teacher tapped into a broader misogynistic discourse in contemporary Chinese popular culture, wherein the phrase "money-worshipping women" is a common denunciatory saying, while the notion of any corresponding "money-worshipping man" (*baijin nan*) remains completely unspoken and unthought. Even an official *China Daily* editorial entitled "We Are on the Wrong Path of Money Worship"[37] tellingly only cites examples of women worshipping money, portraying men as victims of "young girls' mercenary attitude toward marriage" and predicting nothing less than the resulting "degradation of our society." Yet if we take a deep breath and a step back to look at society as a whole, rather than focusing upon women's money worship as potentially degrading society, it would be more accurate to argue that contemporary Chinese society is in many senses a money-obsessed society that therefore naturally contains a number of money-worshipping women, as well as the often overlooked money-worshipping men. In recent decades, the revolutionary capital that played such an essential role in self-presentation and self-promotion in the Maoist era has been replaced by monetary capital, which plays an equally important role in self-presentation; correspondingly, the announcement and celebration of each supernatural accomplishment of the spiritual atomic bomb of Mao Zedong Thought has been replaced by the perpetual announcement and celebration of new celestial economic figures and new over-the-top displays of wealth. Power and money are intertwined. Within this social context, the widely discussed "money-worshipping women" are only part of a larger money-worshipping society. Yet by transferring this discomfiting fact "onto women's bodies and female sexuality,"[38] the uncomfortable truth of a money-worshipping society is denied and reversed, misrecognizing the product and producer by projecting blame onto women as the source of all problems, while by extension portraying the man, the only other component in society, as the eternally innocent victim. I should add, as a side note, that I was not surprised to learn during my stay that all three of the male teachers at this ladies' academy were single. "I like rural women," the founder and main teacher told me one evening, "but if they've gone off to college [*daxue*] to be trained in the inferior way [*xiao dao*], I can't even stand to talk with them!"

Although women are targeted as the source of all problems in contemporary society by the academy's teachers, we should remember that they are also the academy's only students. Claiming to have found the source of a wide range of contemporary social issues in imbalanced gender relations and in modern women in particular, the solution to these issues according to the academy's teachers could also only be found through women. Women, in their analysis, are to be transformed from modern misrepresentations of womanhood into real ladies (*shunü*), so that modern China, which can only ever be a corruption of the ideal of China, might be transformed into the real China.

What, then, is a lady? One early morning, I asked the academy's main teacher this question following the daily tea ritual. Unsurprisingly, he was certain that he had the answer, and could provide very clear standards to which a lady must "conform." He listed five core characteristics:

1. Diligent (*qinlao*)
2. Kind (*shanliang*)
3. Has a sense of right and wrong, knows "her place" (*you guiju, zhitiandi*)
4. Has a tradition to continue, or heritage from the past to deliver to the future (*you chuancheng*)
5. Pure (*chunjie*)

Reviewing these five points, the vision of a "lady" presented here is clearly limiting, based solely upon obligations rather than any type of rights. Each is a social obligation that is judged by external observers: whether one is diligent or not, whether one is kind or not, whether one is pure or not, whether one knows one's place or not, whether one passes tradition from the past to the future—and thus whether one's sense of culture conforms to the "appropriate" standards as determined by the teachers at this academy. Enacting this judgment, the teachers unabashedly presumed that these characteristics of the lady were lacking at the precise moment that they were articulated, and that they thus needed to be cultivated at their academy.

But how are these missing values to be realized? There are two revealing features of this academy that stand out from my time conducting research there: the first is that none of the teachers at this "ladies' academy" are actually ladies. Ironically, they are all men, teaching women how to be ladies. The ideal of the lady is envisioned, inculcated, and judged by men, and the relationship between male and female is thus transformed into a blatantly paternalistic relationship between teacher and student, superior and inferior: even, or rather particularly, in the matter of lady-hood. A second characteristic that the teachers continually emphasized during our discussions is that the school is designed to be like a home: although this "home," upon further discussion, happened to have another quite illuminating layer of meaning.

Explaining his conception of the school as a home one afternoon during my stay, the academy's main teacher drew this graph in my notebook, microanalyzing the Chinese characters that formed the terms "education" and "awakening":

家

教		育	(=Education)
學		覺	(=Awakening)
陽		陰	(Male/ Female)

Home

Teaching		Development	(=Education)
Learning		Sense	(=Awakening)
Yang		Yin	(Male/ Female)

Upon completing this graph, he informed me that education in the past took place in homes, or private academies (*sishu*), creating an all-encompassing sphere of learning in which one would not only study but also live and thereby grow. He contrasted this ideal with the large schools and universities of the present, enacting what he called their "Western industrialized model of education" (*xifang gongyehua jiaoyu moshi*), designed for being a businessman (*zuo shengyi*) rather than truly being a person (*zuo ren*). Based in this ideal of the all-encompassing sphere of learning, this ladies' academy was located in a traditional courtyard setting, and was supposed to be like a "new home" for a new vision of society, in opposition to the society locked safely away outside. In this graph, immediately below the character for "home," the ideal of the school, the teacher wrote *jiaoyu* (education) as two separate characters, aiming to emphasize the distinction between *jiao* and *yu*. *Jiao*, he told me, is the process of teaching. *Yu*, by contrast, refers to the learning process or the environment through which this process is nurtured. The goal of education, he told me, is not only to provide teaching but also to provide a proper environment to *fayu*, to develop. He then paused, looked at me intently, and said, "an environment to develop, just like a baby in a uterus." Thus, *jiao* as education relates to *yang*, the concept associated with masculinity, while *yu* as the environment for development relates to *yin* or femininity. The two characters of *xue* and *jue*, making up the word "awakening," similarly reflect this binary division. *Xue* is a process of learning, but it also has to rely on *jue*, which refers to one's sense of one's environment, or one's experience of this uterus-like space that is to sustain one and support one's development. Encompassing both sides of the graph was this new "home" that the academy's male teachers had founded and overseen.

This was all quite puzzling. Yet perhaps the most puzzling aspect was the combination of, on the one hand, all-male teachers and, on the other hand, the metaphor of an educational uterus: the intersection of men and their control over a ladies' educational institution as control over an imaginary uterus giving birth to a newly balanced society unable to be produced through conventional means of birth, which must inevitably pass through the presumed source of pollution. The male teachers had created a space in which they incorporated both sides of this graph, both *yin* and *yang*, both the masculine and the feminine, under their own male control. This ladies' academy was then envisioned as a home without mothers or even a uterus outside of a mother. It was a pure space controlled by all male teachers, who biologically cannot give birth and who inevitably come from women, instead giving birth to new women, or ladies, to save society from the women of the present. Hence, despite its stated goal of educating women, this ladies' academy is in fact the ultimate misogynistic fantasy in which all problems are attributed to women, who are out of their natural place; and all of the solutions are in the hands of the men, whose job is to put everything back into its proper place: to return to the idealized balance between *yin* and *yang* through their encompassment and control of both.

To provide proof of the happy and healthy babies emerging from their educational uterus, the teachers showed me two pictures before I departed, smiling like proud parents. One was of a fairly attractive young woman with a big smile on her face: her black hair was dyed platinum blonde, and she wore a very short jean skirt and a tank top revealing a belly button ring. A second picture showed a woman dressed in all white Han Clothing, looking sternly at the camera without a smile, standing next to an older woman in a button-down white shirt. Returning to the motif of side-by-side images from which this chapter began, although the women in the two pictures indeed looked completely different, I was informed that they were in fact photos of a single graduate of this academy. The first photo had been taken prior to the young lady's education at the academy. The teachers told me that she had been living a "wild life," creating all types of trouble, and that her parents had no idea how to respond and resolve this situation. Desperate to find a solution to this dilemma, her parents forcibly sent her to this ladies' academy. And although she ran away at first, she eventually came back, and was able to develop within the environment of the ladies' academy, to rediscover her "true self" in lady-hood, eventually quitting her partying ways and taking up the very ladylike hobby of embroidery. In light of my corrupted nontraditional tastes, it is perhaps no surprise that I found the first image considerably more attractive than the second. Yet in light of their preferences, it is also no surprise that the three teachers at the academy could not have been prouder of the second image. One teacher pointed to the second picture, telling me that for the sake of my research I needed to remember that image. "This is how a lady should look," he said.

In discussions with the three female students living at this academy during my time there, they showed not even the slightest hint of disagreement. Besides its inherently limiting nature, the other most striking aspect of the academy's representation of women was the degree to which it was embraced and celebrated by the academy's students in the classroom as well as in dialogue. Although I never found myself in a situation in which I was able to discuss the academy's ideal of "the lady" with students beyond the presence of a supervising male teacher, the three women I knew at the academy repeatedly emphasized to me, in all seeming sincerity and with stunning consistency, their excitement for their newfound ties to tradition, embodied in such practices as sewing, *guqin* mastery, and a deep appreciation of the classics, which thereby transformed them into pure ladies, buying into the masculinist ideology of the traditional lady. Yet this enthusiasm, as suggested by the link between contemporary concerns and the deployment of "eternal" tradition highlighted in Chapter 2, was not natural but was primarily based in the use of tradition for more practical matters in the present: in particular, exercising mastery over the volatile marriage market. Following Bourdieu's analysis of the symbolic violence of masculine domination, it was precisely through "submission" that the ladies of the ladies' academy found a "position,"[39] ironically sacrificing oneself to mastery by the opposite sex as a means to master the opposite sex in the marriage market.

Illustrating this trend, a young woman who came from rural Sichuan all of the way to the east coast of China to learn how to be a lady was completing her month of intensive study at the academy during my research visit. Over a celebratory dinner during her last night at the academy, one of the teachers asked what she planned to do upon returning to her village. She said that she planned to stay at home, pursuing her new lady-like hobbies, while the men of her village lined up outside her home, eager to marry her. The main teacher explained to me all too directly that this student had been unable to find a boyfriend for years, on account of her "rough" (*cu*) nature. Eager to blossom into a true lady in order to appeal to men, she had come to the ladies' academy, and in her brief tenure there had begun wearing Han Clothing on a daily basis, mastered the intricacies of traditional etiquette, studied the Chinese classics, and learned to play the *guqin*. Yet these very traditional aspects of "lady-hood" in all of their ancient allure were directed towards the very contemporary and immediate concerns of finding an ideal partner and getting married. As was the case with much of the traditionalism that I encountered throughout my fieldwork, the notion of the "lady," for both its male promoters and female initiates, was more of a response to contemporary anxieties and uncertainties than a continuation of an actual lasting tradition. Belying this often perplexing mixture of the past and the present, this young lady from Sichuan asked over dinner whether upon graduation she might be issued an official "ladies' license" (*shunü zheng*), which she could show to potential suitors to verify that she was in fact a lady. The academy's teachers agreed that they would consider this possibility, but soon thereafter reconsidered and asserted that true lady-hood was a beauty that, as noted above, could only "shine from the inside out."

Caught between imaginings of the past and the realities of the present, I agreed with the founders and teachers of this academy that there are countless problems in contemporary Chinese society, as is true of any social system. In their reflections upon the current state of urban society, they indeed have recognized issues that need to be examined more closely. Yet in their eagerness to find a single cause for these issues, in a process that echoes the Han Clothing Movement's Manchu conspiracy theories, they have misrecognized their origins. And in their self-congratulation at finding a solution to all of contemporary society's dilemmas in a misogynistic fantasy of the impure modern woman and her opposite, the carefully constructed lady, I could not help but feel that they might only be creating a new problem.

PRINCE

In the final days of my research, the Guangzhou Han Clothing Movement was scheduled to perform at a Tourism Festival for Zhu Village on the remote outskirts of Guangzhou. Collaborating with the local tourism bureau, participants in the festival enjoyed a few perks: a block of motel rooms with semifunctional air conditioning had been reserved across the street from the festival for participants to cool off and nap during the day, as well as to rest overnight in preparation for the two-day festival that, as I had already come to expect, began all too bright and early at 8:00 A.M. on a Saturday morning. In return for these amenities, the entire tourism festival was built not around Zhu Village but rather around Han Clothing performances. This is likely because Zhu Village, upon closer inspection, did not offer many other features that might draw visitors. Granted, there were stories of fairies and other magical events from the past, advertised with colorful illustrations hanging on the outer gates of the park where the festival was held. But as I wandered beyond the park through the narrow alleyways of the village, dodging motorcycles and breathing in the second-hand smoke of those walking in front of me, I could not help but notice that these fairies were long gone. In their place, performers from the Guangzhou Han Clothing Movement had arrived to reenact the certain yet experientially all too distant magic of the past.

Because this was a two-day festival, the organizers solicited ideas from participants for performances in the preceding weeks. Perhaps because the Han Clothing Movement as a whole is based precisely in such a desire to display oneself in the performance of identity, the response was overwhelming, providing sufficient fodder to fill an entire day with performances from 8:00 A.M. to 6:00 P.M. A number of performances were the usual Han Clothing Movement sketches, modeled upon the framework of minority ethnic performance in China: the showcase of different styles of Han Clothing, an acted dialogue explaining Han Clothing to the uninitiated, the display of male and female etiquette, the *guqin* performance, and the calligraphy display. Exhausted by the blistering August sun of Southern China, most participants spent the day crowded in the slightly cooler rooms in the motel across the street, descending to the festival below only at their designated performance time. Occasionally visiting the motel rooms to chat with friends and cool off, I nevertheless spent the majority of my time observing performances alongside the residents of Zhu Village, who seemed genuinely puzzled and amused by the nostalgic performances of their urban neighbors.

While sweating profusely under the blazing August sun of Southern China, I came across a new face in the local Han Clothing Movement, who was also not spending his time in the motel across the street. Heavily made-up with foundation, blush, and lipstick, and wearing light pink Han Clothing, bright red socks, and ballet shoes, "Prince" (*Wangzi*), as he called himself, did not match the stereotypical vision of the true Han man, the "*haohan*," which many fellow Han Clothing enthusiasts embraced. Prince told me that he worked in an office job in downtown Guangzhou, and that he had discovered Han Clothing while searching the Internet at work. He had immediately fallen in love with Han Clothing, he said, on account of its elegance and beauty. As his interest continued to deepen in recent months, he had purchased two sets of Han Clothing, including the light pink outfit that he was wearing that day. Yet he told me that he had been hesitant to join in the movement activities frequently held in Guangzhou. Only when he saw the online announcement seeking performers for this tourism festival did he decide that he was ready to join. The one thing that he loved more than Han Clothing, he said, was dancing, and he was prepared to bring his two loves together that afternoon in a dance performance, finally joining fellow enthusiasts in their celebration of Han Clothing and culture.

When the time arrived for Prince to perform later that afternoon, the host of the show introduced his dance with an awkward smile, saying, "Here's Prince, a new participant. He is going to dance for us this afternoon." As the music began, filling the stuffy afternoon air with a longing female voice singing

FIGURE 17. Prince dancing for the residents of Zhu Village.

against a melody that combined symphonic flair and synth-pop rhythms, Prince proceeded to engage in a dance that, to say the least, did not conform to standard movement imaginings of the traditional man. His interpretation of the song seemed to more closely resemble modern dance than anything "traditional," although he did add a few pirouettes into the mix for good measure. Fluttering across the stage with a dramatic and determined look upon his face, Prince seemed absorbed in the music and completely unfazed by the largely confused glances of the audience and the growing anxious giggles and eager whispers of his fellow Han Clothing enthusiasts. Reaching a dramatic climax in step with the concluding crescendo of the music, Prince stood briefly frozen in his position, standing on his toes with his arms extended upwards into the air, as the host proceeded onto the stage and said with a giggle, "Thank you very much for your dance, Prince. You danced very pretty" (*tiaode hen piaoliang*). Prince smiled and bowed towards the audience in the traditional style taught earlier that day, while the Han Clothing Movement participants standing around me smiled knowingly to one another.

Prince did not join in the group dinner that evening, departing the festival soon after his dance. He did return the next afternoon for his second performance, which received similarly superficial support from the group, combined with the usual awkward laughter. And then, again, he left. A few casual comments among movement participants that afternoon earned some laughs at Prince's expense behind his back, calling him "Queen" (*Nüwang*) rather than Prince (*Wangzi*), and suggesting that "he is clearly trying to hang out with the wrong group" and was not representing "traditional Chinese values." My sympathy with Prince and suggestions that others engage with him just like any other participant were deemed to be reflections of my unrealistic "Western" attitude, ignoring the very real complexity of the history of sexuality in China, as well as its equally real complexity today. "You might have people over there in America who act like that. But here, we don't act like that." When I asked what was meant by "that," my acquaintance could only reply, "just . . . just like that."

This response is, in the end, the real tragedy of the Han Clothing Movement. The Movement provides a rare space of solace for some of the many who feel excluded or alienated from the rapid and often disorienting change of recent years in China. Throughout the course of my fieldwork, I met people who were unemployed or who toiled away their days in dead-end jobs, people whose emotional lives and love lives were reliably unstable, people who faced unrealistic pressures from family members or significant others, people who were alienated, disheartened, and even outraged by the current sociopolitical milieu, and people who simply may have never been made to feel that they were special or even wanted. In the time that I spent with Han Clothing enthusiasts, I came to feel a strong sense of sympathy for participants and the motivations that were bringing them into this movement, despite the fact that I disagreed strongly with the results of their participation. Yet I recognize that in light of the uncertainties, challenges, and indignities that they faced, nothing could be more reassuring than the idea that they were members of an oppressed yet righteous minoritized majority, prevented by intruding outsiders from realizing the true splendor of their existence, and that the social world in which they lived was not in fact the "real China," an idea that kept their imaginary real China on perpetual life support. This search for the imaginary real China was in reality a search for a whole and redeeming self.

Yet despite the fact that the Han Clothing Movement is in the end a massive living metaphor for a feeling of having been excluded from the ideal of China, the ideal image constructed and enacted by movement participants in response to this exclusion was based upon an even more totalizing and exclusionary logic, developing a rigid and homogenizing vision that was all too certain of its own characteristics and all too eager to pronounce, as the inform-ant described above stated, "We don't act like that." From the paranoid myths surrounding the Manchus and their purported preferential treatment of minority nationalities, to the possessive and puritan ideals of the "proper" Han lady, to the almost reflexive mockery and exclusion of "Prince," the other side of the Han Clothing Movement's perpetual search for an ideal identity is far too often a forcible homogenization and exclusion of those who do not abide fully by the rules of proper identity: dividing and excluding Han through a singular idea of Han-ness. As a result, a movement whose partici-pants sought solace from the present all too often devolved into a new medium of exclusion in this present. And as a result, my sympathies for participants often stopped at their proud appropriation of Han-ness as a simultaneous means of imaginary self-realization and marginalization of multiple others.

As stated in the previous section's discussion of the ladies' academy, the Han Clothing Movement as a whole has indeed emerged from very real chal-lenges and tensions in the experience of contemporary Chinese society. Yet there remains a fundamental distinction between recognizing a problem, responding to a problem, and actually solving a problem. And sometimes, as in this case, the solution proposed becomes a problem itself. The Han Clothing Movement, which responds to discrepancies between the ideals and the experience of the nation through a reaffirmation of the ideals of national identity, is a classic example of precisely such a dilemma, reaffirming a problem through its illusory solution.[40]

As has been demonstrated in the preceding chapters, nations are com-posed of immensely complex spaces and experiences that do not yield to our imaginings or hopes, and never will. By responding to the resulting dilemmas of national and personal identity with yet another affirmation of national (and by extension personal) identity, presenting in this case an even more rigid and unyielding vision in the hope of a final resolution, participants in the Han Clothing Movement are tasting the hair of the dog that bit them. Ironically, the primary result is a perpetuation of the dilemmas that moti-vated their participation in the first place, alongside the opening up of new zones of subjugation and exclusion for those who do not conform to the standards of the heterosexual and patriotic Han man (*haohan*) or the demure and virginal Han woman (*shunü*). The hopes and realities, thrills and disap-pointments, and inclusions and exclusions of the nation and identity thus become the primary engine of their reproduction over time, despite, or rather precisely because of, their perpetually elusive nature.

Conclusion

NEOTRADITIONALISM IN CHINA TODAY

THE PRECEDING CHAPTERS HAVE TRACED the complex, uncertain, and self-reproducing processes ongoing behind such seemingly eternal and stable concepts as the Han race and the Chinese nation. Viewed as essentially the same by Han Clothing Movement participants, Han-ness and Chineseness are intertwined with magnificent visions of identity that are reliably larger than life: the land of rites and etiquette, five millennia of tradition, the oldest uninterrupted civilizational state, a rising China, a new superpower, the Great Han, and the splendor of Chinese culture. These grand visions, which form nationalist identity thought as fantasy, are nevertheless fundamentally removed from actual experience as Han within the geographic space currently labeled as China. The fantasies surrounding notions of the nation and identity are never in the end able to correspond to the actual experience of this identity, which can only ever be a pale and fleeting imitation of these concepts' wonder. Yet the disappointments of experience, in turn, lead to a reinvestment in these ideas and ideals as supplements to the disappointments that they have created in the first place, thereby transforming identity into a perpetually deferred but perpetually desired ideal, reproduced in its own impossibility.

The Han Clothing Movement is symptomatic of these tensions, while at the same time attempting to provide a fleeting cure. Cultural manifestations of the movement, from the clothing, ritual, and photography analyzed in Chapter 4, to the conspiracy theories unfolded in Chapter 5 and the ladies' academy investigated in Chapter 6, are attempts to suture this perpetual lack in the experience of the Great Han through the construction of sacred spheres within a profane environment. The Great Han, viewed as an eternal and timeless truth by Han Clothing Movement participants, is then in reality an eternal process generating new problems in its solutions, perpetually self-deconstructing and self-reproducing in the desire produced in the gaps between ideals and the dictatorship of the real.

In an anthropological spirit, this concluding chapter examines a series of structurally comparable phenomena in contemporary Chinese society in light of the framework developed in the preceding chapters. Through these brief studies, on the one hand, I aim to demonstrate that the Han Clothing Movement is not an isolated anomaly in the current sociohistorical context: numerous emerging movements in China today promote an essentialist vision of race and nation, while appropriating tradition to close the gap between ideals and realities. On the other hand, through this survey of neotraditionalisms, I aim to show how the preceding analyses may illuminate a broader spectrum of sociocultural developments in contemporary China and beyond.

VISITING A CONFUCIAN ACADEMY

During a visit to the southern city of Haikou to make a presentation, I set aside a few days to visit a recently established Confucius Academy. The academy's guiding principle is to create an environment to "promote education in the classics and build a harmonious society." Reaffirming neotraditionalists' notable tendency to start the day early, the founder of the academy, Bao, insisted on picking me up from my motel in downtown Haikou at 7:30 A.M. on the first day of my visit. When he arrived in a van with the school's name plastered on the side, I learned that every day at the Confucius Academy began at 5:30 A.M., so I was already running quite late. As Bao recounted his own training and the founding and growth of the school, we drove at terrifyingly high speeds from the center of the city for over an hour, until we arrived at a community of dusty villas located between the dual vastness of fields and the ocean. Cars parked outside shared the lot with roosters, ducks, and most unexpectedly a very large cow. "We grow and raise all our own food, organically. That's the only way to be healthy," Bao explained as I wandered past the livestock into the school building.

Proceeding into the academy, our first stop was a classroom, where a cacophony of voices immediately overwhelmed me. During my stay at this institution, all of the students were reading the *Book of Changes*, which is not light reading for the school's target student base between the ages of 2 and 10.

As I glanced into the classroom, its walls covered in calligraphy, students recited one section of the *Book of Changes* over and over, incessantly. I soon learned that the academy's curriculum had divided the classics into brief sections, which students spent their days reading and rereading aloud one hundred times each. Upon completion of the hundredth reading, students would then proceed onward to the next section of the *Book of Changes*, which would be similarly recited a hundred times. This process would be repeated one passage at a time until the entire book had been read, at which point everyone was scheduled to proceed to another page-turner, the *Classic of History*.

Yet it was not only the cyclical recitation of the *Book of Changes* that produced this overwhelming cacophony. For the reading of the classics in this school was also accompanied by two recordings, played at high volume from tape players in two corners of the room. One recording featured classical Chinese music. Listening closely, I noticed that the second recording was a recitation of poetry in British English: as I strained to decipher the words, Bao informed me that I was listening to a recitation of Shakespeare's Sonnets. When I jokingly asked if he worried that students might have headaches from this unruly sonic environment, he cited "studies in neuroscience" to argue that children are uniquely adept at absorbing input from their environment. Children from birth through the age of 13 are like sponges, he told me, taking in whatever surrounds them; and his job was to provide the "input." Drawing upon this metaphor of the all-absorbent sponge, he had set up all of the classrooms on this triple-classical model: students were to read the classics, while at the same time absorbing classical music and classical English poetry. Depending upon one's perspective, the result was either auditory chaos or a stimulating, or perhaps even overstimulating, educational environment. Regardless of one's perspective, all the students at the academy spent nearly nine hours between 5:30 A.M. and 8:30 P.M. six days a week engaged in this "learning" environment.

Although this Confucius Academy would at first glance appear to be based in the past and "tradition," like the Han Clothing Movement its origins and priorities are to be found in the present, particularly in the concerns surrounding contemporary education. During discussions in the academy's office, Bao told me that education is without a doubt the greatest concern facing the citizens of China today. For decades, people have torturously fretted over how to resolve the dilemmas in the educational system, characterized by rote memorization, unnecessary pressures and competition, and a single-minded focus upon test scores. Most disconcertingly, Bao recounted a meeting that he held with middle-school teachers in a nearby town, who in the preceding months had seen two of their students commit suicide. "There are children selling organs for iPads, or selling themselves for money," he declared with sincere dismay in his voice: what kind of a system, he asked, drives middle-school students to such behavior? Again, we see here neotraditionalism responding to real and very pressing social issues today: as with Han Clothing, the source of the fascination with the past is to be found in the present and its discontents.

And again, as with Han Clothing, we see a confident solution, traditional Chinese education, providing a seemingly certain panacea to any and all problems of the present. This solution, the academy's educational model, was first developed and promoted by Taiwanese scholar Wang Tsai-kuei, a jovial and charismatic individual who has been promoting his eccentric views on pedagogy for nearly two decades in Taiwan and China. Wang has compiled a collection of Chinese classics for the modern student, consisting of the *Great Learning*; the *Doctrine of the Mean*; the *Analects*; selections from the writings of Lao-Tzu, Chuang-tzu, and Mencius; the *Book of Odes*; the *Book of Changes*; the *Classic of History*; the *Yellow Emperor's Classic on Internal Medicine*; the *Classic of Filial Piety*; *Standards for Being a Good Student*; and the *Three-Character Classic*, alongside Shakespeare's *Midsummer Night's Dream* and *Sonnets*. The academy in Haikou is but one branch of the larger traditional education movement based in this curriculum that has risen to prominence in the past decade and offers private educational options in cities throughout China. The goal of this educational program, represented by the always colorful Wang, who oversees the training of all academy heads in Beijing, is to provide the type of broad and well-rounded humanistic education imagined to have been realized in the past, covering philosophy, history, religion, literature, and science. The product of such an education, cultivated in this pure sphere, is expected to be nothing less than pure genius, rising far above one's contemporaries. Repeating a familiar assertion that I had heard so many times throughout my research, Bao declared that "our ancestors were considerably more intelligent than any of us nowadays. They already had solutions to many of the crises that we face today."

The goal, then, is to recapture this imagined genius, its answers, and the splendor thus produced. Yet where was the downfall from this magic moment? In place of the depredations of the Manchus as imagined by the Han Clothing Movement, or the Western notion of gender equality criticized by the ladies' academy's teachers, Wang and his followers attribute the collapse of Chinese education, and by extension China as a whole, to the antitraditionalist New Culture and May Fourth Movements. Prior to the New Culture Movement, they claim, all educated people could read and write in Classical Chinese, and thus had a connection to a culture extending across five millennia. This cultural wealth, presumed to be unparalleled relative to the rest of the world, provided the foundation for the equally unparalleled intelligence and thus charmed existence in the past. Yet the May Fourth Movement's emphasis opposing tradition, promoting a type of Chinese Englightenment, along with the use of vernacular language in writing, promoted as a means of expanding literacy, were in fact a step towards the desacralization of traditional Chinese knowledge as a whole, and thus the disenchantment of Chinese culture and existence itself. The best of intentions thus produced the worst of results, according to this narrative, insofar as "the Chinese" as a whole were cut off from their cultural tradition and national essence, transforming an imagined traditional land of supernatural powers and serenity, the middle kingdom, into just another place on the modern world map. Whereas Lu Xun had been concerned with awakening the masses sleeping in a burning iron house of Confucian orthodoxy,[1] Bao and others like him now feel that the fire was a false alarm, and are distressed to have lost their keys when they stepped outside, leaving them permanently locked out of what appears in retrospect to be a uniquely stable iron structure. Traditional culture, once perceived as the source of all of China's dilemmas, was now, in a complete inversion, perceived as the panacea for all of China's dilemmas.[2]

Providing another example to explain the limitless power of traditional education for a nation, Bao suddenly took the discussion in a direction that I had not expected: employing anti-Semitic conspiracy theories to promote his traditional educational model. Bao asserted with a polite smile that although "the Jews" make up only 0.3 percent of the world's population, they have won over 30 percent of Nobel Prizes. And despite the fact that "the Jews" are a clear minority in comparison to other considerably more populous nationalities of the world, he declared with confidence, they nevertheless clearly control the entire global finance system and run the world. So, how do "the Jews" do it, he asked. According to Wang's educational philosophy, the perceived "magic of the Jews" can be traced back to their reading the classics. From a young age, he asserted, all Jewish children read and memorize the Torah. This activates their brains, maintains their connection with their national essence, and promotes their national spirit, which then empowers them to play a decisive role in such weighty adult matters as running the world. The point to be derived from this example, according to Bao, is that if China wants to be strong and play an important role in the world, then China must do the same. Of course, he added with a hearty laugh, he does not mean that Chinese children should study the Torah! Instead, in order to be like "the Jews," but better, Chinese students must study their own classics, which are of course, he emphasized, more numerous and culturally richer than the Torah.

To re-create this ideal classic educational environment, the academy is located in a remote rural setting without access to television, newspapers, computers, or other contemporary forms of entertainment. The academy is self-sustaining by right of its own organic farm, from which each meal is prepared and in which all students work every Sunday afternoon. From this immunized base, a Confucianized new Yenan, the revitalization of traditional education is to produce the revitalization of traditional culture, reversing the disenchanting turn of modernity. Such imaginary supernatural achievements, in Wang's logic, could only be produced by a truly fantastic educational program. After all, many Chinese students study science, but how many of them study science through the Yellow Emperor's Classic on Internal Medicine? Many Chinese students study English, but how many begin from Shakespeare's Sonnets? The mysticism inherent within Wang's pedagogical approach, presumed to be tapping into a magical and long-lost essence, a lost era of genius, fosters the mysticism of its imagined results, generating a traditionalist educational Great Leap Forward. Bao asserted that, upon completing the course of studies provided at the Confucian Academy, a student could do anything and test into anywhere. His eyes suddenly brightened as an example sprang into his mind: they could probably even skip high school and test directly into Peking or Tsinghua University, he asserted. In a pattern seen throughout my research, what was lacking in evidence for these traditionalist panacea was supplemented by confidence.

During my days at the academy, I attempted to abide by the study patterns of the average student, despite being over twenty years their senior, so as to develop a clearer understanding of the effects of this curriculum. As mentioned above, the day begins at 5:30 A.M. Bao claims that Chinese medicine has proven that it is beneficial to wake up early in the morning: as he said, it makes one stronger. After everyone has arisen, students proceed to the central hall of the academy to pay their respects to Confucius. One student first lit incense before an image of Confucius hanging from the wall, and then proceeded to bow three times towards the image. The entire student body would then follow this student's example. A teacher would then step forward to read an excerpt from the *Analects*, which would in turn be repeated line by line by the students. Finally, everyone would turn to bow before the image of Confucius yet again, marking a sacred start to the day.

With the exception of meals from the school's farm and a calligraphy class in the afternoon, the rest of the day is occupied by reading the classics, as described above. From my observations, the effect of being in class as a section of the obscure *Book of Changes* was read over and over was nothing short of hypnotic. At first, one can follow the characters word by word, and can attempt to make some sense of what is read, particularly as each phrase is repeated a hundred times, repeatedly cycling these puzzling words within one's head. But then as they continue to read, students would often begin tapping on the tables or tapping their feet, seemingly to keep the rhythm of the text. And as they tap along with the rhythm of the reading, the rhythm ever so gradually accelerates and then decelerates, before finally accelerating again. Combined with the classical Chinese music and the Shakespearean sonnets playing out of tape players on either side of the room, everything comes together into one spellbinding cacophony. Then suddenly, the teacher leading the recitation would come to a sudden stop, announcing that they have completed their hundred readings of that section. And we would then proceed to the next section, which would be repeated over and over, bringing us back into the hypnosis of the classical text.

The unyielding repetition that is the central daily experience at this academy, parallel to the repetition of identity performance within the Han Clothing Movement, brings us back to the point from which this study began, namely, the distinction between the ideas or images of identity and its actual experience. Here, the classics with their mystical and purportedly timeless wisdom embody the ideal that must be brought into reality to close this gap between ideals and experience. And the unending and indeed compulsive repetition characteristic of the experience of the classics at this academy, reminiscent of the repeated performances of pure and proper Han-ness within the Han Clothing Movement, embodies the insistence of this elusive signifier, and the determination of those who live in the shadow of these ideas to fuse communication with reality.

Alongside this repetition, the bodily comportment required of students literally embodies this utopian desire to organize and arrange everything perfectly down to the most specific details, despite the reliable resistance of the real world. In each classroom in the academy, a sign posted on the wall reads:

> Place your feet on the ground, and sit up straight
> Sit properly, with your left hand holding the book
> Follow the words with your right hand, and don't let your eyes stray
> Read out loud, read according to the standards.

The micromanagement of every detail, from the placement of feet, hands, and eyes, to the compulsive repetition of the classics, belies the eagerness to exercise control over every detail within this detached and safely self-enclosed sphere, thereby creating an alternate reality embodying the "real China" against the real China, one mystical sentence at a time.

JIANG QING'S CONFUCIAN CONSTITUTIONALISM

One of the most high-profile proponents of traditionalism in China today is Jiang Qing, whose vision of Confucian constitutionalism has graced the Op-Ed page of the *New York Times*[3] and has most recently been published by Princeton University Press's new Princeton-China Series.[4] Jiang's argument that China, on account of its uniquely Confucian cultural heritage, must find its political path forward through such Confucian cultural heritage naturally appeals to those eager to recognize and celebrate national cultural uniqueness. Yet this uniqueness is, again, considerably more complex than Jiang claims.

The primary target of Jiang's Confucian critiques is the idea of "Western" liberal democracy. Jiang contends that "every current of political thought in China assumes that democracy is the way ahead for China," and that this presents an unprecedented "challenge" for China as a whole.[5]

First, Jiang argues, democracy is a thoroughly Western institution without roots in Chinese civilization, which not only means that it could not be successful, but also that any attempt to make it successful would be a fundamental betrayal of cultural tradition. The supposed hegemony of democracy in political expectations, according to Jiang, means that the people of China are no longer able to use their own cultural guidelines to think through politics: a situation which Jiang considers a travesty. [6] Cultures in Jiang's interpretation are not only mutually incompatible systems incapable of being influenced by one another, but even more importantly fundamentally closed-off spheres that must be protected, and even actively defended.

Second, beyond this lack of cultural correspondence, Jiang also emphasizes that democracy is in practice a fundamentally flawed system. According to Jiang, democracy is solely legitimized through and thus reliant upon the will of the people, a potentially misdirected and even disastrous will. The "extreme secularization" of democratic politics[7] ignores moral obligations, promoting a system of rights and thus solely of self-interest, which overlooks "much of ordinary morality that has been in human society for hundreds and thousands of years."[8] Jiang argues that "the exaggerated importance given to the will of the people leads to extreme secularization, contractualism, utilitarianism, selfishness, commercialism, capitalization, vulgarization, hedonism, mediocratization, this-worldliness, lack of ecology, lack of history, and lack of morality."[9] Jiang argues that democratic politicians thus rely upon "pandering to human desires,"[10] producing a system in which the immediate and short-sighted priorities of the electorate are given precedence over longer-term concerns and moral reasoning. Democracy is thus an inferior political system of secular values and petty desires innately unfit for implementation in a land of longstanding civilization and morals.

In light of this perceived sad state of affairs, Jiang has taken it upon himself to develop an alternative that not only corresponds to China's cultural traditions, but that also surpasses and indeed even encompasses democracy as a form of government. Jiang has given this alternative political ideal the not so humble title of the Way of the Humane Authority (*wang dao*),[11] which would be more accurately and thus less benignly translated as the Kingly Way or the Sovereign Way.[12] This Way emerged during the rule of the mythical ancient sage kings of the first three dynasties, Xia, Shang, and Zhou, and presents a tripartite approach, founded upon the ancient cosmological vision of the world as composed of heaven (*tian*), earth (*di*), and man (*ren*). Jiang's political program aspires to unify these three components (*tianren heyi*), via three distinct yet intertwined and mutually reinforcing forms of political legitimacy corresponding to these three elements. The legitimacy derived from the concept of heaven refers to "a transcendent, sacred sense of natural morality," which Jiang calls "sacred legitimacy." The legitimacy corresponding to the earth is a legitimacy "that comes from history and culture because cultures are formed through history in particular places," which he calls "cultural legitimacy." And finally, the legitimacy corresponding to the human is the legitimacy of the will of the people, which he calls "popular legitimacy."[13]

Yet how are sacred, cultural, and popular legitimacies to be realized in practice? Jiang has famously proposed a tricameral legislature, with one house corresponding to each of the three forms of legitimacy, each mapped onto one component of the unity of heaven and humanity. The House of Ru (also rendered as a "House of Exemplary Persons" in other translations)[14] embodies sacred legitimacy derived from heaven: this House is to be populated by Confucian scholars who are either nominated from among fellow scholars, or who have completed a course of study in the "Four Books and Five Classics" at a state-run Confucian Academy. This House is overseen by what Jiang calls "a great scholar" nominated by fellow scholars. The House of the People embodies popular legitimacy derived from the people: its members are to be selected, Jiang asserts, "according to the norms and processes of Western democratic parliaments."[15] Finally, the House of the Nation embodies cultural legitimacy derived from national history and tradition: its members are "selected by hereditary criteria and by assignment."[16] The leader of this house must be a direct descendant of Confucius, who in turn oversees the selection of the House's members "from among the descendants of great sages of the past, descendants of the rulers, descendants of famous people, of patriots, university professors of Chinese history, retired top officials, judges, and diplomats, worthy people from society, as well as representatives of Daoism, Buddhism, Islam, Tibetan Buddhism, and Christianity."[17]

In order for bills to become law, they must pass at least two houses. The House of Ru/Exemplary Persons, according to Jiang, has final executive veto power. Revealing the troubling side of such cultural conservatism, Jiang's example of said veto power is not particularly reassuring, and one might note not even very authentic in relation to the realities of traditional Chinese sexual culture: "A bill, such as one permitting homosexuals to found a family, that passes the House of the People but is against the Way of heaven will be vetoed by the House of Ru."[18] Through this equilibrium between the three houses representing three divergent yet unified forms of legitimacy, Jiang argues that he has envisioned a system that is better than democracy and that accords with "the eternal and unchanging principle of legitimization" established by "China's ancient sages."[19]

The similarities between Jiang Qing's Confucian Constitutionalism and the Han Clothing Movement are revealing. Both are founded upon an ideal vision from the distant past that is at once lacking in the present, yet which at the same time represents the one and only true China. In the place where we once found the land of rites and etiquette (*liyi zhi bang*) as imagined and celebrated within the Han Clothing Movement, we now find the land of the humane authority and the unity of heaven and earth. And as exemplars grounding these transcendent ideals, both movements claim heritage from the remote mythical ancestors of the Chinese people: the civilizing progenitor Yellow Emperor in the case of Han Clothing and the early sage kings in the case of Confucian Constitutionalism.[20] Both thus rely upon the unrestrained imagining of a traditionalist fantasy representing the one and only "real China," towards which each aim to proceed as the natural yet perpetually elusive conclusion of identity.

In place of the Manchus, the outside threat that mischievously enters and pollutes an otherwise pure polity, Jiang considers the greatest threat to China today to be an imagined consensus on democracy as the country's future. Jiang portrays democracy, the perceived primary opponent of Confucian Constitutionalism, as "Western," "secular," and based solely in "desire." I analyze these three accusations in turn below, arguing that they reveal more about Jiang's own desires and anxieties than about actual democratic practice.

With regards to the first aspect of his characterization of democracy, note that Jiang invariably adds the descriptor "Western" before the term "democracy" in a compulsive act of distancing through labeling as other, similar to the type of externalizing labels ("Manchu," "barbarian") popular within the Han Clothing Movement. Enforcement of such a rigid and absolute distinction between China and the rest, while undoubtedly appealing to the yearning for identificatory pride within its subjects, is nevertheless completely ignorant of the realities of cultural processes. On the one hand, Jiang's portrayal of singular cultures existing in opposition to one another fundamentally overlooks the long history of exchange and mutual learning within and between any and all supposedly singular "cultures." On the other hand, despite Jiang's insistent claims to the contrary, there is no singular cultural tradition that must or even can represent his imaginarily singular China. Confucianism undoubtedly played an important role in Chinese tradition, but to say that China's political and cultural traditions are primarily Confucian, and that Confucianism must now be the dominant principle of any return to tradition is not only a quite blatant form of Han-ism but also suffocates other currents within the broad and historically diverse rubric of "Chinese culture." The proposals that Jiang has suggested would be no different from me as a white, Christian (for the sake of imagining) male proposing that on account of the purportedly unique Christian heritage of "the West," our nation's Constitution must be rewritten to match Christian laws and that we should find descendants of Jesus to rule over the nation. Such cultural conservatism would be (and when it emerges, usually is) dismissed as narrow minded, exclusionary, and retrogressive. It is only within the context of cross-cultural interactions that such essentialist programs become normalized, on account of the presumed absolute difference and thus homogeneity of those on the other side of the imagined binary, through which totalizing visions of self and other are constructed.

Jiang skillfully employs this binary in his claim to be countering hegemony for the purpose of independent thinking, stating that "a glance over China's current world of thought shows that Chinese people have already lost their ability to think independently about political questions."[21] I could not agree more with the urgency of new and innovative ideas for a resolution to China's current political stasis. Yet in the very next sentence, Jiang makes all too clear what he means by independent thinking:

> In other words, Chinese people are no longer able to use patterns of thought inherent in their own culture—Chinese culture—to think about China's current political development. This is a great tragedy for the world of Chinese thought! It is, therefore, necessary to go back to the inherent patterns of Chinese culture to ground the development of Chinese political thought, rather than simply following the Western trends and forgetting our own culture.[22]

Independent thinking, in Jiang's view, is only independent in relation to "the West." Domestically, thinking is unified around "inherent patterns," of which Jiang is conveniently the self-appointed interpreter. In a pattern parallel to the Han Clothing Movement's construction of Han identity against mainstream culture today, Jiang encourages people to think outside the box, yet then immediately returns their thoughts to another even darker box. In countering "Western hegemony" and its supposedly limiting political expectations, Jiang reinstitutes a far more stifling hegemony in the name of "culture" and "Confucianism" with even more rigid expectations: after all, the idea that China's future must inevitably be found in its past is neither a model of independent thinking nor a particularly liberating view of politics. Anyone who proposed a similar framework for the future of a "Western" country, or even for such traditionally Confucian neighbors as South Korea, Japan, or Taiwan, simply would not be taken seriously.[23]

Secularism is the second component of Jiang Qing's critique of democracy. According to Jiang, democracy's separation of church and state "den[ies] the value of the sacred"[24] such that a democratic system can only rely upon pandering to "the common man" and "head counting" with "no regard for morality."[25] As a result of these all-too-worldly operations, worldly desires are "not restrained by sacred legitimacy or universal morality," and democracy as a whole thereby "lacks morality," giving rise to "imperialism, fascism, and hegemonism."[26] In contrast to the disenchantment of modern secular politics, Jiang proposes the enchanted notion of the Way of the Humane Authority, purportedly descended from the ancient sage kings, whose mythical nature means that their feats and accomplishments thankfully are not bound by the restrictions of reality.

Daniel Bell's introduction to *A Confucian Constitutional Order: How China's Ancient Past Can Shape its Political Future* retraces Jiang Qing's eventful intellectual development from a Marxist to a political Confucianist. The thread linking Jiang's multiple pursuits within this intellectual history is the search for a final and complete answer to the human condition. For example, during his time as a truck repairman during the Cultural Revolution, Jiang reportedly "read Karl Marx's *Das Kapital* in his spare time and became convinced that Marx's masterpiece would lead him to the final truth about human society."[27] Yet he soon thereafter became disillusioned with Marxism and began reading the works of "Western classical liberal philosophers such as Locke and Rousseau," in hopes that their "different perspectives could be integrated into a coherent liberal Marxist doctrine that could save China from turmoil."[28] Moving onwards toward the study of Taoist, Buddhist, and Christian spirituality, he eventually discovered Confucianism, in which he found "the way ahead for China."[29] In each case, the sacred is a philosophy that promises to provide the final answer to everything, producing a marked structural similarity within the quite varied intellectual and philosophical approaches pursued in Jiang's lifetime. Each is, following Peter Berger's analysis of religion, a sacred canopy providing an otherwise lacking order and meaning,[30] or, following Niklas Luhmann's analysis of religion, a contingency formula, providing a reason for why everything is not the way one would like it to be and transforming the indeterminable into the determinable.[31]

If Jiang Qing's intellectual project is a perpetual search for a final and complete answer, seeking out a final closure and thus transcendent reenchantment of society, it is not surprising that he is disillusioned by and alienated from democratic theory and the uncertainty and disharmony characteristic of its disenchanted "open society."[32] As Yannis Stavrakakis explains in his analysis of the implications of Lacanian theory for politics, the real yet disillusioning advantage of democratic practice is its recognition of the fundamental division, antagonism, and incompleteness of the human condition. Stavrakakis writes: "Democracy does not produce the ambiguity and the lack characterizing the human condition; it does not produce the irreducible division and disharmony characterizing every social form. It only attempts to come to terms with them by recognizing them in their irreducibility, thus producing a new post-fantasmic form of social unity."[33] Democracy as political practice thereby incorporates the incompleteness of society and the human condition into its political system. Yet politics based solely upon people is all too worldly: the disillusioning recognition of the fundamental impossibility of the human condition spurs the search for a return to the sacred. Jiang Qing's intellectual project, founded upon the search for a final, sacred answer characteristic of so many intellectual and political projects preceding it, meets the disenchantment of the world with its determined reenchantment.

Implicit within Jiang's articulation of the preceding two characteristics of democracy, we are able to see notable traces of the third target of his critique, namely, desire. As stated above, Jiang claims that the worldliness of democratic practice means that it is driven by "a secularized, limited, and narrow collection of human desires," which he contrasts with the "sacred, exclusive, [and] supreme" nature of political Confucianism's sacred authority.[34] On account of his frequent denigrating statements regarding human desire,[35] Jiang would appear to be absolutely opposed to the workings of desire in politics. Yet upon closer inspection of his critiques and his proposals, this repeated dismissal of the role of desire in politics is not an actual renunciation of desire, but rather an anxious repression of and compulsive self-distancing from desire, which in fact infuses his own political program, in a style reminiscent of Han Clothing Movement participants' anxious self-distancing from cosplay and Brother Emperor. In his critique of the "foreign" and "secular" nature of democracy, Jiang is in fact acting out and rationalizing his own desire for a pure and thoroughly enchanted Chinese identity, expressed through an imaginary indigenous and sacred politics.

Despite all of his negative assessments of democratic politics, Jiang's political framework incorporates democracy through the House of the People while at the same time, as he describes it, "surpass[ing]" democracy.[36] While democracy is portrayed as a Western and nonsacred political system, Jiang Qing's political Confucianism is importantly able to hierarchically encompass this system within its indigenous and sacred politics. And if the former represents, in his analyses, "the West," and the latter represents "China," then this subordinating incorporation of democracy into what Jiang himself not so humbly characterizes as a "superior" system represents a national victory over the supposed hegemons,[37] whose hegemony is thus undeserved. The desire from which Jiang continually distances himself is then the cultural-nationalist desire for a pure and superior identity within a world in which this pure and superior identity is perceived as not having been given full recognition. Naturally, as the self-proclaimed interpreter of the Confucian political tradition, Jiang has much to gain from the construction of such a political identity. And on account of the resentment-based nature of nationalist propaganda in contemporary China, Jiang's program will appeal to many of those whom it would disenfranchise, expressing a desire for a pure, unique, sacred, and eternally stable identity in what can only be described as an Oriental Orientalism.[38]

THE NEW LEFT AS NEOTRADITIONALISM:
FROM RITES TO REVOLUTION

This next addition to our review of neotraditionalisms may be unexpected. For many with similar political sympathies, the loose coalition of Chinese intellectuals labeled as "the New Left" stands on the front lines of the global struggle against capitalism and neoliberalism, and is thus on the cutting edge of political progress. In an enthusiastic yet still quite informative introduction to this intellectual movement in the recent volume *China and New Left Visions: Political and Cultural Interventions*, Ban Wang and Jie Lu characterize New Leftists as "shar[ing] an intellectual consensus based on their fundamental concerns with social inequality, justice, and China's neoliberal model of development."[39] These are indeed pressing issues in contemporary China, worthy of being raised and seriously discussed. Yet beyond raising these issues, how does the New Left propose to resolve them?

New Leftist thought is not easily characterized as a singular whole, and many of its proponents distance themselves from this label. Nevertheless, there are discernible patterns to this thought, and the editors of *China and New Left Visions* usefully list four primary fields around which New Leftist thinkers coalesce: social justice, capital and power, democracy, and modernity. In the field of social justice, the New Left attributes China's growing inequality to capitalism/ neoliberalism, and thus aims to combat these trends by "maintaining public ownership of the means of production" and promoting a larger state role in market operations.[40] On the topic of capital and power, rather than seeing the Chinese state as controlling and benefiting from the capitalist development of recent years, New Leftists view Chinese political power as having "been capitalized by global capitalism."[41] On the question of democracy, the New Left "advocates participatory democracy by calling for a repoliticization and mobilization of Chinese society."[42] And finally, on the question of modernity, the editors cite Wang Hui's suggestion of "a modern society that can be produced in a way different from the historical form of capitalism, or a self-reflexive process of modernity."[43] Across these fields, New Leftists are unanimous in their support for drawing upon "Chinese revolutionary and socialist legacies" in search of solutions.

This is where, I argue, a movement dedicated to so-called radical ideals becomes intertwined with the types of neotraditionalisms that are the topic of this book. For despite the surface distinctions between the vocabularies of New Leftism and the Han Clothing Movement, these two movements' structural imaginaries are in fact surprisingly similar. New Leftism constructs an image of an ideal time in the (not so) distant past in response to the shortcomings of the present, constructs an enemy that is deemed responsible for the disappearance of this utopia, enforces a very limiting vision of identity as the sole proper form of behavior, and aims to reconstruct their ideal image in the present as the "true China."

Tradition

New Leftism, despite its nominally internationalist leanings, is structured around another ideal vision of the local past, the Maoist era, which is viewed as epitomizing the real, "revolutionary" China. As was the case in other neotraditionalist movements, this romanticization is more an inversion of the present than a reflection of the actual Maoist past, which anyone able to take an emotionally detached look at history can recognize as far from ideal. Yet thanks to its conclusion four decades ago, Maoism increasingly benefits from the romanticization through distance that produces the idealization of the era of the "three sage kings" in other neotraditionalist movements.

In response to the rapidly growing inequality and social conflicts of the present, the Maoist era is imagined as a period of greater equality and solidarity. In response to the corruption and nepotism of the present, the Maoist era is imaginarily remembered as a period of clean government in which officials served the people. In response to the wasteful, state-sponsored face projects of the present, the Maoist era is imagined as a period in which state funds were used solely for the betterment of society. In response to the growing moral crisis, pervasive mistrust, and alienation of the present, the Maoist era is imagined as a time when people worked together and helped one another. And perhaps most importantly, in response to the widespread dissolution of a sense of national mission and values, the Maoist era is imagined as a period characterized by strong moral values, transcendent political ideals, and a seemingly genuine sense of meaning. Yet again, in the national imaginary, what is lacking in the present is discovered in the past, which is perpetually home to the "real China," this time a China of revolutionary socialist values, or a revolutionary "tradition."[44]

Yet in the end, these imaginings can only be based in a willed blindness to the realities of the Maoist era. The problems of the present were not resolved in the Maoist era, they were just better hidden. To imagine the Maoist era as an era of equality is to forget that the glaring urban–rural divide is precisely the product of the Mao-era *hukou* system, as is the stark division of rulers and ruled in the name of "the people."[45] To imagine the past as an era free from exploitation is to ignore the fact that Maoist socialism was nothing less than a harshly enforced state capitalism overseen by vigilant cadres in the false name of "liberation." To imagine the past as an era of clean governance is to forget the state bureaucracy's emergence as a new class of rulers,[46] which replaced one elite group with another[47] that managed to exercise an unprecedented degree of control over the ruled, down to even the most basic of goods: a power that brought with it many privileges. To imagine the past as an era in which state funds were used for the betterment of society is to forget the expropriation of harvests for ideological face projects far more disastrous than those of the present. To imagine the past as an era in which people worked together and helped one another is to forget the persistent paranoid search for the "class enemies" and "counterrevolutionaries" that reemerged as scapegoats for the evasiveness of communist paradise every few years throughout this period, from the beginning of land reform through the end of the Cultural Revolution. And to imagine the Maoist era as a period of strong moral values and political ideals is to forget precisely how often those values and ideals were violated in practice. It is only through a forceful forgetting and covering over of these realities that Wang Hui is able to discuss a "socialist tradition" and "socialist values,"[48] that Daniel Vukovich is able to celebrate the Marxist politics of commitment and intensity,[49] that Kong Qingdong is able to argue that "Mao Zedong Thought can attain victory in any and all battles,"[50] and that Han Deqiang is able to assert that "in my heart, Chairman Mao is our Muhammad."[51] Here, we once more see the desire for a national tradition of which one can be proud without regard for realities: "the real China," again.

Self–Other

The first sentences of the *Selected Works of Mao Zedong* are: "Who are our enemies? Who are our friends? This is a question of the first importance for the revolution." Simple questions produce simple answers, which provide an appealing sense of certainty, and New Leftism accordingly eagerly embraces this binary mapping of the world. Like the other traditionalisms examined in this book, the New Left naturally has an enemy (or two) to explain the lack of correspondence between their ideal vision of China and their experiential reality, as well as plenty of suggestions to realize the identity of reality and their "real" China.

The prime culprits in New Leftist rhetoric are capitalism and "neoliberalism."[52] According to Wang Hui, "in all of its behaviors, including economic, political, and cultural—even in governmental behavior—China has completely conformed to the dictates of capital and the activities of the market."[53] The externalizing undertones of this sentence, portraying China as conforming to capital's "dictates," implicitly suggest that capitalism is external to "China" and that there exists a China that should not and could not conform. We can find similar sentiments in the suggestion, mentioned above, that the Chinese state, rather than overseeing and benefiting from capitalism, has instead "been capitalized by global capitalism."[54] Here, we find another case of self-comforting externalization, wherein the injustices and exploitation characteristic of the current system are alienated not as something that people within China, whether the government or "capitalists," do to one another, but rather as something that "capitalism" or "neoliberalism" as external powers do to the Chinese people through a type of possession, reminiscent of the Manchu conspiracy theories peddled among Han Clothing Movement participants.

The shattering of Maoist ideals in the reform era then becomes a violation of the imagined fundamental spirit of the nation. New Leftist commentators, in their outrage at this development, inevitably overlook the fact that such ideals had already been set aside during Mao's reign. As such, there is arguably no better continuation of the Maoist tradition than an amoral regime that ignores Mao's stated ideals. Yet this irony is overlooked in New Leftist analysis, which somehow, despite repeated contradictory evidence, still continues to believe in Maoist rhetoric as existing in identity with the realities of the Maoist era, an identity that was never achieved, and never will be.

This urge to externalize, embodied in the repetition of the labels of capital, neoliberalism, and of course the familiar scapegoat of "the West," as well as in the suggestion in New Leftist texts that the current situation is a betrayal of China's supposed true revolutionary heritage, aims to deny the extent to which capitalism is systematically intertwined in a self-reproducing cycle with people's desires in China, and is thus arguably as "indigenous" as any other form of socioeconomic organization. Yet again, as was seen in Confucian constitutionalism, the denial of such seemingly crude desire is central to the New Left's articulation of its illusorily more lofty desire, which is rendered as nondesire through its simultaneous condemnation of desire and its expression through the localized language of identity. Similar to the rhetoric of the Han Clothing Movement, or of Jiang Qing, both Mobo Gao and Daniel Vukovich have dramatically described the struggle against the renunciation of Maoism in the possessive nationalist language of "the battle for China's past."[55] The Utopia (*wuyou zhiziang*) website, the leading online New Left forum, is revealingly described in its own words not in terms of leftism or international solidarity, but rather as "China's largest patriotic online bookstore."[56] In this regard, highlighting the synergies between nationalism and Maoism, wherein China was not only a central kingdom with a lengthy and revered past, but also the central kingdom of a new revolutionary global future,[57] New Leftism operates as a traditionalist nationalism, inflated through the universalist ambitions of Marxism, and rationalized through the naturalizing yet unattainable ideal of pure identity, relying upon the strict enforcement of a politically correct vision of Chinese identity in the present for the exaltation of the past.

Identity

This identity-based traditionalist nationalism is on display in prominent New Leftist commentator Wang Hui's writings, wherein the analysis of "imperialism" and "neoliberalism" walks a fine line between romanticized "resistance" and simplistic scapegoating. An example of the latter can be found in Wang's "The 'Tibetan Question' East and West: Orientalism, Regional Ethnic Autonomy, and the Politics of Dignity," originally composed in the aftermath of tensions in Tibet that preceded the 2008 Beijing Olympics.[58] The first section of Wang's lengthy essay is an extended reflection upon Western colonialism, Orientalist knowledge, and the formation of the Chinese nation-state. Wang asserts that "Western knowledge of Tibet is deeply rooted in an Orientalist mind-set,"[59] which, he alleges, produces contemporary support in "the West" for the Tibetan independence movement. This movement, he furthermore claims without providing any evidence, could not exist without Western support.[60] Wang thus contends that the crux of the "Tibet issue" is that "Tibet must liberate itself from the images held by Westerners and the myths of Shangri-la before it can make genuine progress."[61] The logic of this argument is quite perplexing: are we really to believe that the primary challenge facing modern Tibet could be a few paragraphs from Kant, or the Theosophy of Helena Petrovna Blavatsky cited by Wang as evidence of Western Orientalism?[62] Such an argument can only make sense through its predetermined conclusion, abiding by state-enforced narratives that require the source of the current Tibet conflict to be found outside of China, in a comfortably externalizing excuse that Wang calls "the West" or "imperialism," his Manchu.

Orientalism and the imperialist incursions that it has produced in turn become the rationalization for New Leftism's identity, an inviolable "national unity." According to Wang, "'the Chinese nation' refers not just to the national entity in itself that gradually took shape over the course of several thousand years, but also to what political resistance to the Western powers over the past century transformed into a self-conscious political body."[63] As a result, in Wang's view, Chinese nationalism's "emphasis on the principle of 'one Chinese nation' represents a response to the crisis of disintegration brought about by imperialist aggression."[64] Such an analysis of the founding of the Chinese nation-state as a response to the wound of imperialism elicits undeserved sympathy for the idea of the unified nation-state, thereby quite ironically rendering any Tibetan grievances as betrayals of the struggle against imperialism. Or, to phrase this another way, just because we all know that imperialism is bad, this does not mean that the unity of the nation-state is inherently good, particularly when a nation-state is a product of precisely such imperial projects. Such a framing of the issue along the China–West binary furthermore all too conveniently overlooks the fact that the Tibet issue is primarily a matter of the China–Tibet binary; and the focus upon Western imperialism all too conveniently overlooks the considerably more real imperialism that occurs across this axis, which similarly relies upon the type of Orientalist knowledge that Wang feigns to condemn. The will to externalization on display in Chapter 5's analysis of Manchu conspiracy theories is thus again on display in Wang's reflections on "imperialism" and the nation, legitimizing an otherwise unattainable internal harmony (Tibet=China) under the falsely unifying auspices of external enemies.

A similarly incorporating identity logic can be seen in the final section of Wang's paper. Finally moving beyond outdated Orientalist citations to address present-day Tibet, Wang argues that "the Tibetan question cannot be explained as being completely unique or exceptional—it must, rather, be analyzed in the context of the entirety of China's current social transformation."[65] By "the entirety of China's current social transformation," Wang means depoliticization and neoliberalism, the two keywords of his New Leftist analysis. It is thus through this mode of argumentation that, soon after bringing the realities of contemporary Tibet into his analyses, Wang promptly leaves behind these realities to act as if the problems in today's Tibet are exactly the same as problems in any other region of the People's Republic today. This flattening, nationalistic attempt to deny the unique challenges in China's occupied frontiers erases the ethnic and historical component of the Tibet conflict, pretending as if all problems in contemporary Tibet can be understood solely through Western imperialism and neoliberalism, and thus as if the protests that occurred across the Tibetan plateau in 2008 could have just as easily occurred in Hefei, Hangzhou, or Wuhan without out the slightest hint of difference.[66] This is an extremely myopic interpretation with highly selective historical amnesia, and indeed a majoritarian act of analytical violence, but it is an interpretation that matches Wang's desire to affirm, in the end, the nationalist argument that Tibet is part of China, and will always remain so. His concluding remarks praising the international counterprotests supporting the 2008 Beijing Olympics reveal as much: in the often nasty hypernationalism of the anti-CNN youth protecting the "sacred" Olympic torch (*sheng huo*) in its journey around the world, Wang perplexingly manages to see promises of a world perspective and internationalism, even suggesting the "birth of a new politics."[67] Behind Wang's condemnation of "neoliberalism" thus lies a deeply conservative and narrow nationalism, and behind his critique of "imperialism" lies a rationalization of actually existing imperialism that is not to be discussed in the name of a homogenizing "leftist," "internationalist" ideal.

Similar to the Han Clothing Movement, the New Left is a utopian ideology based upon the imagining of a magical moment in the past, rationalizing the distance between their ideal and their reality through self-affirming externalization, and attempting to enforce a constraining identity constructed around opposition to "the West" and the embrace of China's "revolutionary" heritage. New Leftism is then, in conclusion, an unexpected neotraditionalism under the guise of a forward-looking "resistance."

REBUILDING THE PAST IN WENCHUAN

Before leaving China in 2011, I visited the Wenchuan area of Sichuan Province. On May 12, 2008, a massive 7.9 earthquake devastated this area, killing nearly 70,000, injuring hundreds of thousands, and leaving millions homeless.[68] In the years since, the many towns that were destroyed in this quake have been gradually rebuilt, with some towns newly designated as tourism areas.[69]

Tourism is an unexpected choice for a region with as tragic a recent history as Wenchuan. There has been considerable controversy surrounding the earthquake and its victims, particularly on account of the concentration of deaths in collapsed elementary and middle schools. Many school buildings, such as the Fuxin No. 2 Primary School in Mianzhu, the Xinjian Elementary School in Dujiangyan, and the Beichuan Middle School in Beichuan, collapsed into rubble during the first tremors, trapping schoolchildren inside, while adjacent buildings remained standing with minimal damage. In one disturbing example, in all of Beichuan County, the Beichuan Middle School was the only building to collapse.[70] These irregular patterns led bereaved parents, many of whom had lost their only child in the quake, to reasonably assume that the schools had been constructed poorly, using subpar materials and failing to meet relevant building standards.[71] The government's sole response to such claims has been to assert that the earthquake was simply "too big," and that the collapse of buildings can in the end only be blamed on the quake itself.[72] In response to the state's refusal to examine or even acknowledge these potential issues, parents and activists such as Tan Zuoren, Huang Qi, and Ai Weiwei promoted a citizen's investigation into the collapsed schools. Both Tan and Huang have been given lengthy and clearly arbitrary prison terms for their efforts, while Ai has faced unrelenting harassment from the authorities.

Such heated controversies were only present implicitly during my visit, in the form of a variety of carefully constructed images of national unity and victory over tragedy under the leadership of the Communist Party. As we drove through the mountainous terrain leading from Chengdu to Wenchuan, propaganda billboards littered the countryside with such slogans as "No challenges could ever conquer the heroic Chinese people," "Resoluteness brings a smile to the faces of the Chinese people in times of hardship," and "Let's show off Wenchuan's new face." Glancing out the window as we sped past one sign after another, we soon arrived in Shuimo Old Town. We began by visiting an earthquake museum in an elaborately reconstructed pagoda at the edge of town, where we viewed images of state leaders visiting and delivering speeches in the rubble, as well as ethnic minorities in their national clothing happily dancing in the aftermath of reconstruction. Shuimo is, after all, a town inhabited by members of both the Han and the Qiang nationality, both of whom were thereby represented in this exhibition. Proceeding forward into the central thoroughfare in town, I was greeted by a seemingly endless stream of national flags hanging from both sides of the street. The placement of flags at every store along the lane, and even in spaces in between, seemed almost obsessive, covering over the complex recent history of the town through a carefully orchestrated patriotic spectacle whose uncertainty was hinted by its very insistence, and fully revealed by the equal frequency of closed-circuit television cameras on the streets.

The center of town was occupied by a square appropriately called "Harmony Square" (*Hexie Guangchang*). "Harmony" has emerged over the past decade as a keyword of former leader Hu Jintao, who had claimed that harmony (*hexie*) is a longstanding tradition of the Chinese people and the number one goal of his administration. In popular use, these positive culturalist connotations have been replaced by the idea's all-too-apparent political implications, such that the word can be used as a verb, "harmonized" (*bei hexie*) to refer to acts of state suppression: the deletion of Internet posts, erasure of media reports, closure of blogs and newspapers, and even arrests are now jokingly referred to as "harmonization." And correspondingly, any discussion of the contentious recent history of this region had received similar treatment in its all too harmonious reconstruction as a patriotic tourist destination, with Harmony Square at its core. A clumsily blunt poster on the edge of Harmony Square showing smiling local "nomads" giving the thumbs-

FIGURE 18. Poster features smiling residents declaring "The Communist Party is good!"

up sign expressed the message all too directly: "The Communist Party is good!"

Yet what was most striking in this town was not the carefully constructed discourse of national unity and victory under the leadership of the Communist Party, which was after all only to be expected in a multiethnic region with a painful recent past. What was most striking about Shuimo Old Town was that despite its name, nothing about the town was in fact old: everything was new. The town itself, after having been destroyed in the earthquake, had been rebuilt anew, but in an "old" style, in the years since 2008.

Prior to the earthquake, the actually existing old town of Shuimo had been built around heavy industry, with a number of machine parts factories along the river at the base of the town, resulting in insidious water pollution. According to the history presented to us at the local museum, when these factories and the lifestyle that had been built around them were destroyed along with the rest of the village in the 2008 earthquake, they were not rebuilt. Instead, this town that was once an embodiment of the modernist vision with its rows of factories and army of workers was rebuilt anew as an old-style town with a "traditional" feel and "ethnic" flavor. This old town was then not old in the genuine sense, but rather in an imaginary sense: its oldness was very new, envisioning an old town as it should be, with elaborate and elegant architectural designs, expansive thoroughfares free from overcrowding, and a carefree, natural feel.

The town's main street was lined with sturdy, solid stone blocks: precisely the type of materials that could reassure my friend in Shenzhen who bemoaned the unreliability of contemporary building structures. The wide thoroughfare stood in stark contrast to the narrow lanes and alleys of Guangzhou as well as nearby Chengdu, as did the noticeably effective enforcement of the ban on motorcycles and motor-scooters on the walking street. Behind the rows of flags on either side of the main street were two- to three-story buildings, made from wood rather than the concrete and tiles that are all too familiar in modern Chinese cities, and employing traditionalist architectural elements to provide a distinctive feel. The windows on the second floor of each building were decorated with elaborately carved wooden window frames, while the sweeping and overhanging roof styles evoked the powerful aesthetics of traditional architecture. A large arch marked the transition from the central thoroughfare into Harmony Square, whose south side was occupied by a reconstructed traditional terrace that had not been destroyed in the earthquake: in fact, the arch had already been torn down in the 1990s, but was promptly rebuilt in the aftermath of 2008, adding to the aesthetic feel of the town as a whole. If one were to remove the flags from the scene, this space resembled precisely how one might imagine premodern China. It was as if the past century was all but a dream, which had now been surpassed to return to a more peaceful past.

Large stone steps led up to the small stores that occupied these structures, selling traditional souvenirs and snacks. To my surprise, having traveled from my main field site in Guangzhou to the other side of the country, I found that many stores on this main thoroughfare were studios featuring both traditional and ethnic clothing for rent. Interested visitors could have their photographs taken in various ethnic styles or in imagined traditional clothing,

FIGURE 19. "Old-Style Clothing Photography" in Shuimo Old Town, Wenchuan County.

which resembled Han Clothing. As I strolled down the town's main lane, store owners stood in their doorways, each asking if I wanted to have some pictures taken. I chose to visit a store with the very direct name "Old-Style Clothing Photographs" (*Guzhuang Sheying*).

Entering the store, visitors are presented with a number of clothing options to choose from. I was promptly asked which type of "old style" clothing I might like to wear: minority clothing (*minzu fuzhuang*) or traditional style Chinese clothing (*Zhongguo gudai fushi*)?

I decided to wear the ethnic clothing of the Qiang, described as a "nomadic" minority group resident in this region of Sichuan. Taking advantage of the time preparing for my picture and fitting myself into an outfit that was a few sizes too small for me, I asked the owner about her life and business. She told me that business was profitable despite the many similar studios on this road, and that life as a whole was looking positive. "We have had some tragic events. Let's not talk about that. We've rebuilt. Now people come here from all over the country. It's fun to dress up, smile a little, and have a few pictures taken with beautiful Shuimo Old Town in the background."

Traveling to the other side of China, I found myself in a brand new "old town" surrounded by ethnic clothing. Here, where everything had been destroyed in a matter of minutes with the tremors of a massive earthquake, a new town had been rebuilt as old, illusorily burying the painful memories of the recent past through the exaltation and perpetual reenactment of a distant and glorious past. Victory was not only a victory over the tragic earthquake that devastated this region. Victory was also over a mundane modernity, the unending rows of factories, the smothering pollution, the interminable and repetitive work in the name of development, the anxieties, the narrow alleys, the uncertainty, the overcrowding, and the buzzing motor-scooters. All of that, the bustle and confusion of the present and its recent past, was erased, to be replaced with an image of a traditional and harmonious existence. Here, a town was able to be rebuilt in an image that was portrayed as eternal and natural, a reconstructed real China, while visitors were similarly able to rebuild themselves in ethnic and traditional clothing studios, producing images that froze their moment of transformation in time.

Everything looked just right, as if this was how everything was always supposed to be, and always had been. Yet as has been true throughout the cases examined in this book, these ideal images presented as everlasting and eternal were in fact products of considerably more recent developments and challenges. And as has also been true throughout the cases examined herein, the underlying dilemmas remained, unresolved, and barely hidden beneath the new surface presented as eternal, glorious, and unchanging.

NOTES

INTRODUCTION

1. Kevin Carrico, "Recentering China: the Cantonese in and beyond the Han," in *Critical Han Studies: The History, Representation, and Identity of China's Majority*, ed. Thomas Mullaney, James Leibold, Stephane Gros, and Eric Vanden Busche (Berkeley: University of California Press, 2012).

2. William Callahan, *China: The Pessoptimist Nation* (Oxford: Oxford University Press, 2010); Peter Hays Gries, *China's New Nationalism: Pride, Politics, and Diplomacy* (Berkeley: University of California Press, 2004); Christopher Hughes, *Chinese Nationalism in the Global Era* (London: Routledge, 2006).

3. Frank Dikötter, *The Discourse of Race in Modern China* (Oxford, Oxford University Press, 2015).

4. Stevan Harrell, "Introduction: Civilizing Projects and the Reaction to Them," in *Cultural Encounters on China's Ethnic Frontiers*, ed. Stevan Harrell, 3–36 (Seattle: University of Washington Press, 1995), 23.

5. Ma Rong, *Zuqun, minzu, guojia jiangou—dangdai Zhongguo minzu wenti* [Ethnicity, Nationality, and Nation-Building—Ethnic Issues in Contemporary China] (Beijing: Social Sciences Academic Press, 2012).

6. Fei Xiaotong, *Zhonghua minzu duoyuan yiti geju* [The Pattern of Diversity in Unity of the Chinese Nation] (Beijing: Central Nationalities University Publishing, 1999); Xu Jieshun, "Understanding the Snowball Theory of the Han Nationality," in *Critical Han Studies: The History, Representation, and Identity of China's Majority*, ed. Thomas Mullaney, James Leibold, Stephane Gros, and Eric Vanden Busche (Berkeley: University of California Press, 2012).

7. Don Kulick's critique of masochistic anthropology provocatively analyzes the libidinal economies latent within such identifications, highlighting how relationships to the Other are "not only about the Other but also about the self and the self's relation not only to the Other but to its own academic and social structures." See Don Kulick, "Theory in Furs—Masochist Anthropology," *Current Anthropology* 47, no. 6 (2006): 943.

8. See, for example, Daniel Vukovich's recent *China and Orientalism: Western Knowledge Production and the PRC* (London: Routledge, 2012), which discovers and rediscovers Orientalism everywhere from scholarship on the Great Leap Forward famine to representations of Tiananmen, reimagining these all-too-real tragedies as somehow the product of "Western knowledge production."

9. Allen Chun, "Fuck Chineseness: On the Ambiguities of Ethnicity as Culture as Identity," *Boundary 2* 23, no. 2 (1996): 111–38.

10. Ghassan Hage, *White Nation: Fantasies of White Supremacy in a Multicultural Society* (London: Routledge, 2000).

11. Antonia Finnane, *Changing Clothes in China: Fashion, History, Nation* (New York: Columbia University Press, 2008).

12. Jyrki Kallio, *Tradition in Chinese Politics: The Party-state's Reinvention of the Past and the Critical Response from Public Intellectuals* (Helsinki: Finnish Institute of International Affairs, 2011).

13. James Leibold, "More than a Category: Han Supremacism on the Chinese Internet," *China Quarterly* 203 (2010): 539–59.

14. Leibold, "More than a Category," 550.

15. Gries, *China's New Nationalism*, 4.

16. Jacques Lacan, "The Mirror Stage as Formative of the *I* Function, as Revealed in Psychoanalytic Experience," *Ecrits* (New York: Norton, 2006), 75–81.

17. Lacan, "The Mirror Stage," 78.

18. Niklas Luhmann. *Theory of Society, Volume 1* (Stanford, CA: Stanford University Press, 2012); Niklas Luhmann. *Theory of Society, Volume 2* (Stanford, CA: Stanford University Press, 2013).

19. Niklas Luhmann. *Political Theory in the Welfare State* (Berlin: De Gruyter, 1990), 105, 111.

20. Lacan. "The Mirror Stage."

21. Peter Sloterdijk, *Bubbles: Spheres I, Microspherology* (Los Angeles: Semiotexte, 2011); Peter Sloterdijk, *Globes: Spheres II, Macrospherology* (Los Angeles: Semiotexte, 2014); Peter Sloterdijk, *Foams: Spheres III, Plural Spherology* (Los Angeles: Semiotexte, 2016).

CHAPTER I

1. Zhou Qing. *Min yi he shi wei tian- Zhongguo shipin anquan xianzhuang diaocha* [What Kind of God? A Survey of the Current Safety of China's Food] (Beijing: China Worker's Publishing House, 2007).

2. He Xin, *Shei tongzhizhe shijie? Shenmi Gongqihui yu xin zhanzheng xiemi* [Who Rules the World? Revealing the Mysterious Freemasons and the New War] (Hong Kong: CNHK, 2010).

3. The notion of "zhenzheng" is translated here as "real," but also carries with it further connotations of "correct," "authentic," or "true." This phrase "bu shi zhenz-

heng de Zhongguo" suggests that China is not "as it should be," but remains based in the belief that China can be rectified to achieve its true status again.

4. Benedict Anderson, *Imagined Communities: Reflections on the Origin and Spread of Nationalism* (London: Verso, 1983), 5–6.

5. Anderson, *Imagined Communities*, 35.

6. Anderson, *Imagined Communities*, 26–27, 33.

7. Anderson, *Imagined Communities*, 35.

8. Peter Sloterdijk, *Stress and Freedom* (London: Polity, 2016), 3.

9. Jonathan Rée, "Internationality," *Radical Philosophy* 60 (1992): 4.

10. Michael Billig, *Banal Nationalism* (London: Sage, 1995).

11. Niklas Luhmann, *The Reality of the Mass Media* (Stanford, CA: Stanford University Press, 2000).

12. Lyn Spillman, *Nation and Commemoration: Creating National Identities in the United States and Australia* (Cambridge: Cambridge University Press, 1997).

13. Xu Guoqi, *Olympic Dreams: China and Sports, 1895–2008* (Cambridge, MA: Harvard University Press, 2008).

14. Rée, "Internationality," 4.

15. Dylan Evans, *An Introductory Dictionary of Lacanian Psychoanalysis* (London: Routledge, 1996), 20, 82–84.

16. Anthony Smith, *The Nation in History: Historiographical Debates about Ethnicity and Nationalism* (Hanover, NH: Brandeis University Press, 2000), 66.

17. Anderson, *Imagined Communities*, 7.

18. Anderson, *Imagined Communities*, 57–58.

19. Anderson, *Imagined Communities*, 58.

20. Peter Berger and Thomas Luckmann, *The Social Construction of Reality: A Treatise in the Sociology of Knowledge* (Garden City, NY: Doubleday, 1966).

21. Maurice Godelier, *The Mental and the Material* (London: Verso, 1986); Maurice Godelier, *The Enigma of the Gift* (Chicago: University of Chicago Press, 1999.

22. William Callahan, *China Dreams: 20 Visions of the Future* (Oxford: Oxford University Press, 2013).

23. Liu Xiaobo, *Dan ren du jian: Zhongguo minzu zhuyi pipan* [A Poisonous Blade: A Critique of Chinese Nationalism] (Taipei: Broad, 2006); Gries, *China's New Nationalism*.

24. Ziad Fahmy, *Ordinary Egyptians: Creating the Modern Nation through Popular Culture* (Stanford, CA: Stanford University Press, 2011).

25. Luhmann, *The Reality of the Mass Media*, 112–16.

26. Boris Groys, *The Total Art of Stalinism: Avant-Garde, Aesthetic Dictatorship, and Beyond* (London: Verso, 2011), 113.

27. Helmuth Plessner, *The Limits of Community: A Critique of Social Radicalism* (New York: Humanity Books, 1999); Luhmann, *Political Theory in the Welfare State*.

28. Groys, *The Total Art of Stalinism*, 3.

29. Smith, *The Nation in History*, 66.

30. Godelier, *The Enigma of the Gift*.

31. Sloterdijk, *Stress and Freedom*, 52.

32. Ferdinand de Saussure, *Course in General Linguistics* (LaSalle, IL: Open Court, 1986), 66.

33. Jacques Lacan, *Écrits* (New York: Norton, 2006).

34. Jacques Lacan, *The Four Fundamental Concepts of Psychoanalysis* (New York: Norton, 1978), 141, 206–7; Lacan, *Écrits*, 416.

35. Theodor Adorno, *Negative Dialectics* (New York: Seabury, 1973), 150–51.

36. Peter Sloterdijk, *Critique of Cynical Reason* (Minneapolis: University of Minnesota Press, 1987), 205.

37. Adorno, *Negative Dialectics*, 150.

38. Callahan, *China: The Pessoptimist Nation*.

39. Adorno, *Negative Dialectics*, 149.

40. Niklas Luhmann, *Observations on Modernity* (Stanford, CA: Stanford University Press, 1998), 50–55.

41. Luhmann, *Observations on Modernity*, 54.

42. Berger, Peter. *The Sacred Canopy: Elements of a Sociological Theory of Religion* (Garden City, NY: Doubleday, 1967).

43. Luhmann, *The Reality of the Mass Media*, 94.

44. Bruce Kapferer, *Legends of People, Myths of State* (Washington, DC: Smithsonian Institution, 1988); Wilhelm Reich, *The Mass Psychology of Fascism* (New York: Farrar, Strauss, & Giroux, 1970).

45. This is a term borrowed from Berezin's discussion of the ritual reconstruction of Italian identity under fascism. See Mabel Berezin, *Making the Fascist Self: The Political Culture of Interwar Italy* (Ithaca, NY: Cornell University Press, 1997), 27–30.

46. Plessner, *Limits of Community*, 115.

47. Peter Sloterdijk, *Thinker on Stage: Nietzsche's Materialism* (Minneapolis: University of Minnesota Press, 1989), 46.

48. Adorno, *Negative Dialectics*, 148.

49. Luhmann, *Observations on Modernity*, 105.

50. Niklas Luhmann, "Why Does Society Describe Itself as Postmodern?" *Cultural Critique* 30 (1995): 171–86.

51. Jonathan Rée, "National Passions," *Common Knowledge* 2, no. 3 (1993): 51.

52. In his Lacanian analysis of politics, Stavrakakis uses this phrase "that's not it" to represent the perpetual search for desire and its displacement, showing how it is precisely denial that perpetuates desire. See Yannis Stavrakakis, *Lacan and the Political* (London: Routledge, 1999), 45.

CHAPTER 2

1. This tradition was only broken in 2011, when participants at the APEC summit to be held in Hawaii were either not asked to dress in the "aloha" shirts often

associated with the islands, or, perhaps explicitly asked to refrain from doing so. According to Barack Obama's reflections on aloha shirts and APEC, "I got rid of the Hawaiian shirts because I looked at pictures of some of the previous APEC meetings and some of the garb that appeared previously and I thought this might be a tradition that we might want to break." See Adam Taylor, "APEC's Silly Shirts: The Awkward Tradition that Won't Go Away," https://www.washingtonpost.com /news/worldviews/wp/2014/11/10/apecs-silly-shirts-the-awkward-tradition-that -wont-go-away/?utm_term=.d692bf88d122. A series of photographs of the history of this political-sartorial practice can be found in the online article, "APEC Summits: What the Leaders Wore—In Pictures." http://www.guardian.co.uk/world /gallery/2011/nov/14/apec-summits-what-leaders-wore-in-pictures#/?picture=38182 5716&index=5.

2. Matthew Chew, "Contemporary Re-emergence of the Qipao: Political Nationalism, Cultural Production and Popular Consumption of a Traditional Chinese Dress," *China Quarterly* 189 (2007): 148–49.

3. Hazel Clark, *The Cheongsam* (New York: Oxford University Press, 2000).

4. Sites include www.ctcc-web.cn, www.tianhan.com.cn, www.hanweiyang.cn, www.hanyifang.com, www.confucianism.com.cn, and http://tieba.baidu.com /f?ie=utf-8&kw=%E6%B1%89%E6%9C%8D&fr=search. Cited in Jiang Yuqiu, Wang Yixuan, and Chen Feng. *Hanfu* [Han Clothing]. (Qingdao: Qingdao Publishing House, 2008), 161.

5. Groys, *The Total Art of Stalinism*.

6. Michael Puett, "Classical Chinese Historical Thought," in *A Companion to Global Historical Thought*, ed. Prasenjit Duara, Viren Murthy, and Andrew Sartori, 34-46 (Oxford: Wiley-Blackwell, 2014).

7. Albert Feuerwerker, "China's History in Marxian Dress," *American Historical Review* 66, no. 2 (1961): 323–53.

8. Callahan, *China: The Pessoptimist Nation*.

9. Eric Hobsbawm and Terence Ranger, eds., *The Invention of Tradition* (Cambridge: Cambridge University Press, 1983).

10. Edward Rhoads, *Manchus and Han: Ethnic Relations and Political Power in Late Qing and Early Republican China, 1861–1928* (Seattle: University of Washington Press, 2000), 61.

11. Rhoads, *Manchus and Han*, 62.

12. Although movement associations generally consist of about 50% men and 50% women, the carefully prescribed gender roles for each diverge greatly, as discussed in Chapter 6.

13. Perry Link, "China: The Anaconda in the Chandelier," *New York Review of Books*, April 11, 2002.

14. Jiang, Wang, and Chen, *Hanfu*.

15. "Representative to the People's Consultative Conference Recommends Designating Han Clothing as National Clothing (*Zhengxie weiyuan jianyi ba Hanfu dingwei guofu*)." www.confucianism.com.cn/html/A00030007/1540733.html.

16. Jiang, Wang, and Chen, *Hanfu*, 167.

17. "100 Scholars Issue a Joint Statement: Make Han Clothing the Olympic Outfit (*Bai ming zuezhe fachu lianhe changyi: Hanfu wei Aoyun liyi fuzhuang*)." http://news.xinhuanet.com/society/2007–04/05/content_5935634.htm.

18. "CPPCC Member Suggests Designing Official Han Ethnic Costume." http://www.womenofchina.cn/womenofchina/html1/special/15/379–1.htm; "Beijing Holds 12th NPC First Session Press Conference." http://www.womenofchina.cn/html/womenofchina/report/150414–1.htm. Thanks to James Leibold for bringing these recent cases to my attention.

19. Stevan Harrell, *Ways of Being Ethnic in Southwest China* (Seattle: University of Washington Press, 2001). 202–3.

20. Thomas Mullaney, *Coming to Terms with the Nation: Ethnic Classification in Modern China* (Berkeley: University of California Press, 2011), xix.

21. Fredrik Barth, ed. *Ethnic Groups and Boundaries: The Social Organization of Culture Difference* (Long Grove, IL: Waveland, 1969), 14.

22. Barth, *Ethnic Groups and Boundaries*, 15.

23. Susan Blum, *Portraits of "Primitives": Ordering Human Kinds in the Chinese Nation* (Lanham, MD: Rowman & Littlefield, 2001); Dru Gladney, "Representing Nationality in China: Refiguring Majority/ Minority Identities," *Journal of Asian Studies* 53, no. 1 (1994): 92–123; Harrell, "Introduction."

24. Magnus Fiskesjö, "Rescuing the Empire: Chinese Nation-building in the Twentieth Century," *European Journal of East Asian Studies* 5, no. 1 (2006): 15–44.

25. Gladney, "Representing Nationality in China."

26. Harrell, "Introduction," 27.

27. Susan McCarthy, *Communist Multiculturalism: Ethnic Revival in Southwest China* (Seattle: University of Washington Press, 2009), 130.

28. Harrell, "Introduction," 27.

29. Dru Gladney, *Dislocating China: Reflections on Muslims, Minorities, and Other Subaltern Subjects* (Chicago: University of Chicago Press, 2004), 13.

30. Harrell, "Introduction."

31. Dru Gladney, "Introduction: Making and Marking Majorities," in *Making Majorities: Constituting the Nation in Japan, Korea, China, Malaysia, Fiji, Turkey, and the United States* (Stanford, CA: Stanford University Press, 1998), 1–9.

32. Kalpana Seshadri-Crooks, *Desiring Whiteness: a Lacanian Analysis of Race* (London: Routledge, 2000).

33. This phrase "the Han man's burden" is derived from Pál Nyíri's "The Yellow Man's Burden: Chinese Migrants on a Civilizing Mission," *China Journal* 56 (2006): 83–106.

34. This term is derived from Judith Butler's articulation of "gender trouble." See Judith Butler, *Gender Trouble: Feminism and the Subversion of Identity* (New York: Routledge, 1990).

35. Song Qiang, et al., *Zhongguo keyi shuo "bu"—lengzhan hou shidai de zhengzhi yu qinggan jueze* [China Can Say "No"—Political and Emotional Choices in the Post–Cold War Era] (Beijing: China Industry and Commerce Joint Publishing House, 1996).

36. Katherine Palmer Kaup, *Creating the Zhuang: Ethnic Politics in China* (Boulder, CO: L. Rienner, 2000).

37. Gladney, "Representing Nationality in China."

38. Gerd Baumann, "Conceptualising Identities: Anthropological Alternatives to Essentialising Difference and Moralising about Othering," in *Grammars of Identity/Alterity: A Structural Approach* (New York: Berghahn Books, 2004), 20.

39. Gladney, "Introduction," 1.

40. This yearning for a lost innocence in tradition, prior to the disorienting process of "explication" and knowledge's paradoxical desecuring, is compellingly analyzed in Sloterdijk's *Foams*, 184–92.

41. Fred Davis, *Yearning for Yesterday: A Sociology of Nostalgia* (New York: Free Press, 1979), 34.

42. Yuan Weishi, *Wenhua yu zhongguo zhuangxing* [Culture and China's Transition] (Hangzhou: Zhejiang University Publishing, 2012), 46.

43. Hobsbawm and Ranger, *The Invention of Tradition.*

44. Arthur Waley, *The Analects of Confucius* (New York: Vintage Books, 1989).

45. Davis, *Yearning for Yesterday*, 34.

46. Stephanie Coontz, *The Way We Never Were: American Families and the Nostalgia Trap* (New York: Basic Books, 1992).

47. Sloterdijk describes modernity as existing within atmospheres that can no longer be taken for granted. Han Clothing and other neotraditionalist movements recognize this discomfiting homelessness, and aim to reconstruct the comforting "containers" of tradition. See Sloterdijk, *Foams*, 180.

48. Carrico, "Recentering China."

49. Xu, "Understanding the Snowball Theory of the Han Nationality," 113, 126.

50. Sloterdijk, *Foams.*

51. Qin Shao, *Shanghai Gone: Domicide and Defiance in a Chinese Megacity* (Lanham, MD: Rowman & Littlefield, 2013).

52. Zhou, *Min yi he shi wei tian.*

53. Elizabeth Economy, *The River Runs Black: The Environmental Challenge to China's Future* (Ithaca, NY: Cornell University Press, 2010).

54. He Qinglian, *Media Control in China* (New York: Human Rights in China, 2007).

55. Movement participants were reliably disappointed in most official media portrayals of the movement, which tended to downplay the ethnic and cultural aspects of the movement, portraying it instead as primarily a nostalgic fashion movement, or even suggesting that participants wished they could travel across time. One example of such a portrayal can be found at http://nie.163.com/news/2012/8/3/440_337977.html.

56. Davis, *Yearning for Yesterday.*

57. Davis, *Yearning for Yesterday*, 29.

58. "Suture" is employed here in a Lacanian sense, meaning a measure that, however temporarily, closes the gap between the imaginary and experience.

59. André Nusselder, *Interface Fantasy: A Lacanian Cyborg Ontology* (Cambridge, MA: MIT Press, 2009), 96.

60. Nusselder, *Interface Fantasy*, 6, 112–13.

61. The title of this section is a variation on the title of Harrell's *Ways of Being Ethnic in Southwest China* (University of Washington Press, 2001).

CHAPTER 3

1. Mark Lilla, *The Shipwrecked Mind: on Political Reaction* (New York: New York Review of Books, 2016), 137.

2. I propose this admittedly harsh yet linguistically honest translation in light of the proximity of this term to *shengcai* or *shengfan*, the word for culinary leftovers. The term "female leftovers" thus seems to more accurately render the abrasiveness of the original Chinese saying.

3. Mayfair Mei-hui Yang, *Gifts, Favors, and Banquets: The Art of Social Relationships in China* (Ithaca, NY: Cornell University Press, 1994).

4. Like Tsin Village, Kangle Village is also an urban village providing housing for migrant workers. One of the earliest urban villages in the city of Guangzhou, Kangle is notoriously "chaotic" (*luan*), home to cramped factories, a lively sex trade, and hundreds of winding alleys producing a superurban village south of Xingang Road that extends for miles towards neighboring Ke Village.

5. John Friedmann, *China's Urban Transition* (Minneapolis: University of Minnesota Press, 2005).

6. David Bandurski, *Dragons in Diamond Village, and Other Tales from the Backalleys of Urbanizing China* (Sydney: Viking, 2015).

7. Bandurski, *Dragons in Diamond Village*.

8. Bandurski, *Dragons in Diamond Village*.

9. Bandurski, *Dragons in Diamond Village*.

10. Verna Yu, "Guangzhou Slum Residents Battle Police," *South China Morning Post*, August 14, 2010.

11. Yu, "Guangzhou Slum Residents Battle Police."

12. Blum, *Portraits of "Primitives,"* 10.

13. Berger, *The Sacred Canopy*, 54.

14. Steven Sangren, "Women's Production: Gender and Exploitation in Patrilineal Mode," in *Chinese Sociologics: An Anthropological Account of the Role of Alienation in Social Reproduction* (London: Athlone, 2000), 153–85.

15. Franck Billé argues in his study of Sinophobic attitudes in Mongolia that the desire to imaginarily distance Mongolia from "Asia" is an attempted denial of Mongolia's undeniable ties to Asia. See Franck Billé, *Sinophobia: Anxiety, Violence, and the Making of Mongolian Identity* (Honolulu: University of Hawaii Press, 2015).

CHAPTER 4

1. Ludwig Feuerbach, *The Essence of Christianity* (Mineola, NY: Dover Publications, 2008).

2. For a comparative discussion of utilitarian and psychoanalytical readings of clothing, see James Flugel, *The Psychology of Clothes* (London: Hogarth, 1930).

3. Feng Yingzhi. *Hanzi yu fushi wenhua* [Chinese Characters and Sartorial Culture] (Shanghai: Donghua University Publishing, 2008).

4. Anne Hollander, *Sex and Suits* (New York: Knopf, 1994), 18.

5. Finnane, *Changing Clothes in China*.

6. Boris Groys, *On the New* (London: Verso, 2014).

7. Godelier, *The Enigma of the Gift*, 171.

8. Godelier, *The Enigma of the Gift*, 124.

9. Godelier, *The Enigma of the Gift*, 115.

10. Godelier, *The Enigma of the Gift*, 116.

11. Godelier, *The Enigma of the Gift*, 115.

12. James Harrison, *The Communists and Chinese Peasant Rebellions: A Study in the Rewriting of Chinese History* (New York: Atheneum, 1971).

13. Eugénie Lemoine-Luccioni, *La robe: essai psychoanalytique sur le vêtement* [A Psychonalytical Essay on Clothing] (Paris: Seuil, 1983).

14. Denis Fleurdorge, "Du vêtement en général . . . et de celui de l'exclusion en particulier [On Clothing in General . . . and Exclusionary Clothing in Particular]." *Le Sociographe* 17 (2005): 20.

15. The Onion, "Boss's Clout Evaporates After He's Seen in Shorts at Company Picnic," News in brief, June 25, 2015. http://www.theonion.com/article/bosss-clout-evaporates-after-hes-seen-shorts-compa-50757.

16. Flugel, *The Psychology of Clothes*, 183.

17. One alternative explanation of the meaning of this ritual is the association between hair and sexual maturity established in a number of papers in Hiltebeitel and Miller's *Hair*. In this regard, it is important to note that this is a coming-of-age ceremony, and the binding of the hair could thereby represent the desire to control female sexuality. The corresponding male ceremony forms the hair into a dominant phallic bun protruding directly from the top of the head. See Alf Hiltebeitel and Barbara D. Miller, eds., *Hair: Its Power and Meaning in Asian Cultures* (Albany: State University of New York Press, 1998). For further discussion of the sexual politics of the Han Clothing Movement, see Chapter 6.

18. Adam B. Seligman, Robert P. Weller, Michael J. Puett, and Bennett Simon, *Ritual and its Consequences: An Essay on the Limits of Sincerity* (Oxford: Oxford University Press, 2008), 28.

19. Arnold van Gennep, *The Rites of Passage* (Chicago: University of Chicago Press, 1960).

20. Victor Turner, *The Ritual Process: Structure and Anti-structure* (Ithaca, NY: Cornell University Press, 1977), 94.

21. Jing Jun makes a similar point in his ethnographic and historical study of self-proclaimed descendants of Confucius in Gansu amid the vicissitudes of cultural iconoclasm and restoration from the Maoist to the reform era. Observing the reconstruction of sacred rites based upon informants' childhood memories from decades ago, Jing Jun notes the cultural capital associated with both traditional characters and classical Chinese by right of their virtual elimination in the Maoist era. See Jing Jun, *The Temple of Memories: History, Power, and Morality in a Chinese Village* (Stanford, CA: Stanford University Press, 1996).

22. Seligman et al., *Ritual and Its Consequences*, 20.

23. Angela Zito, *Of Body & Brush: Grand Sacrifice as Text/Performance in Eighteenth-Century China* (Chicago: University of Chicago Press, 1997).

24. See Chapter 3, "Animism, Magic and the Omnipotence of Thoughts" in Sigmund Freud, *Totem and Taboo* (New York: W.W. Norton, 1989).

25. Seligman et al., *Ritual and Its Consequences*, 31.

26. Catherine Bell, *Ritual Theory, Ritual Practice* (New York: Oxford University Press, 1992), 129.

27. Seligman et al., *Ritual and Its Consequences*, 28.

28. This comment relates to Peter Gries's discussion of the perceived inversion of the proper global hierarchy within the discourses of modern Chinese nationalism, wherein the former "teacher" (i.e., China) has become a "student" to countries like the United States and Japan, producing a cognitively dissonant situation in need of resolution. See Gries, *China's New Nationalism*, 34, 39.

29. If it is indeed ritual that distinguishes people as people, the civilization–barbarian dichotomy is even starker in the contrast of ethnic performance and Han ritual described at the end of Chapter 2.

30. On the formation of political communities through ritual, see Mabel Berezin's study of ritual in Italian fascist politics, as well as Denis Fleurdorge's analyses of the role of ritual in constructing presidential (2001) and political (2005) power. Denis Fleurdorge, *Les rituels du président de la* République [The Rituals of the President of the Republic] (Paris: Presses Universitaires de France, 2001); Denis Fleurdorge, *Les rituels et les représentations du pouvoir* [Rituals and Representations of Power] (Paris: Editions Zagros, 2005).

31. Edmund Leach, *Political Systems of Highland Burma: A Study of Kachin Social Structure.* (London: London School of Economics and Political Science, 1954), 16.

32. George Homans, "Anxiety and Ritual: The Theories of Malinowski and Radcliffe-Brown," *American Anthropologist* 43, no. 2 (1941): 164–72.

33. Bell, *Ritual Theory, Ritual Practice*, 150.

34. Cited in Seligman et al., *Ritual and its Consequences*, 27.

35. Bruce Kapferer, *The Feast of the Sorcerer: Practices of Consciousness and Power* (Chicago: University of Chicago Press, 1997), 178.

36. Kapferer, *The Feast of the Sorcerer*, 180.

37. Turner, *The Ritual Process*, 125.

38. Seligman et al., *Ritual and Its Consequences*.

39. This analysis of the narcissistic nature of ritual action is derived from Steven Sangren's analysis of Nezha and his more recent work on the family as instituted fantasy. See Steven Sangren, *Chinese Sociologics: An Anthropological Account of the Role of Alienation in Social Reproduction* (London: Athlone, 2000); Steven Sangren, "Masculine Domination: Desire and Chinese Patriliny," *Critique of Anthropology* 29, no. 3 (2009): 255–78; and Steven Sangren, "The Chinese Family as Instituted Fantasy: or, Rescuing Kinship Imaginaries from the 'Symbolic,'" *Journal of the Royal Anthropological Institute* 19, no. 2 (2013): 279–99.

40. John Gillis, *A World of Their Own Making: Myth, Ritual, and the Quest for Family Values* (New York: Basic Books, 1996), 108.

41. Kristofer Schipper, *The Taoist Body* (Berkeley: University of California Press, 1993), 24.

42. Seligman et al., *Ritual and Its Consequences*, 42.

43. Susan Sontag, *On Photography* (New York: Farrar, Straus and Giroux, 1977), 141.

44. François Laruelle, *The Concept of Non-photography* (Falmouth, UK: Urbanomic, 2011).

45. Pierre Bourdieu, *Photography: a Middle-brow Art* (Stanford, CA: Stanford University Press, 1990), 76.

46. Sontag, *On Photography*, 13.

47. Bourdieu, *Photography*, 19.

48. Bourdieu, *Photography*.

49. Sontag, *On Photography*, 3.

50. Bourdieu, *Photography*, 76.

51. Roland Barthes, *Camera Lucida: Reflections on Photography* (New York: Hill and Wang, 1981), 5.

52. Laruelle, *The Concept of Non-photography*.

53. Sontag, *On Photography*, 63–64.

54. André Bazin, *Qu'est-ce qu le cinéma? 1: ontologie et langage* (Paris: Éditions du cerf, 1958).

55. Bourdieu, *Photography,* 30.

56. Bonnie Adrian, *Framing the Bride: Globalizing Beauty and Romance in Taiwan's Bridal Industry* (Berkeley: University of California Press, 2003), 204.

57. Sontag, *On Photography*, 116.

58. Barthes, *Camera Lucida*, 87.

59. Karl Marx and Friedrich Engels, *The German Ideology* (New York: International Publishers, 1972), 42.

CHAPTER 5

1. Theodor Adorno, *The Stars Down to Earth and Other Essays on the Irrational in Culture* (London: Routledge, 2002), 154.

2. Chew, "Contemporary Re-emergence of the Qipao."

3. Rhoads, *Manchus and Han*, 61.

4. James Lee and Robert Y. Eng, "Population and Family History in Eighteenth Century Manchuria: Preliminary Results from Daoyi, 1774–1798," *Qingshi wenti* 5, no. 1 (1984): 1–55, pg. 8, quoted in Rhoads, *Manchus and Han*, 18.

5. See also James Leibold's discussion of Manchu conspiracy theories within this Han-ist Movement, and their occasionally violent repercussions, in Leibold, "More than a Category."

6. Richard Hofstadter, *The Paranoid Style in American Politics* (New York: Vintage, 2008), 24, 36.

7. In an attempt to reflect movement discourses for the reader, the following paragraphs will use the terms "the Manchus" and "the Han" without quotation marks or other clearly necessary disclaimers, despite the inherently complex and uncertain nature of these two seemingly simple and straightforward words.

8. Dikötter, *The Discourse of Race in Modern China*, 3.

9. Uradyn Bulag, *The Mongols at China's Edge: History and the Politics of National Unity* (Lanham, MD: Rowman & Littlefield, 2002).

10. Cited in Dikötter, *The Discourse of Race in Modern China*, 12.

11. Mi Chu Wiens, in his study of anti-Manchu thought in the early Qing, characterizes early anti-Manchuism as "the prototype of Chinese nationalism," highlighting the significance of "*minzu*" (nationality/ ethnicity/race) in the word for nationalism (*minzu zhuyi*). See Mi Chu Wiens. *Anti-Manchu Thought During the Early Ch'ing*, Papers on China, from Seminars at Harvard University (Vol. 22A), (Cambridge, MA: East Asia Research Center, Harvard University, 1969), 20.

12. As discussed in Chapter 2, historian Edward Rhoads notes that Han adoption of Manchu clothing in the Qing was only required of the male scholar-official elite. See Rhoads, *Manchus and Han*. Rhoads's argument can then only be "explained" by including Rhoads's research as part of the Manchu conspiracy.

13. Cited in Kong Xiangji and Murata Yujiro, "*Sun Yixian yanshuo yu miehan zhengce- dui Riben dangan zhong liangfen zhongyao fanman wenxian zhi kaocha* ["Speeches of Sun Yat-sen" and "Policies to Eliminate the Han"—an Examination of Two Important Anti-Manchu Documents from the Japanese Diplomatic Files]," in *Jinian Sun Zhongshan danchen 140 zhounian guoji xueshu yantaohui lunwen ji* [Collection of Papers from an International Academic Seminar Marking the 140th Anniversary of Sun Yat-sen's Birth] (Beijing: Chinese Academy of Social Sciences, 2006), 121–23.

14. Kong and Murata, "*Sun Yixian yanshuo.*"

15. Norman Cohn, *Warrant for Genocide: The Myth of the Jewish World Conspiracy and the Protocols of the Elders of Zion* (London: Serif, 1967); Léon Poliakov, *The History of Anti-Semitism, Volume 4: Suicidal Europe, 1870–1933* (Philadelphia: University of Pennsylvania Press, 1985).

16. Tsou Jung, *The Revolutionary Army: A Chinese Nationalist Tract of 1903* (Paris: Mouton & Co., 1968).

17. *Mandu yundong zuijin da shiji* [Major Events in the Manchu Independence Movement], December 2011 (Last accessed February 12, 2013). http://www.xinhan

minzu.com/dv_rss.asp?s=xhtml&boardid=45&id=19782&page=1. Same document available at http://blog.boxun.com/hero/201306/jianshen/11_1.shtml.

18. Henry Ford, *The International Jew* (Minneapolis: Filiquarian Publishing, 2007), 8.

19. *Hanjun* bannermen are Han soldiers who fought in support of the Manchu Qing Dynasty.

20. Michael Barkun, *A Culture of Conspiracy: Apocalyptic Visions in Contemporary America* (Berkeley: University of California Press, 2013), 70.

21. Billé has found similar conspiratorial narratives in Mongolia of "Chinese" businesses operating under Mongolian guise. See Billé. *Sinophobia*, 63.

22. Niklas Luhmann, "Limits of Steering," *Theory, Culture, & Society* 14, no. 1 (1997): 41–57.

23. Ford, *The International Jew*, 237.

24. The name "queue films" ties these contemporary films directly to the humiliating bodily marker of Manchu domination from which the historical downfall of the Han began.

25. Barkun, *A Culture of Conspiracy*, 35.

26. "Gay Tinky Winky Bad for Children," BBC News, February 15, 1999. http://news.bbc.co.uk/2/hi/276677.stm.

27. Kathleen Stewart, "Conspiracy Theory's Worlds," in *Paranoia Within Reason*, ed. George Marcus (Chicago: University of Chicago Press, 1999), 15.

28. See, for example, Michael Barkun, *Religion and the Racist Right: The Origins of the Christian Identity Movement* (Chapel Hill: University of North Carolina Press, 1994); Mark Fenster, *Conspiracy Theories: Secrecy and Power in American Culture* (Minneapolis: University of Minnesota Press, 1999); Brian Keeley, "Of Conspiracy Theories," *Journal of Philosophy* 96, no. 3 (1999): 109–26; Peter Knight, *Conspiracy Nation: The Politics of Paranoia in Postwar America* (New York: New York University Press, 1999); Hoon Song, *Pigeon Trouble: Bestiary Biopolitics in a Deindustrialized America* (Philadelphia: University of Pennsylvania Press, 2010); and Harry West and Todd Sanders, *Transparency and Conspiracy: Ethnographies of Suspicion in the New World Order* (Durham, NC: Duke University Press, 2003).

29. For example, see Li Xiguang and Liu Kang, *Yaomohua Zhongguo de beihou* [Behind the Plot to Demonize China] (Beijing: China Social Sciences Publishing, 1996).

30. Karl Popper, *The Open Society and Its Enemies, Vol. 2: Hegel and Marx* (Princeton, NJ: Princeton University Press, 1963), 94–95.

31. The most incisive analysis of the desires and identifications implicit in the Marxist worldview is to be found in the third chapter of Jean-Francois Lyotard's *Libidinal Economy*, "The Desire Named Marx," in which he argues that "every political economy is libidinal." Jean-Francois Lyotard, *Libidinal Economy* (London: Athlone, 1993), 108.

32. Michael Schoenhals, "Demonizing Discourse in Mao Zedong's China: People vs. Non-people," *Totalitarian Movements and Political Religions* 8, no. 3–4 (2007): 465–82.

33. James Siegel, *Naming the Witch* (Stanford, CA: Stanford University Press, 2006).

34. Susan Harding and Kathleen Stewart, "Anxieties of Influence: Conspiracy Theory and Therapeutic Culture in Millennial America," in *Transparency and Conspiracy: Ethnographies of Suspicion in the New World Order*, ed. Harry G. West and Todd Sanders (Durham, NC: Duke University Press, 2003).

35. Luhmann, "Why Does Society Describe Itself as Postmodern?" 173.

36. Reflecting the mirroring relationship between the Manchus and the Han within this conspiracy theory, the argument that Manchus are dedicated to revitalizing the Qing Dynasty in turn produces an argument in support of the revitalization of the pre-Qing imperial order as a pure "Han" order.

37. Carrico, "Re-centering China."

38. Hofstadter, *The Paranoid Style in American Politics*, 4.

39. Hofstadter, *The Paranoid Style in American Politics*, 36.

40. John Gibson, *The War on Christmas: How the Liberal Plot to Ban the Sacred Christian Holiday Is Worse Than You Thought* (New York: Sentinel, 2005).

41. Jared Taylor, *White Identity: Racial Consciousness in the 21st Century* (Oakton, VA: New Century Foundation, 2011).

42. On this topic, see Michael Hechter's fascinating recent book *Alien Rule*, wherein he argues that alien rulers can be legitimate, and even proposes an international leadership marketplace, wherein countries might compete to draw in the most talented leaders from around the globe. Michael Hechter, *Alien Rule* (Cambridge: Cambridge University Press, 2013).

43. Marshall Sahlins, "The Stranger-King or, the Elementary Forms of the Politics of Life," *Indonesia and the Malay World* 36, no. 105 (2008): 177–99.

44. Song Hongbing, *Huobi zhanzheng* [Currency wars] (Beijing: CITIC Publishing, 2009).

45. He, *Shei tongzhi zhe shijie?*

46. Alain Badiou, *The Meaning of Sarkozy* (London: Verso, 2008), 3, 16.

47. Laruelle's *Anti-Badiou* usefully deconstructs Badiou's "anti-democratic, even aristocratic style," arguing that "Badiou is one of the most conservative and regressive philosophers that could be, dressed in the deceptive habits of modernity" (24, 35). See François Laruelle, *Anti-Badiou: On the Introduction of Maoism into Philosophy* (London: Bloomsbury, 2013).

48. Barkun, *A Culture of Conspiracy*.

49. Robert Costa, "Gingrich: Obama's Kenyan, Anti-Colonial Worldview," *National Review*, September 11, 2010. http://www.nationalreview.com/corner/246302/gingrich-obama-s-kenyan-anti-colonial-worldview-robert-costa.

50. Allen Chun, "Toward a Postcolonial Critique of the State in Singapore," *Cultural Studies* 26, 5 (2012): 670–87.

51. Chun, "Toward a Postcolonial Critique of the State in Singapore," 679.

52. Sadik Al-Azm, "Orientalism and Conspiracy," in *Orientalism and Conspiracy Theory: Politics and Conspiracy Theory in the Contemporary Islamic World*, Essays

in Honor of Sadik J. Al-Azm, ed. Ardnt Graf, Schirin Fathi, and Ludwig Paul (London: IB Tauris, 2011).

53. Chun, "Toward a Postcolonial Critique of the State in Singapore," 677.

54. Chun, "Toward a Postcolonial Critique of the State in Singapore," 685.

55. Edward Said, *Orientalism* (New York: Vintage Books, 1979), 45.

56. Gerd Bauman and Andre Gingrich's *Grammars of Identity/Alterity* insightfully expands Said's approach beyond the East–West binary into three grammars: orientalizing, segmentation, and encompassment. The result is a considerably more nuanced structural vision of identity as a process not burdened by geographical locations. See Bauman, "Conceptualizing Identities."

57. Said, *Orientalism*, 41.

58. Chun, "Toward a Postcolonial Critique of the State in Singapore," 685.

59. Here I am thinking of Siegel's discussion of the figure of the witch as simultaneously "revealing" and "concealing" in its stand-in as an explanation for the incomprehensible. See Siegel, *Naming the Witch*.

60. Song Qiang, et al., *Zhongguo bu gaoxing: da shidai, da mubiao, ji women de neiyou waihuan* [Unhappy China: The Great Time, Grand Vision, and Our Challenges] (Jiangsu: Phoenix Publishing, 2009); Song Qiang et al., *Zhongguo keyi shuo "bu."*

61. Song, *Huobi Zhanzheng*.

62. He, *Shei tongzhi zhe shijie?*

63. Lang Xianping. *Lang Xianping shuo xin diguo zhuyi zai Zhongguo: xiandai diguo zhuyi zhen mianmu yiji fengkuang de lueduo xingwei* [Lang Xianping Discusses Neo-imperialism in China: The True Face of Modern Imperialism and its Crazy Plundering Behavior], (Beijing: Red East, 2010).

64. Zeng Xun, *Kong Qingdong xianxiang pipan* [A Critique of the Kong Qingdong Phenomenon] (Beijing: China Fortune, 2012).

65. Harding and Stewart, "Anxieties of Influence."

CHAPTER 6

1. Erich Fromm, *The Sane Society* (New York: Rinehart, 1955), 58.

2. Cynthia Enloe, *Bananas, Beaches, and Bases: Making Feminist Sense of International Politics* (Berkeley: University of California Press, 1990).

3. Pierre Bourdieu, *Masculine Domination* (Stanford, CA: Stanford University Press, 2001), 33.

4. Nira Yural-Davis, "Gender and Nation," *Ethnic and Racial Studies* 16, no. 4 (1993): 627.

5. Bourdieu, *Masculine Domination*.

6. Nira Yural-Davis, "Women and the Biological Reproduction of 'the Nation,'" *Women's Studies International Forum* 19, no. 1/2 (1996): 17–24.

7. Farrer discusses the persistence of this closed virginity complex within the process of "opening." See James Farrer, *Opening Up: Youth Sex Culture and Market Reform in Shanghai* (Chicago: University of Chicago Press, 2002), 240–42.

8. Bourdieu, *Masculine Domination*, 48.

9. Sigmund Freud, *The Psychology of Love* (New York: Penguin Books, 2007), 174.

10. Afary examines similarly gendered traditionalist ideologies in Islamism and the debates that these ideologies have provoked. See Janet Afary, "The War against Feminism in the Name of the Almighty: Making Sense of Gender and Muslim Fundamentalism," *New Left Review* 224 (1997), 89–110.

11. The site was formerly located at the address www.ypzc.net, but has been closed since early 2012.

12. Yuan, *Wenhua yu Zhongguo zhuanxing.*

13. Afary, "The War against Feminism in the Name of the Almighty;" Elizabeth Zechenter, "In the Name of Culture: Cultural Relativism and the Abuse of the Individual," *Journal of Anthropological Research* 53 (1999): 319–47.

14. Handler, *Nationalism and the Politics of Culture in Quebec*, 50.

15. "Single men" here is literally written as "bare branches" (*guanggun*), a psychosexually suggestive term used commonly in Chinese popular culture to refer to single males.

16. "*Zhongguo guang gun tuanjie qi lai, bie rang yangren, heiren qiang Zhongguo nüren!*" [Single Men of China Unite, Stop Foreigners and Black People from Stealing Chinese Women!]. http://bbs.hanminzu.org/forum.php?mod=viewthread&tid=293030&extra=page%3D3.

17. Claude Lévi-Strauss, *The Elementary Structures of Kinship* (Boston: Beacon, 1969).

18. This metaphorical "protection of resources" reveals the foundational violence that subsequent commentators have noted in Lévi-Strauss's construction of the "exchange of women." See Gayle Rubin, "The Traffic in Women: Notes on the 'Political Economy' of Sex," in *Toward an Anthropology of Women*, ed. Rayna Reiter (New York: Monthly Review, 1975), 157–210. In "Gender and Nation," Yural-Davis also incisively notes that the core of this phenomenon is not so much "exchange" as control.

19. Although the correct terminology would be "indigenous" or "native," for the sake of accurately reflecting the tone of the original article, I have kept the term "Indian" as used therein (*yindi'an*). The same is true of the essay's repeated references to "black people," wherein the English phrasing, although coarse, may still be somewhat more polite than the connotations presumed by the original author.

20. Yinghong Cheng's research on racism in China convincingly argues that Chinese understandings of ethnicity or nationality are based in biological metaphors. See Yinghong Cheng, "From Campus Racism to Cyber Racism: Discourse of Race and Chinese Nationalism," *China Quarterly* 207 (2011): 561–79.

21. Xu, "Understanding the Snowball Theory of the Han Nationality."

22. Bourdieu, *Masculine Domination*, 19.

23. Sangren, *Chinese Sociologics.*

24. Fascinatingly, in his study of Sinophobic discourses in Mongolia, Franck Billé finds popular conspiracy theories claiming that "the Chinese state has programs encouraging Chinese men to go to Mongolia and have sex with Mongolian women in order to produce Chinese babies." Mirrored sexual anxieties are thus present on both sides of the border. See Billé, *Sinophobia*, 25.

25. Joane Nagel, "Masculinity and Nationalism: Gender and Sexuality in the Making of Nations," *Ethnic and Racial Studies* 21, no. 2 (1998): 252.

26. In a recent issue of *Positions*, William Callahan notes the centrality of the figure of the decapitated male and the raped woman in Chinese national self-representation. See William Callahan, "Textualizing Cultures: Thinking beyond the MIT Controversy," *Positions* 23, no. 1 (2015): 131–44. The portrayal of China as a raped woman is also noted by Peter Hays Gries in his *China's New Nationalism* (2004, 10), as well as in Rong Cai's analysis of Mo Yan's *Large Breasts and Full Hips*. See Cai Rong, "Problematizing the Foreign Other: Mother, Father, and the Bastard in Mo Yan's *Large Breasts and Full Hips*." *Modern China*. 29, no. 1 (2003): 108–37.

27. Freud, *Totem and Taboo*, 38.

28. Yural-Davis "Women and the Biological Reproduction of 'the Nation,'" 17.

29. Bourdieu, *Masculine Domination*, 13.

30. Bourdieu, *Masculine Domination*, 7.

31. Katherine Carlitz, "The Social Uses of Female Virtue in Late Ming Editions of Lienü Zhuan," *Late Imperial China* 12, no. 2 (1991): 117–48.

32. Bourdieu, *Masculine Domination*, 2.

33. Nagel, "Masculinity and nationalism," 254.

34. George Mosse, *Nationalism and Sexuality: Middle-Class Morality and Social Norms in Modern Europe* (Madison: University of Wisconsin Press 1985), 100.

35. Bourdieu, *Masculine Domination*.

36. Sloterdijk, *Foams*.

37. Gao Qihui, "We Are on the Wrong Path of Money Worship," *China Daily*, June 24, 2010. http://www.chinadaily.com.cn/opinion/2010–06/24/content _10013634.htm.

38. Zhong Xueping, *Masculinity Besieged? Issues of Modernity and Male Subjectivity in Chinese Literature of the Late Twentieth Century* (Durham NC: Duke University Press, 2000), 13.

39. Bourdieu, *Masculine Domination*, 37.

40. On the relationship between problems and solutions, and in particular the possibility of solutions as problems in and of themselves, see Luhmann, *Political Theory in the Welfare State*.

CONCLUSION

1. Gloria Davies, *Worrying about China: The Language of Chinese Critical Inquiry* (Cambridge, MA: Harvard University Press, 2007).

2. Gloria Davies makes a similar point in her analysis of the reversal of thought currents on China within Chinese critical discourse: "whereas the predicament (*kunjing*) of modern China had previously been explained through depictions of China as a 'land of darkness' over which the oppressive forces of Confucianism and traditional Chinese culture held sway, those depictions are now regarded as seriously flawed and a cause of the 'predicament' itself. Conversely, the preoccupation of many present-day intellectuals is with recovering China's cultural integrity or even civilizational grandeur." See Davies, *Worrying about China*, 9.

3. Jiang Qing and Daniel Bell, "A Confucian Constitution in China," *New York Times*, July 11, 2012.

4. Jiang Qing, *A Confucian Constitutional Order: How China's Ancient Past Can Shape its Political Future* (Princeton, NJ: Princeton University Press, 2012).

5. Jiang, *A Confucian Constitutional Order*, 37.

6. Jiang, *A Confucian Constitutional Order*, 27.

7. Jiang, *A Confucian Constitutional Order*, 29

8. Jiang, *A Confucian Constitutional Order*, 54.

9. Jiang, *A Confucian Constitutional Order*, 33.

10. Jiang, *A Confucian Constitutional Order*, 29.

11. Jiang Qing, *Zhengzhi Ruxue—dangdai Ruxue de zhuanxiang, tezhi yu fazhan* [Political Confucianism—The Orientation, Characteristics, and Development of Contemporary Confucianism] (Taipei: Yang Cheng Tang Media, 2003).

12. The use of the phrase "Way of the Humane Authority" is quite an imaginative way, in my reading, to make an anachronistic and authoritarian concept sound somewhat more pleasant.

13. Jiang, *A Confucian Constitutional Order*, 28.

14. Jiang and Bell, "A Confucian Constitution in China."

15. Jiang, *A Confucian Constitutional Order*, 41.

16. Jiang, *A Confucian Constitutional Order*, 41.

17. Jiang, *A Confucian Constitutional Order*, 41.

18. Jiang, *A Confucian Constitutional Order*, 41.

19. Jiang, *A Confucian Constitutional Order*, 42.

20. Jiang, *A Confucian Constitutional Order*, 186.

21. Jiang, *A Confucian Constitutional Order*, 27.

22. Jiang, *A Confucian Constitutional Order*, 27.

23. Although such a proposal would be quite unrealistic for China's democratic neighbors, Jiang Qing still attempts to incorporate such a recommendation into his program. His suggestion reads: "Since democracy manifests the flaw of the sole sovereignty of popular legitimacy and excludes cultural legitimacy, the political development of these countries [i.e., India, Japan, and Turkey] has turned its back on their own historical and cultural traditions. They have created a political system that is in rupture with their own tradition and without roots. This type of rootless system lacks the nourishing sustenance of the resources of the past millennia. In contrast, the Way of the Humane Authority can provide historical-cultural legitimacy, and so

non-Western countries will be able to draw on their own rich resources for their political development." Jiang's critique of democracy as hegemonic within Asia is then clearly not opposed to allowing his supposedly indigenous Chinese political system to assume a similarly hegemonic position within "the East" as a whole. See Jiang, *A Confucian Constitutional Order*, 39.

24. Jiang, *A Confucian Constitutional Order*, 29.

25. Jiang, *A Confucian Constitutional Order*, 34.

26. Jiang, *A Confucian Constitutional Order*, 34.

27. Jiang, *A Confucian Constitutional Order*, 2.

28. Jiang, *A Confucian Constitutional Order*, 3.

29. Jiang, *A Confucian Constitutional Order*, 27.

30. Berger, *The Sacred Canopy*.

31. Niklas Luhmann, *A Systems Theory of Religion* (Stanford, CA: Stanford University Press, 2012), 86, 111.

32. Popper, *The Open Society and its Enemies, Vol. II*.

33. Stavrakakis, *Lacan and the Political*, 125.

34. Jiang, *A Confucian Constitutional Order*, 48.

35. Jiang, *A Confucian Constitutional Order*, 29, 33, 34, 35, 36, 37, 48, 49, 66, 73, 75, 79.

36. Jiang, *A Confucian Constitutional Order*, 40.

37. Jiang, *A Confucian Constitutional Order*, 37.

38. This evocative phrase was used by Allen Chun to describe Kuomintang constructed political culture in postwar Taiwan. See Allen Chun, "An Oriental Orientalism: the Paradox of Tradition and Modernity in Nationalist Taiwan," *History and Anthropology* 9, no. 1 (1995): 27–56.

39. Ban Wang and Jie Lu, *China and New Left Visions: Political and Cultural Interventions* (Lanham, MD: Lexington Books, 2012), x.

40. Wang and Lu, *China and New Left Visions*, xi.

41. Wang and Lu, *China and New Left Visions*, xi.

42. Wang and Lu, *China and New Left Visions*, xi.

43. Qt. Wang and Lu, *China and New Left Visions*, xi.

44. Raymond Aron first observed the nostalgic nature of the Marxist exaltation of revolution, arguing that this nostalgia was a product of a complex mix of inevitable social imperfection, optimism, and impatience. See Raymond Aron, *The Opium of the Intellectuals* (Garden City, NY: Doubleday, 1955), 64–65.

45. In response to a paper by Gan Yang that describes the Maoist tradition as one of "equality," Yuan Weishi revealingly comments, "Gan Yang says that he wants to continue the 'equality' of the first 30 years of the People's Republic. But could he be a little more specific about what that equality consisted of? Declaring, based upon the *Quotations from Chairman Mao*, that some of our citizens were enemies? Transforming the majority of our population, including the peasants, into targets of "education" and thought reform? Is this real equality? Were peasants stuck in the countryside through the hukou system equal to everyone else? Were they celebrating China's 'capability to lead the world'?" See "*Yi shijie gongmin de yanguang shenshi*

yiqie (Consider Everything from the Viewpoint of a Global Citizen)," *Southern Weekly*, April 15, 2009, http://www.infzm.com/content/26991.

46. Milovan Djilas, *The New Class: an Analysis of the Communist System* (New York: Praeger, 1957).

47. Aron, *The Opium of the Intellectuals*.

48. Wang Hui, *The End of the Revolution: China and the Limits of Modernity* (London: Verso, 2009).

49. Daniel Vukovich, "The Battle for Chinese Discourse and the Rise of the Chinese New Left: Toward a Postcolonial Politics of Knowledge," in *China and New Left Visions: Political and Cultural Interventions*, ed. Ban Wang, and Jie Lu (Lanham, MD: Lexington Books, 2012), 74.

50. Kong Qingdong, "Mao Zedong Thought Can Attain Victory in Any and All Battles" (videotaped speech on the occasion of Mao's 119th birthday). http://v.youku.com/v_show/id_XNDkzMjc2OTYo.html.

51. Guan Jun and Zhang Lei, "Han Deqiang: Mao Is My Teacher," *Southern People Weekly*, October 12, 2012. www.nfpeople.com/News-detail-item-3730.html.

52. The use of such stock phrases in teleological analysis is described best by Raymond Aron, who stated "nothing will prevent people from clinging to the same old words—Capitalism, Imperialism, Socialism—to describe realities which have become quite different. And the words enable them, not to explain scientifically the course of history, but to lend it a significance which is fixed in advance. Thus the catastrophes are transfigured into means of salvation. In search of hope in an age of despair, the philosophers settle for an optimism based on catastrophe." See Aron, *The Opium of the Intellectuals*, 106.

53. Wang Hui, *China's New Order: Society, Politics, and Economy in Transition* (Cambridge, MA: Harvard University Press, 2003), 141.

54. Wang and Lu. *China and New Left visions*, xi.

55. Gao Mobo, *The Battle for China's Past: Mao and the Cultural Revolution* (London: Pluto, 2008); Vukovich, "The Battle for Chinese Discourse and the Rise of the Chinese New Left."

56. See the Utopia website, http://www.wyzxsd.com/index.php.

57. Robert Elegant, *The Center of the World: Communism and the Mind of China* (New York: Funk and Wagnalls, 2008).

58. Wang Hui, "The 'Tibetan Question' East and West: Orientalism, Regional Ethnic Autonomy, and the Politics of Dignity," in *The Politics of Imagining Asia* (Cambridge, MA: Harvard University Press, 2012).

59. Wang, "The 'Tibetan Question,'" 138.

60. Wang, "The 'Tibetan Question,'" 161.

61. Wang, "The 'Tibetan Question,'" 153.

62. Wang, "The 'Tibetan Question,'" 143, 147.

63. Wang, "The 'Tibetan Question,'" 188.

64. Wang, "The 'Tibetan Question,'" 179.

65. Wang, "The 'Tibetan Question,'" 199.

66. Engaging in further externalization, Wang proposes that the debate about the Sinification of Tibet could really be seen as a debate about Westernization, globalization, or capitalism. Even when the Western imperialist is physically absent, Wang can still develop a path to find him wherever necessary.

67. Wang, "The 'Tibetan Question,'" 226.

68. Xiaoming Ai, dir., *Women de wawa* [Our Children] (Hong Kong: University Service Center for Chinese Studies, Chinese University of Hong Kong, 2009).

69. "Wenchuan Tourism: Quake Town Reborn from Ashes," CCTV English, February 27, 2012. http://english.cntv.cn/program/newshour/20120227/114837.shtml.

70. Ai, *Women de wawa*.

71. Liao Yiwu, *Quand la terre s'ouverte au Sichuan: journal d'un tragedie* [When the Ground Opened in Sichuan: Journal of a Tragedy] (Paris: Buchet/ Chastel, 2010).

72. Ai, *Women de wawa*.

CHARACTER GLOSSARY

AYI 阿姨

AOQUN 襖裙

BAGUA 八卦

BAIJIA JIANGTAN 百家講壇

BAIJIN NAN 拜金男

BAIJIN NÜ 拜金女

BAIJIU 白酒

BAINIAN GUOCHI 百年國恥

BAOFAHU 暴發戶

BEI HEXIE 被和諧

BI WOMEN HAI HUA 比我們還華

BIANZIXI 辮子戲

BIAOYAN 表演

BU SHI ZHENSHI DE ZHONGGUO 不是真實的中國

BU SHI ZHENZHENG DE ZHONGGUO 不是真正的中國

CHENGREN 成人

CHENGREN LI 成人禮

CHENGZHONGCUN 城中村

CHOUFENG 抽風

CHUNJIE 純潔

CHUNJIE 春節

CU 粗

DA'AO 大襖

DAHAN 大漢

DAHAN ZHI FENG 大漢之風

DAXUE 大學

DI 地

DIGOUYOU 地溝油

DU 毒

DUJING 讀經

DUOYUAN YITI 多元一體

FANDANG FAN SHEHUI ZHUYI 反黨反社會主義

FANRI YOUXING 反日遊行

FUCONG 服從

FUQIANG 富強

FUZHUANG 服裝

GUDAI FUSHI 古代服飾

GUQIN 古琴

GUZHUANG SHEYING 古裝攝影

GUANXI 關係

GUANGGUN JIE 光棍節

GUANJIE 關節

GUOFU 國服

GUO JIERI 過節日

HANFU 漢服

HANFU YUNDONG 漢服運動

HANFU ZAISHEN, PING'AN YISHENG 漢服在身, 平安一生

HANJIAN 漢奸

HANJUN 漢軍

HANMINZU 漢民族

HANMINZU ZHUYI 漢民族主義

HANYU 漢語

HAOHAN 好漢

HAO LUOHOU 好落後

HEXIE 和諧

HEXIE GUANGCHANG 和諧廣場

HEIGUI 黑鬼

HEIREN 黑人

HONGWU SHEN JIAN 洪武神劍

HUREN 胡人

HUA 華

HUAXIA 華夏

HUAYI ZHI BIAN 華夷之辨

HUO HUASHI 活化石

JILI 筓禮

JINÜ 妓女

JITUO 寄托

JIZHE 筓者

JIANG DAOLI 講道理

JIAOYU 教育

JIE 節

LI 禮

LIYI ZHANSHI 禮儀展示

LIYI ZHI BANG 禮儀之邦

LIANGYI 兩儀

LUAN 亂

LUOPAN 羅盤

MAGUA 馬褂

MAIGUOZEI 賣國賊

MANFU 滿服

MEIGUO BAIREN WENHUA 美國白人文化

MIANQIANG QUANJIU 勉強勸酒

MIEHAN ZHENGCE 滅漢政策

MINZU 民族

MINZU FUZHUANG 民族服裝

MINZU ZHUYI 民族主義

NANZHUANG 男裝

NEIZHENG 內政

NONGCUN BAOWEI CHENGSHI 農村包圍城市

NÜWANG 女王

NÜZHUANG 女裝

QIANGBI 槍斃

QIANGSHI 強勢

QIPAO 旗袍

QISHI 歧視

QINLAO 勤勞

QINGAITIAO 青艾條

QINGKE 請客

QUJU 曲裾

RENAO 熱鬧

REN 人

REN SUOYI WEI RENZHE, LIYI YE 人之所以爲人者, 禮儀也

RIBEN GUIZI 日本鬼子

RUQUN 襦裙

SANCONG 三從

SAO B 騷 B

SHANLIANG 善良

SHANGSI JIE 上巳節

SHEHUI ZEREN 社會責任

SHENYI 深意

SHENYI 深衣

SHENG NÜ 剩女

SHUNÜ 淑女

SHUNÜ ZHENG 淑女証

SISHU 私塾

TAIJI 太極

TANGZHUANG 唐裝

TIFA YIFU 剃髮易服

TIAN 天

TIANCHAO 天朝

TIANDAO 天道

TIAN REN HE YI 天人合一

TIANZI 天子

TIAO DE HEN PIAOLIANG 跳得很漂亮

WAIGUOREN 外國人

WAIGUO SHILI 外國勢力

WANGDAO 王道

WANGZI 王子

WEIDA 偉大

WEIGUAN 圍觀

WENHUA DI 文化低

WENZI YU 文字獄

WOGUO 我國

WOMEN ZHONGGUO GUNIANG 我們中國姑娘

WUYI LAODONG JIE 五一勞動節

WUZHUDE HANZU MUQIN 無助的漢族母親

XINU 西奴

XIYI 西夷

XIFANG GONGYEHUA JIAOYU MOSHI 西方工業化教育模式

XIZHUANG 西裝

XIAODAO 小道

XIN BU ZAI JIALI 心不在家裏

XUANDUAN 玄端

XUEJUE 學覺

YAPIN ZHENCAO WANG 雅品貞操網

YANG 陽

YANGREN 洋人

YAO 搖

YAOGUN YINYUE 搖滾音樂

YIKAO 依靠

YI SHI ZHU XING 衣食住行

YIN 陰

YINDI'AN 印第安

YOU CHUANCHENG 有傳承

YOU GUIJU, ZHI TIANDI 有規矩, 知天地

YOU NEI WANG WAI DE MEI 由內往外的美

YUMCHA 飲茶

YUNDONG 運動

ZHENCAO NÜSHEN 貞操女神

ZHENGQUE JIAZHIGUAN 正確價值觀

ZHENGSHI 正視

ZHENGSHI KAISHI 正式開始

ZHIDUO 直裰

ZHONGGUO, JIAYOU 中國, 加油

ZHONGGUO MENG 中國夢

ZHONGHUA MINZU 中華民族

ZHONGGUO MINZU WENHUA JIE 中國民族文化節

ZHUANGZHONG YISHI GUOCHENG 莊重儀式過程

ZHIJU 直裾

ZIYUAN 資源

ZIZHI CUN 自治村

ZIZHI QU 自治區

ZIZHI XIAN 自治縣

ZONGZI 粽子

ZOU GUANG 走光

ZUQUN 族群

ZUOREN 做人

ZUO SHENGYI 做生意

BIBLIOGRAPHY

Adorno, Theodor. *Negative Dialectics*. New York: Seabury, 1973.

——. *The Stars Down to Earth and Other Essays on the Irrational in Culture*. London: Routledge, 2002.

Adrian, Bonnie. *Framing the Bride: Globalizing Beauty and Romance in Taiwan's Bridal Industry*. Berkeley: University of California Press, 2003.

Afary, Janet. "The War Against Feminism in the Name of the Almighty: Making Sense of Gender and Muslim Fundamentalism." *New Left Review* 224 (1997): 89–110.

Ai, Xiaoming, dir. *Women de wawa* [Our Children]. University Service Center for Chinese Studies: Chinese University of Hong Kong, 2009.

Al-Azm, Sadik J. "Orientalism and Conspiracy." In *Orientalism and Conspiracy Theory: Politics and Conspiracy Theory in the Contemporary Islamic World, Essays in Honor of Sadik J. Al-Azm*, edited by Ardnt Graf, Schirin Fathi, and Ludwig Paul. London: IB Tauris, 2011.

Anderson, Benedict. *Imagined Communities: Reflections on the Origin and Spread of Nationalism*. London: Verso, 1983.

Aron, Raymond. *The Opium of the Intellectuals*. Garden City, NY: Doubleday, 1957.

Badiou, Alain. *The Meaning of Sarkozy*. London: Verso, 2008.

Bandurski, David. *Dragons in Diamond Village, and Other Tales from the Back Alleys of Urbanizing China*. Sydney: Viking, 2015.

Barkun, Michael. *A Culture of Conspiracy: Apocalyptic Visions in Contemporary America*. Berkeley: University of California Press, 2013.

——. *Religion and the Racist Right: the Origins of the Christian Identity Movement*. Chapel Hill: University of North Carolina Press, 1994.

Barth, Fredrik, ed. *Ethnic Groups and Boundaries: the Social Organization of Culture Difference*. Long Grove, IL: Waveland, 1969.

Barthes, Roland. *Camera Lucida: Reflections on Photography*. New York: Hill and Wang, 1981.

Baumann, Gerd. "Conceptualising Identities: Anthropological Alternatives to Essentialising Difference and Moralising about Othering." In *Grammars of*

Identity/Alterity: A Structural Approach, edited by Gerd Baumann and André Gingrich. New York: Berghahn Books, 2004.

Bazin, André. *Qu'est-ce qu le cinéma? 1: ontologie et langage* (What Is Cinema? Vol. 1: Ontology and Language). Paris: Éditions du cerf, 1958.

Bell, Catherine. *Ritual Theory, Ritual Practice.* New York: Oxford University Press, 1992.

Berezin, Mabel. *Making the Fascist Self: the Political Culture of Interwar Italy.* Ithaca, NY: Cornell University Press, 1997.

Berger, Peter. *The Sacred Canopy: Elements of a Sociological Theory of Religion.* Garden City, NY: Doubleday, 1967.

Berger, Peter, and Thomas Luckmann. *The Social Construction of Reality: A Treatise in the Sociology of Knowledge.* Garden City, NY: Doubleday, 1966.

Billé, Franck. *Sinophobia: Anxiety, Violence, and the Making of Mongolian Identity.* Honolulu: University of Hawaii Press, 2015.

Billig, Michael. *Banal Nationalism.* London: Sage, 1995.

Blum, Susan. *Portraits of "Primitives": Ordering Human Kinds in the Chinese Nation.* Lanham, MD: Rowman & Littlefield, 2001.

Bourdieu, Pierre. *Masculine Domination.* Stanford, CA: Stanford University Press, 2001.

———. *Photography: A Middle-Brow Art.* Stanford, CA: Stanford University Press, 1990.

Breidenbach, Joana, and Pál Nyíri. *Seeing Culture Everywhere: From Genocide to Consumer Habits.* Seattle: University of Washington Press, 2009.

Bulag, Uradyn. *The Mongols at China's Edge: History and the Politics of National Unity.* Lanham, MD: Rowman & Littlefield, 2002.

Butler, Judith. *Gender Trouble: Feminism and the Subversion of Identity.* New York: Routledge, 1990.

Cai, Rong. "Problematizing the Foreign Other: Mother, Father, and the Bastard in Mo Yan's *Large Breasts and Full Hips.*" *Modern China* 29, no. 1 (January 2003): 108–37.

Callahan, William. *China: The Pessoptimist Nation.* Oxford: Oxford University Press, 2010.

———. "Textualizing Cultures: Thinking beyond the MIT Controversy." *Positions* 23, 1 (2015): 131–44.

Carlitz, Katherine. "The Social Uses of Female Virtue in Late Ming Editions of *Lienü Zhuan.*" *Late Imperial China* 12, no. 2 (1991): 117–48.

Carrico, Kevin. "Recentering China: The Cantonese in and beyond the Han." In *Critical Han Studies: The History, Representation, and Identity of China's Majority*, edited by Thomas Mullaney, James Leibold, Stephane Gros, and Eric Vanden Busche. Berkeley: University of California Press, 2012.

Cheng, Yinghong. "From Campus Racism to Cyber Racism: Discourse of Race and Chinese Nationalism." *China Quarterly* 207 (2011): 561–79.

Chew, Matthew. "Contemporary Re-emergence of the Qipao: Political Nationalism, Cultural Production and Popular Consumption of a Traditional Chinese Dress." *China Quarterly* 189 (2007): 144–61.

Chun, Allen. "Fuck Chineseness: On the Ambiguities of Ethnicity as Culture as Identity." *Boundary 2* 23, no. 2 (1996): 111–38.

———. "An Oriental Orientalism: The Paradox of Tradition and Modernity in Nationalist Taiwan." *History and Anthropology* 19, no. 1 (1995): 27–56.

———. "Toward a Postcolonial Critique of the State in Singapore." *Cultural Studies* 26, no. 5 (2012): 670–87.

Clark, Hazel. *The Cheongsam*. Oxford: Oxford University Press, 2000.

Cohn, Norman. *Warrant for Genocide: The Myth of the Jewish World Conspiracy and the Protocols of the Elders of Zion*. London: Serif, 1967.

Coontz, Stephanie. *The Way We Never Were: American Families and the Nostalgia Trap*. New York: Basic Books, 1992.

Cui, Zhiyuan. "Partial Intimations of the Coming Whole: The Chongqing Experiment in Light of the Theories of Henry George, James Meade, and Antonio Gramsci." *Modern China* 37 no. 6 (2011): 646–60.

Davies, Gloria. *Worrying about China: The Language of Chinese Critical Inquiry*. New York: Free Press, 2007.

Davis, Fred. *Yearning for Yesterday: A Sociology of Nostalgia*. New York: Free Press, 1979.

Dikötter, Frank. *The Discourse of Race in Modern China*. Oxford: Oxford University Press, 2015.

Djilas, Milovan. *The New Class: An Analysis of the Communist System*. New York: Praeger, 1957.

Economy, Elizabeth. *The River Runs Black: The Environmental Challenge to China's Future*. Ithaca, NY: Cornell University Press, 2010.

Elegant, Robert. *The Center of the World: Communism and the Mind of China*. New York: Funk and Wagnalls, 1968.

Enloe, Cynthia. *Bananas, Beaches, and Bases: Making Feminist Sense of International Politics*. Berkeley: University of California Press, 1990.

Evans, Dylan. *An Introductory Dictionary of Lacanian Psychoanalysis*. London: Routledge, 1996.

Fahmy, Ziad. *Ordinary Egyptians: Creating the Modern Nation through Popular Culture*. Stanford, CA: Stanford University Press, 2011.

Farrer, James. *Opening Up: Youth Sex Culture and Market Reform in Shanghai*. Chicago: University of Chicago Press, 2002.

Fei, Xiaotong. *Zhonghua minzu duoyuan yiti geju* [The Pattern of Diversity in Unity of the Chinese Nation]. Beijing: Central Nationalities University Publishing, 1999.

Feng, Yingzhi. *Hanzi yu fushi wenhua* [Chinese Characters and Sartorial Culture]. Shanghai: Donghua University Publishing, 2008.

Fenster, Mark. *Conspiracy Theories: Secrecy and Power in American Culture*. Minneapolis: University of Minnesota Press, 1999.

Feuerbach, Ludwig. *The Essence of Christianity*. Mineola, NY: Dover Publications, 2008.

Feuerwerker, Albert. "China's History in Marxian Dress." *American Historical Review* 66, no. 2 (1961): 323–53.

Finnane, Antonia. *Changing Clothes in China: Fashion, History, Nation*. New York: Columbia University Press, 2008.

Fiskesjö, Magnus. "Rescuing the Empire: Chinese Nation-Building in the Twentieth Century." *European Journal of East Asian Studies* 5, no. 1 (2006): 15–44.

Fleurdorge, Denis. *Les Rituels du président de la République* [The Rituals of the President of the Republic]. Paris: Presses Universitaires des France, 2001.

———. *Les rituels et les représentations du pouvoir* [Rituals and Representations of Power]. Paris: Editions Zagros, 2005.

———. "Du vêtement en général . . . et de celui de l'exclusion en particulier [On Clothing in General . . . and Exclusionary Clothing in Particular]." *Le Sociographe* 17 (2005).

Flugel, J. C. *The Psychology of Clothes*. London: Hogarth, 1930.

Ford, Henry. *The International Jew: The World's Foremost Problem*. Dearborn: Dearborn Publishing, 1922.

Freud, Sigmund. *The Psychology of Love*. New York: Penguin, 2007.

———. *Totem and Taboo: Some Points of Agreement between the Mental Lives of Savages and Neurotics*. New York: W.W. Norton, 1989.

Friedmann, John. *China's Urban Transition*. Minneapolis: University of Minnesota Press, 2005.

Fromm, Erich. *The Sane Society*. New York: Rinehart, 1955.

Gao, Mobo. *The Battle for China's Past: Mao and the Cultural Revolution*. London: Pluto, 2008.

Gao, Qihui, "We Are on the Wrong Path of Money Worship," *China Daily*, June 24, 2010.

van Gennep, Arnold. 1960. *The Rites of Passage*. Chicago: University of Chicago Press, 1960.

Gibson, John. 2005. *The War on Christmas: How the Liberal Plot to Ban the Sacred Christian Holiday Is Worse Than You Thought*. New York: Sentinel, 2005.

Gillis, John R. 1996. *A World of Their Own Making: Myth, Ritual, and the Quest for Family Values*. New York: Basic Books, 1996.

Gladney, Dru. *Dislocating China: Reflections on Muslims, Minorities, and Other Subaltern Subjects*. Chicago: University of Chicago Press, 2004.

———. "Introduction: Making and Marking Majorities." In *Making Majorities: Constituting the Nation in Japan, Korea, China, Malaysia, Fiji, Turkey, and the United States*, edited by Dru Gladney, 1–9. Stanford, CA: Stanford University Press, 1998.

———. "Representing Nationality in China: Refiguring Majority/ Minority Identities." *Journal of Asian Studies* 53, no. 1 (1994): 92–123.

Godelier, Maurice. *The Enigma of the Gift*. Chicago: University of Chicago Press, 1999.

———. *The Mental and the Material*. London: Verso, 1986.

Gries, Peter Hays. 2004. *China's New Nationalism: Pride, Politics, and Diplomacy*. Berkeley: University of California Press, 2004.

Groys, Boris. *The Total Art of Stalinism: Avant-Garde, Aesthetic Dictatorship, and Beyond*. London: Verso, 1992.

———. 1992. *On the New*. London: Verso, 1992.

Hage, Ghassan. *White Nation: Fantasies of White Supremacy in a Multicultural Society*. London: Routledge, 2000.

Handler, Richard. *Nationalism and the Politics of Culture in Quebec*. Madison: University of Wisconsin Press, 1988.

Harding, Susan, and Kathleen Stewart. "Anxieties of Influence: Conspiracy Theory and Therapeutic Culture in Millennial America." In *Transparency and Conspiracy: Ethnographies of Suspicion in the New World Order*, edited by Harry G. West and Todd Sanders. Durham, NC: Duke University Press, 2003.

Harrell, Stevan. "Introduction: Civilizing Projects and the Reaction to Them." In *Cultural Encounters of China's Ethnic Frontiers*, edited by Stevan Harrell, 3–36. Seattle: University of Washington Press, 1995.

———. *Ways of Being Ethnic in Southwest China*. Seattle: University of Washington Press, 2001.

Harrison, James. *The Communists and Chinese Peasant Rebellions: A Study in the Rewriting of Chinese History*. New York: Atheneum, 1971.

He, Qinglian. *The Fog of Censorship: Media Control in China*. New York: Human Rights in China, 2007.

He, Xin. *Shei tongzhizhe shijie? Shenmi Gongqihui yu xin zhanzheng xiemi* [Who Rules the World? Revealing the Mysterious Freemasons and the New War]. Hong Kong: CNHK Publications Limited, 2010.

Hechter, Michael. *Alien Rule*. Cambridge: Cambridge University Press, 2013.

Hiltebeitel, Alf, and Barbara D. Miller, eds. 1998. *Hair: Its Power and Meaning in Asian Cultures*. Albany: State University of New York Press.

Hobsbawm, Eric, and Terence Ranger, eds. *The Invention of Tradition*. Cambridge: Cambridge University Press, 1983.

Hofstadter, Richard. *The Paranoid Style in American Politics*. New York: Vintage, 2008.

Hollander, Anne. *Sex and Suits*. New York: Knopf, 1994.

Homans, George C. "Anxiety and Ritual: The Theories of Malinowski and Radcliffe-Brown." *American Anthropologist* 43, no. 2 (Part 1) (1941): 164–72.

Hughes, Christopher. *Chinese Nationalism in the Global Era*. London: Routledge, 2006.

Jiang, Qing. *A Confucian Constitutional Order: How China's Ancient Past Can Shape its Political Future*. Princeton, NJ: Princeton University Press, 2012.

———. *Zhengzhi Ruxue- dangdai Ruxue de zhuanxiang, tezhi yu fazhan* [Political Confucianism—The Orientation, Characteristics, and Development of Contemporary Confucianism]. Taipei: Yang Cheng Tang Media, 2003.

Jiang, Qing, and Daniel Bell. "A Confucian Constitution in China." *New York Times*, July 11, 2012.

Jiang Yuqiu, Wang Yixuan, and Chen Feng. *Hanfu* [Han Clothing]. Qingdao: Qingdao Publishing House, 2008.

Jing, Jun. *The Temple of Memories: History, Power, and Morality in a Chinese Village.* Stanford, CA: Stanford University Press, 1996.

Kallio, Jyrki. *Tradition in Chinese Politics: The Party-State's Reinvention of the Past and the Critical Response from Public Intellectuals.* Helsinki: Finnish Institute of International Affairs, 2011.

Kapferer, Bruce. *The Feast of the Sorcerer: Practices of Consciousness and Power.* Chicago: University of Chicago Press, 1997.

————. *Legends of People, Myths of State: Violence, Intolerance, and Political Culture in Sri Lanka and Australia.* Washington, DC: Smithsonian Institution, 1988.

Kaup, Katherine Palmer. *Creating the Zhuang: Ethnic Politics in China.* Boulder, CO: L. Rienner, 2000.

Keeley, Brian. "Of Conspiracy Theories." *Journal of Philosophy* 96, no. 3 (1999): 109–26.

Kong, Xiangji, and Murata Yujiro. "Sun Yixian yanshuo yu miehan zhengce- dui Riben dangan zhong liangfen zhongyao fanman wenxian zhi kaocha" ["Speeches of Sun Yat-sen" and "Policies to Eliminate the Han"—An Examination of Two Important Anti-Manchu Documents from the Japanese Diplomatic Files]. In *Jinian Sun Zhongshan danchen 140 zhounian guoji xueshu yantaohui lunwen ji* [Collection of Papers from an International Academic Seminar Marking the 140th Anniversary of Sun Yat-sen's Birth]. Beijing: Chinese Academy of Social Sciences, 2006.

Knight, Peter. *Conspiracy Nation: The Politics of Paranoia in Postwar America.* New York: New York University Press, 2002.

Kulick, Don. "Theory in Furs: Masochist Anthropology." *Current Anthropology* 47, no. 6 (2006): 933–52.

Lacan, Jacques. *Écrits: The First Complete Edition in English.* New York: Norton, 2006.

————. *The Four Fundamental Concepts of Psychoanalysis.* New York: Norton, 1978.

————. "The Mirror Stage as Formative of the *I* Function, as Revealed in Psychoanalytic Experience." In *Ecrits*, 75–81. New York: Norton, 2006.

Lang Xianping. 2010. *Lang Xianping shuo xin diguo zhuyi zai Zhongguo: xiandai diguo zhuyi zhen mianmu yiji fengkuang de lueduo xingwei* [Lang Xianping Discusses Neo-Imperialism in China: The True Face of Modern Imperialism and its Crazy Plundering]. Beijing: Red East, 2010.

Laruelle, François. *Anti-Badiou: On the Introduction of Maoism into Philosophy.* London: Bloomsbury, 2013.

————. *The Concept of Non-photography.* Falmouth, UK: Urbanomic, 2011.

Leach, Edmund. *Political Systems of Highland Burma: A Study of Kachin Social Structure.* London: London School of Economics and Political Science, 1954.

Lee, James, and Rorbert Y. Eng. "Population and Family History in Eighteenth Century Manchuria: Preliminary Results from Daoyi, 1774–1798." *Qingshi wenti* 5, no. 1 (1984): 1–55.

Leibold, James. "More Than a Category: Han Supremacism on the Chinese Internet." *China Quarterly* 203 (2010): 539–59.

Lemoine-Luccioni, Eugénie. 1983. *La robe: essai psychoanalytique sur le vêtement* [A Psychoanalytical Essay on Clothing]. Paris: Seuil, 1983.

Lévi-Strauss, Claude. *The Elementary Structures of Kinship*. Boston: Beacon Press, 1969.

Li, Xiguang, and Liu Kang. *Yaomohua Zhongguo de beihou* [Behind the Plot to Demonize China]. Beijing: China Social Sciences Publishing, 1996.

Liao, Yiwu. *Quand la terre s'ouverte au Sichuan: journal d'un tragedie* [When the Ground Opened in Sichuan: Journal of a Tragedy]. Paris: Buchet/ Chastel, 2010.

Lilla, Mark. *The Shipwrecked Mind: On Political Reaction*. New York: New York Review of Books, 2016.

Link, Perry. "China: The Anaconda in the Chandelier." *New York Review of Books*, April 11, 2002.

Liu, Xiaobo. *Dan ren du jian: Zhongguo minzu zhuyi pipan* [A Poisonous Blade: A Critique of Chinese Nationalism]. Taipei: Broad Press, 2006.

Luhmann, Niklas. "Limits of Steering." *Theory, Culture, & Society* 14, no. 1 (1997): 41–57.

———. *Observations on Modernity*. Stanford, CA: Stanford University Press, 1998.

———. *Political Theory in the Welfare State*. Berlin: De Gruyter, 1990.

———. *The Reality of the Mass Media*. Stanford, CA: Stanford University Press, 2000.

———. *A Systems Theory of Religion*. Stanford, CA: Stanford University Press, 2012.

———. *Theory of Society, Vol. 1*. Stanford, CA: Stanford University Press, 2012.

———. *Theory of Society, Vol. 2*. Stanford, CA: Stanford University Press, 2013.

———. "Why Does Society Describe Itself as Postmodern?" *Cultural Critique* 30 (1995): 171–86.

Lyotard, Jean-Francois. *Libidinal Economy*. London: Athlone, 1993.

Marx, Karl, and Friedrich Engels. *The German Ideology*. New York: International Publishers, 1972.

McCarthy, Susan. *Communist Multiculturalism: Ethnic Revival in Southwest China*. Seattle: University of Washington Press, 2009.

Mosse, George L. *Nationalism and Sexuality: Middle-Class Morality and Social Norms in Modern Europe*. Madison: University of Wisconsin Press, 1985.

Mullaney, Thomas. *Coming to Terms with the Nation: Ethnic Classification in Modern China*. Berkeley: University of California Press, 2011.

Nagel, Joane. "Masculinity and Nationalism: Gender and Sexuality in the Making of Nations." *Ethnic and Racial Studies* 21, no. 2 (1998): 242–69.

Narumi, Hiroshi. *Kosupure-suru shakai: sabukaruchā no shintai bunka* [The Cosplay Society: Subculture and Body Culture]. Tokyo: Serika Shobō, 2009.

Nietzsche, Friedrich. *The Birth of Tragedy, and the Case of Wagner*. New York: Vintage Books, 1967.

Nusselder, André. *Interface Fantasy: A Lacanian Cyborg Ontology*. Cambridge, MA: MIT Press, 2009.

Nyíri, Pál. "The Yellow Man's Burden: Chinese Migrants on a Civilizing Mission." *China Journal*, no. 56 (July 2006): 83–106.

The Onion. "Boss's Clout Evaporates After He's Seen in Shorts at Company Picnic." *Onion News in Brief*, June 25, 2015. http://www.theonion.com/article/bosss-clout -evaporates-after-hes-seen-shorts-compa-50757.

Plessner, Helmuth. *The Limits of Community: A Critique of Social Radicalism*. New York: Humanity Books, 1999.

Poliakov, Léon. *The History of Anti-Semitism, Volume 4: Suicidal Europe, 1870–1933*. Philadelphia: University of Pennsylvania Press, 1985.

Popper, Karl. *The Open Society and its Enemies, Vol. 2: Hegel and Marx*. Princeton, NJ: Princeton University Press, 1963.

Puett, Michael. "Classical Chinese Historical Thought." In *A Companion to Global Historical Thought*, edited by Prasenjit Duara, Viren Murthy, and Andrew Sartori, 34–46. Oxford: Wiley-Blackwell, 2014.

Rée, Jonathan. "Internationality." *Radical Philosophy*, no. 60 (1992): 3–11.

———. "National Passions." *Common Knowledge* 2, no. 3 (1993): 43–54.

Reich, Wilhelm. *The Mass Psychology of Fascism*. New York: Farrar, Strauss, & Giroux, 1970.

Rhoads, Edward J. M. *Manchus and Han: Ethnic Relations and Political Power in Late Qing and Early Republican China, 1861–1928*. Seattle: University of Washington Press, 2000.

Rubin, Gayle. "The Traffic in Women: Notes on the 'Political Economy' of Sex." In *Toward an Anthropology of Women*, edited by Rayna Reiter, 157–210. New York: Monthly Review, 1975.

Sahlins, Marshall. "The Stranger-King or, the Elementary Forms of the Politics of Life." *Indonesia and the Malay World* 36, no. 105 (2008): 177–99.

Said, Edward. *Orientalism*. New York: Vintage Books, 1979.

Sangren, Steven. "The Chinese Family as Instituted Fantasy: or, Rescuing Kinship Imaginaries from the 'Symbolic.'" *Journal of the Royal Anthropological Institute* 19, no. 2 (2013): 279–99.

———. *Chinese Sociologics: An Anthropological Account of the Role of Alienation in Social Reproduction*. London: Athlone, 2000.

———. "Masculine Domination: Desire and Chinese Patriliny." *Critique of Anthropology* 29, no. 3 (2009): 255–78.

———. "Women's Production: Gender and Exploitation in Patrilineal Mode." In *Chinese Sociologics: An Anthropological Account of the Role of Alienation in Social Reproduction*, 153–85. London: Athlone, 2000.

de Saussure, Ferdinand. *Course in General Linguistics*. LaSalle, IL: Open Court, 1986.

Schipper, Kristofer. *The Taoist Body*. Berkeley: University of California Press, 1993.

Schoenhals, Michael. "Demonizing Discourse in Mao Zedong's China: People vs. Non-people." *Totalitarian Movements and Political Religions* 8, no. 3–4 (2007): 465–82.

Seshadri-Crooks, Kalpana. *Desiring Whiteness: A Lacanian Analysis of Race.* London: Routledge, 2000.

Seligman, Adam B., Robert P. Weller, Michael J. Puett, and Bennett Simon. *Ritual and Its Consequences: An Essay on the Limits of Sincerity.* Oxford: Oxford University Press, 2008.

Shao, Qin. *Shanghai Gone: Domicide and Defiance in a Chinese Megacity.* Lanham, MD: Rowman & Littlefield, 2013.

Siegel, James. *Naming the Witch.* Stanford, CA: Stanford University Press, 2006.

Sloterdijk, Peter. *Bubbles: Spheres Vol. 1, Microspherology.* Los Angeles: Semiotext(e), 2011.

———. *Critique of Cynical Reason.* Minneapolis: University of Minnesota Press, 1987.

———. *Foams: Spheres Vol. 3, Plural Spherology.* Los Angeles: Semiotext(e), 2016.

———. *Globes: Spheres Vol. 2, Macrospherology.* Los Angeles: Semiotext(e), 2014.

———. *Stress and Freedom.* London: Polity, 2016.

———. *Thinker on Stage: Nietzsche's Materialism.* Minneapolis: University of Minnesota Press, 1989.

Smith, Anthony. *The Nation in History: Historiographical Debates about Ethnicity and Nationalism.* Hanover, NH: Brandeis University Press, 2000.

Song, Hongbing. *Huobi zhanzheng* [Currency Wars]. Beijing: CITIC, 2009.

Song, Hoon. *Pigeon Trouble: Bestiary Biopolitics in a Deindustrialized America.* Philadelphia: University of Pennsylvania Press, 2010.

Song, Qiang, et al. *Zhongguo keyi shuo "bu"—lengzhan hou shidai de zhengzhi yu qinggan jueze* [China Can Say "No"—Political and Emotional Strategies in the Post–Cold War Era]. Beijing: China Industry and Commerce Joint Publishing House, 1996.

Song, Qiang, et al. *Zhongguo bu gaoxing—da shidai, damubiao, ji women de neiyou waihuan* [Unhappy China—The Great Time, Grand Vision, and Our Challenges]. Beijing: Phoenix Media Publishing Group, 2009.

Sontag, Susan. *On Photography.* New York: Farrar, Straus and Giroux, 1977.

Spillman, Lyn. *Nation and Commemoration: Creating National Identities in the United States and Australia.* Cambridge: Cambridge University Press, 1977.

Stavrakakis, Yannis. *Lacan and the Political.* London: Routledge, 1999.

Stewart, Kathleen. "Conspiracy Theory's Worlds." In *Paranoia within Reason,* edited by George Marcus, 13–19. Chicago: University of Chicago Press, 1999.

Taylor, Jared. *White Identity: Racial Consciousness in the 21st Century.* Oakton, VA: New Century Foundation, 2011.

Tsou, Jung [Zou Rong]. *The Revolutionary Army: A Chinese Nationalist Tract of 1903.* Paris: Mouton & Co, 1968.

Turner, Victor. *The Ritual Process: Structure and Anti-structure*. Ithaca, NY: Cornell University Press, 1977.

Vukovich, Daniel. "The Battle for *Chinese* Discourse and the Rise of the *Chinese New Left*: Toward a Postcolonial Politics of Knowledge." In *China and New Left Visions: Political and Cultural Interventions*, edited by Ban Wang and Jie Lu, 61–80. Lanham, MD: Lexington Books, 2012.

———. *China and Orientalism*. London: Routledge, 2012.

Waley, Arthur. *The Analects of Confucius*. New York: Vintage Books, 1989.

Wang, Ban, and Jie Lu. *China and New Left Visions: Political and Cultural Interventions*. Lanham, MD: Lexington Books, 2012.

Wang, Hui. *China's New Order: Society, Politics, and Economy in Transition*. Cambridge, MA: Harvard University Press, 2003.

———. *The End of the Revolution: China and the Limits of Modernity*. London: Verso, 2009.

———. "The 'Tibetan Question' East and West: Orientalism, Regional Ethnic Autonomy, and the Politics of Dignity." In *The Politics of Imagining Asia*. Cambridge, MA: Harvard University Press, 2011.

West, Harry, and Todd Sanders. *Transparency and Conspiracy: Ethnographies of Suspicion in the New World Order*. Durham, NC: Duke University Press, 2003.

Wiens, Mi Chu. *Anti-Manchu Thought during the Early Ch'ing*. Papers on China, from Seminars at Harvard University (Vol. 22A). Cambridge, MA: East Asia Research Center, Harvard University, 1969.

Xu, Guoqi. *Olympic Dreams: China and Sports, 1895–2008*. Cambridge, MA: Harvard University Press, 2008.

Xu, Jieshun. "Understanding the Snowball Theory of the Han Nationality." In *Critical Han Studies: The History, Representation, and Identity of China's Majority*, edited by Thomas Mullaney, James Leibold, Stephane Gros, and Eric Vanden Busche. Berkeley: University of California Press, 2012.

Yang, Mayfair Mei-hui. *Gifts, Favors, and Banquets: The Art of Social Relationships in China*. Ithaca, NY: Cornell University Press, 1994.

Yu, Verna. "Guangzhou Slum Residents Battle Police." *South China Morning Post*, August 14, 2010.

Yuan, Weishi. *Wenhua yu zhongguo zhuangxing* [Culture and China's Transition]. Hangzhou: Zhejiang University Publishing, 2012.

Yural-Davis, Nira. "Gender and Nation." *Ethnic and Racial Studies* 16, no. 4 (1993): 621–32.

———. "Women and the Biological Reproduction of 'the Nation.'" *Women's Studies International Forum* 19, no. 1/2 (1996): 17–24.

Zechenter, Elizabeth. "In the Name of Culture: Cultural Relativism and the Abuse of the Individual." *Journal of Anthropological Research*, no. 53 (1997): 319–47.

Zeng, Xun. *Kong Qingdong xianxiang pipan* [A Critique of the Kong Qingdong Phenomenon]. Beijing: China Fortune Press, 2012.

Zhong, Xueping. *Masculinity Besieged? Issues of Modernity and Male Subjectivity in Chinese Literature of the Late Twentieth Century*. Durham, NC: Duke University Press, 2000.

Zhou, Qing. *Min yi he shi wei tian- Zhongguo shipin anquan xianzhuang diaocha* [What Kind of God? A Survey of the Current Safety of China's Food]. Beijing: China Worker's Publishing House, 2007.

Zito, Angela. *Of Body & Brush: Grand Sacrifice as Text/Performance in Eighteenth-Century China*. Chicago: University of Chicago Press, 1997.

INDEX

abstraction, 15, 120, 128, 130, 178
Adorno, Theodor, 28–29, 131
Adrian, Bonnie, 129
affect, 2, 19, 21, 22, 24, 27, 69, 99
affective system, 29, 31, 32, 59, 84, 143, 152
agency: in ritual, 114–116, as useless, 158
Ai Weiwei, 212
AIDS, 5
alienation, 13, 28, 57, 100, 121, 171, 208
Analects, 54, 112, 194, 197
Anderson, Benedict, 2, 19–22, 23, 24, 25, 32.
    See also imagined communities
anti-CNN, 211
anti-Japanese protests (2010), 103–104
anti-Semitism, 195–196, compared to anti-Manchu-ism, 137–140. *See also* racism
anxiety, 51, 53, 56, 87, 94, 105, 114, 117
Asian Games (2010), 41, 81–82
Asia-Pacific Economic Cooperation (APEC), 35–36, 39, 130, 132
autonomy, majority misunderstandings of, 138
autopoeisis, 19, 143. *See also* social systems theory

banal nationalism, 20
bannermen (Qing Dynasty), 39, 132, 137, 138, 146
bare branches (*guanggun*), 167–168
barbarians, 1, 16, 73; distinction between Chinese and, 3, 4, 7, 67, 118, 134, 144, internalized, 113, 118, 134, 139–140;

minorities as, 35, 52; "Westerners" as, 4, 179
Baruya, 100
baijiu (hard liquor), 70–71, 117
Baiyun Mountain (Guangzhou), 122–124
Barth, Fredrik, 43–44, 46, 49. *See also* ethnic boundaries
Bazin, André, 129
Beijing, 2, 12, 13, 40, 41, 79, 84, 91, 92, 134, 135, 138, 194, 210, 211
Beijing Olympics (2008), 41, 152, 210, 211
Bell, Daniel, 203
Berger, Peter, 87, 203
Blum, Susan, 86, 88
Book of Changes, 78, 192, 193, 194, 197
Book of Rites, 54
Bourdieu, Pierre, 129, 163, 174, 176, 185
Brother Emperor, 61, 88–95, 105, 106, 125, 165

Callahan, William, 29
cancer, 18, 51–53
captation, 21
censorship, 7–9, 152
century of humiliation, 29, 93; as fault of Manchus, 4, 143–144
Chen Xitong, 138
Chengdu, 2, 12, 103–104, 140, 213
China Can Say 'No', 157
Chineseness, 3, 11, 14, 34, 36, 39, 42, 55, 58, 68, 94, 95, 101, 113, 131, 134, 154, 159, 169, 191

gender roles, 160–164; and Han Clothing, 170; and mythology, 177–178

van Gennep, Arnold, 111

Gillis, John, 119

Gingrich, Newt, 150–151

Gladney, Dru, 50

Godelier, Maurice, 100

"Great Han Empire," 140

Great Wind of the Han (*Dahan zhi feng*), 12

Gries, Peter, 12

Groys, Boris, 24, 25, 100

guqin, 50, 66, 72, 73, 89, 174, 175, 185, 187

guanxi, 62, 76

Guangzhou, 2, 5, 12, 41, 42, 45, 50, 59, 63, 66, 76, 77, 78, 79, 80, 89, 102, 108, 121, 122, 131, 144, 154, 167, 169, 172, 186, 187, 215

gutter oil, 18, 139

Hage, Ghassan, 11

Haikou, 2, 12, 192, 194

Han: diversity of, 2, 145; as modern and unmarked, 34, 37, 45, 46, 47, 50, 51; as potential minority, 149; as "snowball," 55–56, 169; standard representations of, 42–46; as true "Chinese," 4; as victim of modernity, 55–56, 57, 86, 145, 149

Han Clothing Movement: and civil society, 189–190; history of, 35–38; as "movement" (*yundong*), 40–42; naming practices of, 61, 75; relations with the party-state, 40–41, 84–86; relations with society, 103–104, 106–108

Han Deqiang, 208

Han trouble, 33, 46–48, 69, 129

Hanminzu.com, 37

hao han, 163

harmony, 8, 213–214

He Xin, 157

Hobsbawm and Ranger (*Invention of Tradition*), 54

Hofstadter, Richard, 133–134, 147

homogeneous, empty time, 20, 22, 25,

homophobia, 187–189

Huang Qi, 212

Hukou, 207

id, 61, 91

identiodicy, 30, 144

identity: as alienated, 13; and boundaries, 43–48; critique of, 11; disappointing experience, 24–29; as fantasy, 19–24, 60; as paradoxical system, 29–32; and politics, 149–151; and postcolonial theory, 151–153; as prison, 152–153; and tradition, 54–44; through clothing, 97–108; through conspiracy theory, 141–146; through ritual, 108–121; through photography, 122–130

imaginary (Lacan), 10, 13, 21, 25–26

imaginary communities, 14, 23–24, 31, 33, 58, 61, 82

imagined communities, 2, 16, 19–24, 25, 32, 33

"Indians," 74, 168, 170

infidelity, 118, 179,

invention of tradition, 51–55, 108–111

Jiang Qing, 198–205, and "independent thinking," 202, life course of, 203. *See also* Confucian Constitutionalism

Jinan University, 63

Kallio, Jyrki, 11

Kapferer, Bruce, 114

Kaup, Katherine Palmer, 48

Kong Qingdong, 157, 208

Kong Xiangji, 135

Kunming, 2, 12, 13, 40, 101

kwaimatnie, 100

Lacan, Jacques, 13, 14, 21, 26–28, 204. *See also* desire; fantasy; imaginary

Ladies' Academy: daily schedule at, 175; as imaginary uterus, 182–184; as misogynistic fantasy, 183–184; students" opinions of, 184–185; teachers viewpoints, 175–180; vision of education, 182–183; vision of lady, 181–182, 184

land of rites and etiquette (*liyi zhi bang*), 2, 39, 40, 60, 61, 63, 67, 96, 116, 191, 200

Lao She, 136

Last Emperor, The, 140

"Lecture Room" (*Baijia jiangtan*), 140

"leftover women," 73–74
Leibold, James, 12
Lévi-Strauss, Claude, 167–168
"Liars" (*pianzi*), 78
Li Bai, 60
Li Bin, 147–148
Luhmann, Niklas, 13, 23, 203. *See also* autopoeisis; social systems theory

magical thinking (Freud), 112
majority-minority representations, 42–48
Malinowski, Bronislaw, 114
Manchus, 36, 176; as baby-killers, 147–148; as core of Han identity, 148–149, 153; as dominating business, government, and culture, 138–140; as genocidal, 134–135, 156; as indiscernible, 144; as oppressing Han, 137; as secret rulers of China today, 132–133
Maoism, 40–42, 180, 206–208
masculine domination, 169–170, 174, 185
May Fourth Movement (1919), 195
meaning, 30, 62, 63, 72, 75, 94, 203, 207; in clothing, 87, 98; as end unto itself, 110–112; in ritual, 110–111, 112, 115–116, 118–119
Mencius, 139, 194
minorities: as basis for Han identity, 48–51; as carefree, 77; as living fossils, 45, 56; as marked 45; as primitive, 7; in stages of history, 45, 49–50; standard representations of, 43–46, 63–65; as ungrateful, 8, 86
minzu: controversies surrounding, 3–4; as core of "nationalism," 1, 2; as "race," 1, 3, 5
misogyny, 166, 177–178
mixed blood, 170
modernity: as boring, 46
money-worshipping women (*bai jin nü*), 180
Murata Yujiro, 135
"my country" (*wo guo*), 23, 32

naming the witch (Siegel), 143
nationalism: ethnosymbolic theories of, 21, 25; as fantasy, 19–24; and Han-ness, 1–3; materialist theories of, 20, 21, 25; and Maoism, 209; and protest, 103–105; and

sex/ sexuality, 159, 163, 166–167, 172–173, 177–178; and Tibet, 210, 211; as a self-reproducing system, 29–32; social construction of, 22; as source of state legitimacy, 84; as split, 24–29
National People"s Congress, 41, 113, 172
"the new" (Groys) 100
new class (Djilas), 207
New Leftism: and identity, 209–212; and self-other distinction, 208–209; as tradition, 206–208
neotraditionalism, 191–192
New Culture Movement (1915), 176, 195
nonfashion, 99–100
nostalgia, 4–5, 55, 58, 60
nouveau riche (*baofahu*), 139
Nüwa, 90, 178

Obama, Barack, 150–151
Olympic torch protests (2008), 211
one-child policy, 146–150, as "crueler than the Japanese," 147–148; as "foreign," 149–150; as genocide, 149; as Manchu plot, 146–147
openness: and sexuality, 162–163
Orientalism, 10, 50, 151, as reproducing East-West binary, 152, and Tibet, 210–211
Oriental Orientalism (Chun), 205

paranoid style (Hofstadter), 133–134
parental pressures, 71, 73–74
Photography, 122–130; compared to clothing and ritual, 128, compared to portraits, 129; and gender roles, 160; as idealizing, 125–126; as movement practice, 122–124; as stabilizing, 127–128; as transcendent, 126; as "true," 126, 128
pleasure principle, 25
"Policies to Eliminate the Han," 134–135, 147
Polo, Marco, 93
postcolonialism, and identity, 151, as a general theory of institutions, 151–152
Practical jokes in the nuptial chamber (*nao dongfang*), 117
prejudice (*qishi*), 5

print capitalism, 19–20
"Protocols of the Elders of Zion," 135. *See also* anti-semitism
Purity, 6, 51, 61, 134, 150, 163, 169, 170, 173, 177
Pu Yi, 136

qipao, 131–132, 155
Qianlong Emperor, 112
Qiang nationality, 213, 214, 216
Qinshihuang, 38, 99
Qing clothing policy, 39
queue order (1645), 39, 134
queue shows (*bianzixi*), 134

race, 1, 3–6, 10, 14, 16, 66–68, 85, 134, 145, 147, 149, 168–170
racism: against minorities, 44–45; anti-black, 5–6, 66–68, 163, 167, 171, anti-Tibetan, 7–8
Radcliffe-Brown, A.R., 114
real China, 2, 9, 14, 17–19, 24, 26, 32, 33, 35, 37, 40, 42, 58–63, 67, 70, 87, 121, 131, 144, 164, 175–176, 181, 189, 198, 201, 207, 208
Rée, Jonathan, 20, 21, 32
renao (hot and noisy), 111, 117
rising China, 9, 23, 57
ritual: and anxiety, 114; as alternate world, 114–115; compared to Christianity in America, 113; as defense against social disintegration, 119; disruption of, 121; as means of control, 115; as ordering, 112–113; 116–117; as outside of society 111; as sacred space, 111–112; vs. performance, 65
rock & roll, 66–68. *See also* "shaking"

sacred, 30, 100–101, vs. profane, 106
Said, Edward, 10, 151, 152. *See also* Orientalism
de Saussure, Ferdinand, 13, 26
Sangren, Steven, 91
Seligman, Weller, Puett, and Simon (*Ritual and its Consequences*), 111, 120
Shakespeare, William, 193
"shaking," 66–68
Shangsi Festival, 109

Shenzhen, 2, 12, 16, 17, 64, 70, 71, 72, 108, 114, 215
Shi Lang, 138
Shuimo Old Town, 213–217
Siegel, James, 143
signifier/ signified, 13, 26, and fantasy/ reality, 26–28
Sloterdijk, Peter, 13, 14, 20, 29. *See also* spheres
Smith, Anthony, 21, 25
Smith, Jonathan, 114
Sontag, Susan, 124, 129
Snow, Edgar, 93
social systems theory, 13–14 29–32. *See also* Luhmann, Niklas
solutions: as problems, 189–190
son of heaven (*tian zi*), 8
spheres, 13, 14, 22, 57, 63, 86, 89, 99, 114, 116, 178, 179, 180, 182, 183, 191, 199. *See also* Sloterdijk, Peter
Splendid China theme park, 49, 64
state media, 23–24, 27, 72
Stewart, Kathleen, 141
stranger king, 150; and assumption of native goodness, 150
Sun Yat-sen University, 73, 76, 89
superego, 60, 61, 91
Supreme Ultimate (*taiji*), 78, 93
symbolic chain, 22, 23, 27, 28, 29

Taizong Emperor, 99
Taiwan Solidarity Union, 137
Taobao, 52
Taoist calendar, 119–120
Tan Zuoren, 212
Tangzhuang: as *magua*, 35, 131–132, 155
tea ceremony, 121
Tea Party, 16
teleportation, 53
test-focused learning, 193–194
theodicy, 29–30
three northeastern provinces, 138
three obediences (*san cong*), 164–165
three sovereigns (*san huang*), 169, 206
Tian Xueyuan, 146, 147
Tibet, 7–8, 210–212
Titanic (1997), 60
Top Gun (1986), 37

tradition, 6–9, 11, 17–18; and education, 192–198; and gender, 160–166, 177–178, 185; and government, 83–84, 198–205; as inversion of the present, 51–55; and leftism, 206–208; and ritual, 108–111; as trap or solution, 99

Tsin (Xian) Village, 80–84

Turner, Victor, 111, 115

Tu Shiyou, 165–166

Unhappy China, 157

unity of heaven and humanity (*tian ren he yi*), 85, 138, 144, 177, 199, 200

unity (*yiti*) and diversity (*duoyuan*), 4, 41, 57

urban villages (*chengzhongcun*), 77, 80–82. *See also* Tsin Village

Virginity, 165–166

Vukovich, Daniel, 207, 209

Wang Ban and Lu Jie, 205–206

Wang Hui, 207, 208, on Tibet, 209–212

Wang Letian, 37

Wang Tsai-kuei, 194

"war on Christmas," 149

Washington, George, 10

Way of the Humane Authority (*wang dao*), 199

weddings, modern 116–117; and photography, 129–130; traditional "Han," 117–118. *See also* ritual

weiguan (surrounding and observing), 107

Wenchuan Earthquake (2008), 212, and tourism, 212–217

"Western media," 7

Xi Jinping, 23

Xia Dynasty, 90

Xiaobei (section of Guangzhou), 5

Xinhai Revolution (1911), 135–136; as permanent revolution, 136

Xu Jieshun, 4

Yan Chongnian, 12

Ye Hongming, 41

Yellow Emperor, 36, 59, 60, 90, 92

yin poison, 179

yin-yang binary, 98, 176, 177, 182

yi shi zhu xing, 17–19

Yuan Mu, 138

Yu the Great, 18

Zhengzhou, 37

Zhou Dynasty, 54–55

Zhu Village, 186–188

Zhu Yuanzhang, 72, 99

Zhuang, 48